T0265663

BUILT IN CHELSEA

———

TWO MILLENNIA OF ARCHITECTURE AND TOWNSCAPE

DAN CRUICKSHANK
UNICORN IN ASSOCIATION WITH CADOGAN

Published in 2022 by
Unicorn, an imprint of Unicorn Publishing Group
5 Newburgh Street
London
W1F 7RG
www.unicornpublishing.org

Text © Daniel Cruikshank
Images © See page 304

ISBN 978-1-911604-96-9

10 9 8 7 6 5 4 3 2 1

Designed by Charlie Smith Design Ltd
Printed in Wales by Gomer Press

CONTENTS

1. Above
Chelsea's waterfront looking west, showing
Cheyne Walk and Chelsea Old Church in the
distance. Painted by Thomas Hosmer Shepherd,
seemingly from the Cadogan Pier, which had
been constructed in 1841. Shepherd captures
a moment, probably in the early 1850s, when
Chelsea village remained a tranquil riverside
enclave. However, all was soon to change when
the Embankment was constructed in the early
1870s, obliterating the ancient waterside and
essentially cutting Chelsea off from the river.

This book tells the story of Chelsea through its buildings. Although such an aim may seem simple, there are complexities because to an extraordinary degree Chelsea has meant very different things to many different people. Partly this is because Chelsea has long been two distinct places. There is the Thames-side village of Chelsea, with the Old Church at its heart, which has probably been the focus of a small trading and manufacturing community since Roman times and then there is inland Chelsea, with the King's Road as its spine, that grew into prominence from the late seventeenth century, and particularly from the late eighteenth century when fields, pastures and gardens were turned into terraces and squares. At this time it was joined by the secondary apex of Sloane Street, with the creation of Hans Town, the first 'New Town' commissioned by the 1st Earl Cadogan.

Early accounts of Chelsea focus, quite naturally, on the ancient riverside village with its established and distinct character. For Samuel Pepys it was a place of delight and bucolic retreat, where he could go 'to take some air', quench his thirst and see the pretty sights – including 'young ladies of the schoole' attending services in Chelsea Old Church. In his diary for August 1661, Pepys records visiting an 'alehouse' in 'Chelsey' where he 'sat and drank' and then walked back to Westminster among trees, 'neat-houses' and market gardens (August 1661 and 22 March 1663, *Diary of Samuel Pepys,* ed. Robert Latham and William Matthews, London: G. Bell and Co., 1970, vol. II, p. 158; vol. IV, p. 82).

Other Londoners appear to have found Chelsea village's somewhat remote location daunting, even dangerous. Sir Richard Steele, writing in the *Tatler* in 1709, in the persona of Isaac Bickerstaff, suggested that journeys from the City were hazardous because they involved passing along 'the Five Fields [now Ebury Street] where robbers lie in wait' (see page 236 and *Tatler*, no. 34, pp. 205–07 of 1754 edition, vol. I, London).

In the early 1720s, Daniel Defoe focused on yet another aspect of the village. He described it as a 'town of palaces', as indeed it was (see page 20 and Daniel Defoe, *A Tour thro' the Whole Island of Great Britain*, London, 1724–7). The sequence of riverside mansions, clustered around the Old Church, included several of high social status and significant architectural quality. There was Shrewsbury House, built to the east of the church by the 12th Earl of Warwick in the late fourteenth century; the Old Manor, of similar date, to the north of the church; Sir Thomas More's early sixteenth-century house – later known as Beaufort House – to the west of the church; the New Manor House, probably built in the early sixteenth century and certainly acquired in 1536 by Henry VIII; Winchester House – in origin the New Manor House's west wing – which was occupied in the mid-seventeenth century by the Bishop of Winchester; the early seventeenth-century Danvers House, a pioneering Palladio-inspired jewel of a building; and the Baroque Lindsey House, built in the 1670s to the west of Beaufort House. There were later and slightly lesser mansions and villas further to the west and east of the church, notably the very early eighteenth-century Gough House.

This miraculous collection of palatial buildings remained largely intact until 1740 when Chelsea's changing fortunes and aspirations, combined with the speculative construction of terrace houses, led to their replacement. Sir Hans Sloane acquired Beaufort House and the New Manor House, both of which were demolished by the mid 1750s, with their sites and grounds forming the nucleus of the Cadogan Estate and subsequently built upon. In fact, the pattern of replacing mansions and their grounds with streets and terraces had started before Sloane's time when Danvers House was demolished, perhaps as early as 1696, with the south end of Danvers Street soon laid out on each side of the drive that had linked the house to the river's edge. The sole survivor of these mansions is the much-altered Lindsey House.

Chelsea village's riverside site made it not only a favoured location for mansions but also, from its earliest recorded times, for quays, wharfs, warehouses, manufactures, inns and taverns. In addition, from the late seventeenth century Chelsea was also home to one of London's more characterful coffee houses, known as Don Saltero's and located on Cheyne Walk.

This mix of diverse establishments attracted City and Westminster revellers, such as Pepys, but also working river folk, such as boatmen, ferrymen and boat-builders. Naturally, this gave riverside Chelsea a most distinctive and varied character.

By the mid-nineteenth century it was a place of wealth and poverty, of promenade and industry. This vivid life and the pure light, which still distinguished riverside Chelsea from the smoke-begrimed city to the east, attracted waves of artists. In about 1846 J.M.W. Turner leased a most modest terrace house on Cheyne Walk, no doubt drawn to Chelsea village by the sparkle of sunlight upon the water and by its quayside life. He lived with his old Margate mistress, Sophia Booth, and called himself Mr Booth, presumably because he wanted to merge with his surroundings, observing without being observed, and be left undisturbed to get on with his work. It was in this Cheyne Walk house that Turner died, on the morning of 19 December 1851. His alleged last words, 'Sun is God', could well have been inspired by the drama of a winter dawn over the Thames, visible from his first-floor bedroom.

In the year of Turner's death, William Holman Hunt was living at 5 Prospect Place, on the corner of Lawrence Street, almost opposite the Old Church, and it is probable that it was here in 1854 that he completed *The Light of the World*. Based on a text in the Book of Revelation, the painting shows the figure of Christ set against dawn light and trees in winter, with what appears to be a distant river. This scene perhaps records the view from Hunt's first-floor studio overlooking the Thames, an uncanny echo of the view that Turner could have seen from his bedroom as he died (*The Victoria County History: A History of the County of Middlesex, volume 12, Chelsea*, ed. Patricia E.C. Croot, London, 2004, pp. 102–08). Other artists soon followed: in 1862, Dante Gabrielle Rossetti took a lease on 16 Cheyne Walk and in 1866 James McNeill Whistler settled into a portion of Lindsey House.

By the time the society painter John Singer Sargent had moved into a large studio house in Tite Street in 1885, Chelsea's distinctive character had evolved. London had long been a city of dramatic contrasts but in the small compass of Chelsea these were extreme. Sloane Street and Cadogan Place had become the focus of aristocratic Chelsea, reinforced during the late 1880s by grand homes in the newly built Cadogan Square. At the same time, the old riverside village and the streets, such as Tite Street and Glebe Place, connecting it to the King's Road became the hub of an idiosyncratic and wayward world inhabited by cultivated but eccentric bohemians and individual artists, including Oscar Wilde, who in 1884 moved into a what is now 34 Tite Street. Arthur Ransome, a writer now best known for his children's stories, confirmed the area's artistically unconventional and adventurous character when in 1907 he wrote in *Bohemia in London* that Chelsea had long waged 'war with the common sense of the multitude' and was a 'battle field ... for art and literature'.

It was not just Chelsea's artistic character that caught the eye, but also its poverty.

Most of the working wharfs and a large number of taverns and humble homes had been swept away when the Chelsea Embankment had been constructed in the early 1870s, but in the late 1880s the philanthropist and social reformer Charles Booth was still able to identify significant areas of mean housing and deprivation in Chelsea. These he duly noted on his colour-coded London 'Poverty Map' of 1889. Booth used black and dark blue to mark the location of communities and households that were, in his opinion, 'vicious, semi-criminal' and 'very poor' suffering 'chronic want', and in Chelsea he identified desperate areas near the river towards the west end of Cheyne Walk and to the north and south of the central portion of the King's Road, around what is now Chelsea Manor Street.

During the first half of the twentieth century these parallel Chelsea worlds survived and, in their ways, thrived. There were consistent and productive campaigns to replace the area's decayed but often ancient and characterful buildings with artisans' model dwellings, but this was offset by the decline of once smart streets into homes that were little better than slums. This gave Chelsea's already complex character another twist or two. The artists who moved into Chelsea from the 1860s tended to be wealthy and successful, and able to commission and occupy the area's remarkable collection of avant-garde studio houses, notably in Tite Street, Glebe Place, Flood Street and along the Embankment. However, in the early twentieth century the new generation of Chelsea artists, on the whole producing work that challenged rather than reflected popular taste, were less commercially successful and less affluent. So Chelsea's pockets of poverty, with their low-rent, run-down and often airy abandoned workshops or stables, such as those along Manresa Road, became the ideal breeding ground for a new type of artistic community.

As Chelsea's old buildings changed into philanthropic dwellings and luxury homes, there was inevitably a reaction from those who wished to preserve Chelsea's distinctive character. The Chelsea Society was founded in 1927 to provide a focus for preservation; it was in fact the first of London's many civic and residents' associations and it remains as ever: consistent, coherent, relevant and effective.

In the mid-twentieth century, Chelsea became an epicentre of fashion as a wave of egalitarian pop culture, fuelled economically by the newly won spending power of young people, made London its temporary world capital. In the early 1960s, the King's Road in Chelsea, along with Carnaby Street in Soho and Portobello Road in Notting Hill, suddenly became internationally significant.

This meant, among many things, that Chelsea came under intense and often quizzical and partly baffled scrutiny. For example, the insightful and articulate architectural critic Ian Nairn appears to have been most confused by the quiet and often undistinguished setting that had become a world stage on which Chelsea's young people displayed themselves. In *Nairn's London*, published in 1966, he dismissed Chelsea's architectural presence as 'only relatively remarkable', being 'made up of a few pretty bits set in an unlovely mixture of the utilitarian and the genteel'. There were, lamented Nairn, 'no eccentric buildings to match the eccentric people.... King's Road (was) full of idiosyncratic life ... yet without anything in the buildings to express it' (Ian Nairn, *Nairn's London*, London: Penguin Books, 1966, p. 134).

However, for Chelsea's great architectural masterpiece, the Royal Hospital, Nairn had most pertinent praise. Constructed from 1682 to the east end of Chelsea, and essentially linking the riverside village to the King's Road, the hospital was the collective work of two of Nairn's great architectural heroes. Of Sir Christopher Wren's building, Nairn observed that it possesses 'not excessive polish but excessive politeness ... courteousness ... wisdom and calm authority', but the stables, added between 1814 and 1817 by Sir John Soane, was something more. For Nairn it was a work of pure genius. For him the stables enshrined 'the rules of scale and proportion, plus the magic quality which converts a literary exercise into a poem'. Contemplation of the stables offered, for Nairn, 'something near a miracle, to be had any day for the asking' (*Nairn's London* p. 136).

I know just what Nairn means. Although he damned Chelsea as a whole with faint praise, I cannot but feel that the two points he made about Soane's stables can be applied to parts of Chelsea. To walk through the Royal Hospital and its grounds, down Swan Walk and past the Physic Garden and along Cheyne Walk to Cheyne Row, is to experience an urban and architectural 'miracle' that is indeed just there 'for the asking'. And along the way – and if you are in the mood – you can observe and ponder upon those varied qualities that, magically, transform mere building into sublime and poetic architecture.

The way in which these memorable buildings and places were created are among the stories this book tells.

Dan Cruickshank
January 2022

2. Above
Chelsea Royal Hospital – designed by Sir
Christopher Wren in 1682 – from the Thames.
This view was painted in c. 1746 by Edward
Haytley who, rather curiously, omitted the long
and narrow canals that flanked the central
path connecting the hospital to the river.
The canals were not filled in until the 1850s.

SWEET THAMES, RUN SOFTLY

3. *Above*
The waterside village of Chelsea from the west,
with, in the distance Battersea Bridge, opened
in 1772, connecting the village to the south bank.
On the north bank, on the left, is Cremorne
House, being remodelled by James Wyatt for Lord
Cremorne at the time this view was painted in
1784 by the maritime artist Thomas Whitcombe.

Chelsea's history is ancient and there is a hint of the enigmatic about it. Chelsea had its origin as a Thames-side village with a wharf, indeed the name Chelsea – Cealchyth – derives from the Anglo-Saxon term for a landing place that is chalky or from which chalk or lime could be collected. The location of this wharf and village is marked today by Chelsea Old Church on Cheyne Walk. Daniel Lysons, in the Middlesex volume of his *Environs of London* of 1795, states that in the most ancient record he had seen, dating from the reign of Edward the Confessor, the village was named Cealchylle and that it started to be written Chelsey in the sixteenth century and in the current fashion from the late seventeenth century. As to its meaning, Lysons writes that he 'would not hesitate a moment in saying that it was so called from its hills of chalk; but as there is neither chalk nor a hill in the parish, the derivation does not prove satisfactory'. Lysons also points out that the name seems to 'have puzzled the Norman scribes' because in the Domesday Book two versions of the name are given, one scribed over the other (Daniel Lysons, *Environs of London, 1795, Volume 2, Middlesex,* London: Cadell & Davies, 1795, p. 70).

So there is some mystery about the meaning of the place name Chelsea, but it would appear to have its origin as a humdrum place of river-borne trade, perhaps with a ready supply of lime or clay rather than chalk useful for the manufacture of mortar or render for building works or for potteries. This speculation was supported by a series of archaeological discoveries made in 1997 at the west end of Cheyne Walk. What was believed to be a seventh- or eighth-century wharf, perhaps established by the Saxon King Offa, was unearthed and then – very near the Old Church – Roman pottery shards were found, suggesting there was a wharf on the site from at least the third century AD. The shards included the remains of storage jars and Samian ware, dated to AD 225–50, that had probably been made in France, and imported Basalt lava used for millstones. Taken together, this suggests there was an ancient wharf in Chelsea when, or just before, the port of Lundenwic, at what is now Aldwych, started to evolve into London's major riverside trading centre. So, for a while, Chelsea was perhaps as important a centre of trade as Lundenwic and remained so until King Alfred resettled the City in the late ninth-century (see Chelsea Society Annual Report for 1997, pp. 23–4).

Other archaeological evidence from sites near Chelsea most strongly suggest that it was not just a centre of river-borne trade but, like many water-side locations

Woodhenge on the Thames — 6,500 years ago the river was a thing of natural, celestial power, with the rise and fall of its tide governed by the movement of the moon.

at the time, regarded as sacred. Indeed, the river itself was probably regarded as a divine being – a god – to be celebrated, thanked and appeased through sacrifice and offerings.

The river was a thing of natural, indeed celestial power, with the rise and fall of its tide governed by the movement of the moon. The river brought life, but not just because it brought water without which no plant could thrive. It also brought physical power through the ebb and flow of its tides that could be utilised by the river folk to operate mills and machines to process crops, to irrigate land and to bring abundance. The Thames was also no doubt sacred in ancient times because – like all great rivers – it marked boundaries and was in a sense a threshold or a place of meeting between peoples and between mankind and the gods. The fact that an alternative name for the Thames, in its uppermost reaches just west of Dorchester, is the Isis, makes one ponder. It is not known how long this has been the

4. Left
The Thames at low tide, looking from the south bank southwest towards Battersea Power Station from the west side of Vauxhall Bridge. The oak piles rising above the water date from c.1,500 BC and supported a causeway to a now lost island or bridge across the river.

case (earliest references date from the mid-fourteenth century), or whether any reference to the great Egyptian goddess Isis, venerated by Rome and associated with Juno, was intended. Perhaps the name is merely a compression of Tamesis, the Latin version of the Celtic name for the Thames.

The evidence that the Thames was once seen as a sacred river – perhaps a highway of souls like the Ganges in India – is strong and intriguing, with significant finds west of Westminster Bridge suggesting that the upper reaches of the Thames, including Chelsea, was regarded in ancient times as particularly holy. Two remarkable things survive in the Thames at Vauxhall. At low tide, in the season of the year when the flow of the Thames is reduced to a trickle and a bold traveller can wade across, miraculous things appear in the gravel and slime of the naked and exposed riverbed. Most astonishing are the stumps of oak posts, immediately north of Vauxhall Bridge, that have been dated, using preserved tree rings, to around 4,500 BC.

This might be the remains of a woodhenge, marking a grove particularly sacred in late Mesolithic times that stood on the riverbank. It is generally accepted that 6,500 years ago the Thames ran slightly to the south and east of its present course.

Just to the southeast of these enigmatic stumps, on the south side of Vauxhall Bridge, is another set of oak stumps. Here two rows run parallel to each other, at right angles to the bank and out towards the centre of the river where they stop. These stumps date from about 1,500 BC, suggesting that during the Bronze Age there was a causeway running from the 'south' bank to a now lost gravel island in the Thames. Or perhaps the causeway continued to the 'north' bank to form London's first known bridge. So the purpose of the structure is uncertain. The piles could be the remains of a bridge or of a causeway to which flat-bottomed barges could be moored mid-stream, thus remaining operational during most low tides, where they could be loaded with vegetables or flowers grown in the verdant marshland and meadows south of the Thames. The only real clue are two Bronze Age bronze-made spearheads found driven deep into riverbed near the piles. The depth of the spearheads suggest they were not simply lost but were votive offerings to the spirit and the power of the river. Indeed, the entire purpose of the causeway could simply have been to provide a connection to the long-lost island that the local people believed was of sacred significance. There is further evidence that during the Bronze Age the Thames was seen as a life-giving and life-taking divinity that demanded offerings. One of the most visually striking and compelling pieces of evidence was found in the river just over half a mile to the east of Chelsea Old Church, and opposite the point where the Westbourne River or Creek joins the Thames.

In 1857, when foundations were being dug for the suspension towers of what became known as Chelsea Bridge, a most remarkable find was made. On the riverbed, near the south side was what appeared to be a military graveyard or site of battle. There were human bones and the remains of weapons that were identified as Roman or of the Roman age. There was great excitement. From Julius Caesar's own brief but pithy account of his second invasion of Britain – undertaken in 54 BC – we know his legions reached the Thames at a ford and that, in Caesar's opinion, the river was 'fordable at one point only, and even there with difficulty' (Julius Caesar, *The Conquest of Gaul*, trans. S.A. Handford, Penguin, 1965, p. 137). This is confusing. Presumably what Caesar meant is that he drew his forces up at the first practicable ford as the river widened and deepened as it flowed towards the estuary. Other fords would have been further west, upstream, but off his preferred route of march. Romans, from Caesar onwards, displayed a keen interest in the Thames and its estuary. The nearer to them they could be the better because – if necessary – the Thames was a highway for supply, reinforcements or safe and speedy extraction if things got difficult. Nearly a hundred years after Caesar, other Roman invaders established Londinium on the first site inland from the estuary where the Thames could be bridged and where there was a natural harbour – the Pool of London – for shipping.

Caesar makes it clear the Thames was a boundary. Cassivellaunus had been chosen by the Britons to lead their combined forces against Rome, and his territory

was, wrote Caesar, 'separated from the maritime tribes by a river called the Thames'. By 'maritime tribes' (Caesar, p. 135) Caesar meant primarily those to the south of the Thames, in Kent, who were Belgic settlers from Gaul and who still had much in common with the continent and so were familiar to the Romans. Hence, by crossing the Thames, Caesar was entering the more alien heartland of his main opponent, with the intention of destroying him in his lair. It was to be victory or destruction. So, in a sense, a crossing of the Rubicon. This, of course, was typically Roman: audacious and fearless.

The evidence found in 1857 seemed to confirm that the ford Caesar used was between Battersea and Chelsea, which surprised few because this had long been accepted as the location of what was arguably London's first Thames ford upstream from the estuary.

Caesar describes the action that would have taken place on, or near, the site of Chelsea Bridge. He records that 'large enemy forces' were 'drawn up on the opposite (Chelsea) bank; which was fenced by sharp stakes fixed along the edge' with 'similar ones ... concealed in the river bed'. Undaunted, Caesar sent his cavalry across and then his infantry that 'went with such speed and impetuosity, although they only had their heads above water', that they struck simultaneously with the cavalry. The result, states Caesar, was that 'the enemy was overpowered and fled from the river-bank' (Caesar, pp. 137–8). More compelling detail was added a couple of hundred years later by a Greek historian named Polyaenus who in his *Stratagems of War* states that Caesar's attacking force was aided by an armoured war-elephant, with archers and soldiers dispersing sling-shot from the tower on the elephant's back. If true (it is possible that Polyaenus was confusing this invasion with Claudius's in AD 43 when elephants were certainly used), it is hardly surprising that the startled Britons broke and fled at the sight of this rampaging death-dealing beast.

Sadly, no elephant bones were found in 1857 and few now believe these human remains to be evidence of the Roman battle at the ford, although it is possible. However, if not evidence of combat, what do these fragments mean? One object found among them suggests the answer. As at Vauxhall, this could have been a place where sacrifices were made to the river gods – of arms and armour – and where the dead were buried. For among the bones and Roman era war material was something far older and more remarkable. Seemingly deposited in the river, perhaps 300 years before the Romans arrived, there emerged from the mud and debris a magnificent and highly ornamented bronze shield. It is now called the Battersea shield because it was found near the south bank, but if a few metres to the north it would no doubt be called the Chelsea shield. The shield bears no marks of combat and may well have been ceremonial and, like the spearheads at Vauxhall, a votive offering. Its ornament offers insights into the religious beliefs of those who made it and those who, in all probability, cast it into the Thames. There are three circles of raised repoussé work, within which are circles, spiral decoration and twenty-seven small round compartments. Each of these compartments was originally filled with red, coral-like enamel set within swirling or swastika forms made of bronze. Traditionally, the swastika is a symbol of solar energy, so this shield – like the sacred river into which it was cast – may have been to do with fertility, with abundance. The shield is dated to between 350 and 50 BC, similar in date to a smaller shield, thought to be another votive offering, found in 1849 in the Thames at Wandsworth.

These discoveries, so near the Anglo-Saxon riverside village of Chelsea, cannot but make one ponder its origin. By the third century AD it was evidently a place involved with river-borne trade and commerce but had it also been, in the Bronze Age or earlier, a sacred place of river sacrifice? Was the parish church built on a sacred pagan site to tame or claim the power for the new religion? Alfred Beaver, in his *Memorials of Old Chelsea,* published in 1892, asserted that the number of finds near 'Chelsea Suspension Bridge … justified [the assumption] that the district generally was inhabited by the Britons'. Beaver was of the opinion 'that a fierce fight between the Britons and the invaders took place at Chelsea is beyond all question' (Alfred Beaver, *Memorials of Old Chelsea: A New History of the Village of Palaces,* Wakefield: E.P. Publishing, 1971, ed. Patricia Meara, pp. 11–13).

The first church in Chelsea was 'probably' built in 799 (Ben Weinreb and Christopher Hibbert, *The London Encyclopaedia*, 3rd edition, London: Macmillan, 2008, p. 154), with the sacred importance of the riverside site in Anglo-Saxon times seemingly confirmed, in a slightly tangential way, by the fact that no fewer that five Church Synods were held in Chelsea in the nearly thirty years between 787 and 816. The first church council was presided over by King Offa of Mercia – whose wharf was nearby – and was possibly attended by papal legates, so a weighty affair.

The church was rebuilt and first documented in 1157, confirming that by this date the riverside community had grown into a village sizeable and important enough to require a new church and for records to be kept. The church was dedicated to All the Saints (surely a match for any lingering pagan spirits, although the dedication might only date from the thirteenth century), and – as with all medieval parish churches – was for the cure of the souls of all within its parish but also to serve as the centre of local government and the means by which the

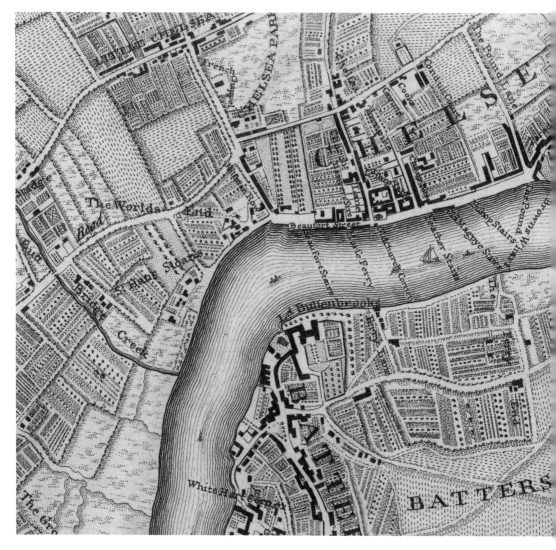

5. Above
A detail of John Rocque's small scale 'Exact Survey of the
Citys of London, Westminster and ye Borough of Southwark
and the Country near Ten Miles Round', begun in 1741 and
published from 1744–6. The riverside village of Chelsea is
clearly shown, although not in great detail. From the left:
Lindsey House can be made out to the east of 'Milman Row';
the Old Church and Old Church Street; the quadrangular
form denotes Shrewsbury House with, set back and to the
east of Cheyne Row, Winchester House or Palace; the site of
the New Manor House (not in fact demolished until 1753);
on Cheyne Walk the terrace built 1717/18 on the site of the
house's 'Great Garden'; then Paradise Row leading to the
north front of the Royal Hospital.

population was controlled by the state through ecclesiastical hierarchies and the means by which church tithes and taxes were assessed and collected. The other rule of law was the manor, which was established by the time of the Norman invasion in 1066. The Domesday Book records it had been held by a man of King Edward the Confessor but by 1086 he had been succeeded by Edward of Salisbury, the Sheriff of Wiltshire and presumably a Norman. By 1115 possession of the manor had passed to Westminster Abbey, with which it was in easy communication by river.

The thread through all this is, of course, the Thames. The river was a highway of trade, communication and ceremony connecting the City with its outlying villages, bringing prosperity but also, for centuries, perceived as a divinity and the source of abundance and – if not appeased – the cause of flood, death and destruction. The Thames gave Chelsea its origin and ancient identity but also much of its enduring character because its growth was first along the river before it sent tendrils inland. It is important to remember that, until the late eighteenth century, as *The Buildings of England* points out, Chelsea remained a riverside village 'as much on its own as Teddington or Laleham further upstream' (Bridget Cherry and Nikolaus Pevsner, *The Buildings of England, London 3: North West,* London: Penguin, 1991, p. 551).

From the late fourteenth century, the village's riverside location – beautiful in itself but also making communication with the city quicker and safer than by road – prompted prominent families to choose Chelsea as the location for their mansions, virtually all spaced along the river's edge and each with its own landing place. The process gained pace in the early Tudor period because Chelsea found itself in the centre of royal, political and merchant power. To its east were the palaces of Westminster, Whitehall,

St James's, the City and the more distant palace of Placentia at Greenwich. To the west were the royal power bases at Richmond and, crucially, from 1529, at Hampton Court. The status of Chelsea increased significantly when Henry VIII acquired the lordship of the manor in the mid-1530s and established himself in a larger house to the east of the Old Manor House.

From Tudor times, and well into the nineteenth century, London was a city of water, with the Thames the main commercial and ceremonial highway. Chelsea, in prime strategic place because of its ease of communication with Westminster and the City – and because of its riverside beauty – became, as Daniel Defoe described it in 1724, a little 'town of palaces' (*A Tour thro' the Whole Island of Great Britain,* London, 1724–7). A little earlier, Dr John King, the Rector of Chelsea between 1694 and 1732, had noted simply that 'Chelsey is a Sweet and pleasant village' set beside 'the noble River Thames' (*Transcript of the Rev. Dr. John King's Manuscript Account of Chelsea, and the Receipts of the Rectory from the Glebe Lands and other sources during is Rectorship, 1694–1732,* Chelsea Public Library, 1902).

Defoe was mostly moved by the expansive grandeur of The Royal Hospital, but he was also impressed by Chelsea's rate of growth that promised to soon make it 'a part of London'. When Chelsea did indeed become physically part of London, which happened soon after Hans Town was developed from the late 1770s (see page 111), Defoe's happy phrase was adapted and Chelsea was characterised not as a town but a 'village' of palaces set within the mighty city (for example, Rev. A.G. L'Estrange, *The Village of Palaces; or, Chronicles of Chelsea,* London: Hurst and Blackett, 1880). The building histories of these riverside palaces are now most enigmatic. The great and early palaces – mostly late medieval and

Tudor – have all gone, leaving virtually no built evidence above ground but, of course, their once mighty presence echoes through the ages in the street pattern and in the balance between open space and buildings. The great buildings were clustered close to Chelsea Old Church, each with its own frontage on the river, and two survivors, along with the terrain others had occupied and where they left their mark in the pattern of streets and gardens, is shown on John Rocque's small-scale London map of 1746 (John Rocque's 'Exact Survey of the Citys of London, Westminster and ye Borough of Southwark and the Country near London ten miles round', published 1744–6, see *The A to Z of Georgian London,* intro. by Ralph Hyde, Guildhall Library, London, 1981, p. vi). This reveals a number of terraces and buildings standing mostly to the north and northeast of the parish church. Here, from west to east, was the Old Manor House, demolished soon after 1687; Shrewsbury House, shown on Rocque's map as a quadrangular block immediately west of Cheyne Row, demolished in 1813; Winchester House or Palace, demolished in 1825 or just before; and the New Manor House, or Chelsea Place. This was not demolished until 1753, but it is not shown on Rocque's map. This is odd, but suggests that he quickly revised the plates and issued an amended edition. Rocque's map also show the terrace houses built from c. 1717 along much of the south frontage of the New Manor House's 'Great Garden' (see page 18).

James Hamilton's map of 1717 appears to show the New Manor House, but only as a long, narrow building. However, a rough survey of c. 1705 by Dr King suggests the New Manor House had a courtyard form with a main elevation towards the river (see page 85). Hamilton's map includes a perspective of the Manor House 'in Cheyne Walk'. Both King and Hamilton suggest the New Manor House was set forward and to the east of its wing of significant scale.

This wing became Winchester House or Palace, which appears on Rocque's map. The 'Great Garden' is named on Hamilton's map and shown without buildings along it south edge. Winchester House – as it is named – appears on Richard Horwood's detailed map of 1799–1819, confirming its location as implied on the Hamilton and Rocque maps.

These palatial buildings to the east of the Old Church were predominately Tudor or late medieval. To the west of the church, between what are now Old Church Street and Milman's Street, and stretching from the river to the King's Road was the estate compiled and acquired just after 1520 by Sir Thomas More and on which his house, later known as Beaufort House, had stood. Rocque shows the estate as largely gardens incorporating avenues of trees because Beaufort House had been demolished between 1738 and 1740. The map shows a terrace on the east side of Milman's Street, stretching as far as the King's Road, named 'Millman Row', and buildings along the eastern portion of estate's riverfront. To the west, set further back from the river and almost at the junction with Millman Row, is a detached building. This must be Lindsey House, built in 1674 for the Earl of Lindsey and now, although long divided into separate dwellings, the sole significant survivor of Chelsea's early riverside mansions.

A good view of More's former estate in its setting is offered by John Kip's birds-eye view of Beaufort House, looking north`, probably made in around 1700 but published in 1707–09 in his *Britannia Illustrata* (*Britannia Illustrata: Views of Several of the Queen's Palaces and also of the Principal Seats of the Nobility & Gentry of Great Britain, 1707–09*, folio of plates by John (Jan) Kip in collaboration with Leonard Knyff). This view includes not only Lindsey House (on the far left, or west) –

built on land that was once part of More's estate – but also reveals that the building on the eastern portion of the estate's river frontage was a long, two-storey structure separated by a public carriageway (originally named Duke Street) from an equally long multi-gabled range rising from the river-edge. Both appear to be sixteenth or early seventeenth century in date. To the west of Duke Street was a large quay, set in front of Beaufort House's front court. The wall separating the court from the quay was terminated by two small tower-like gable-topped lodges that probably dated from More's time. Kip's view also shows a fine large garden to the east, incorporating a circular drive around a lawn, separated from Beaufort House by a wall. This fine garden belonged to Danvers House. This was another Chelsea mansion that, not shown in the view, stood to the south of the circular drive and was to be demolished between 1696 and 1716. The south end of Danvers Street was built in the late 1690s and later extended north to pass centrally through the site of Danvers House.

The land on which Danvers House and its garden were located had been detached by More from his Chelsea estate in 1534 and given to his daughter Margaret and her husband William Roper. They had probably lived on a portion of this property, known as Butts Close, for some time but in 1534 More – the lawyer – wanted to make their occupation legal. Perhaps the transaction was no more than a belated wedding gift, but more likely the intention was to secure them a property if, in the difficult future that More anticipated, the worst came to the worst and his property was forfeit to the Crown. He was, of course, right to be worried. Danvers House had been built in the early 1620s by Sir John Danvers and was a remarkable pioneering classical villa inspired by the works of Palladio and other late Renaissance Italian architects (see page 49).

6. *Right*
Johannes Kip and Leonard Knyff's bird's-eye view of Chelsea village, made c. 1700 but published 1707-09. Lindsey House is on the far left, behind it, Gorges House, then, looking east (right), Beaufort House, with just visible the Inigo Jones designed pedimented gate of 1621 at the north end of the garden and leading on to the King's Road. Then the gardens of Danvers House, demolished shortly before this view was made, with, to their north, the quadrangular set of gardens occupying Dovecot Close that served as the kitchen garden to Beaufort House. In the foreground is Duke Street, a westward extension of Cheyne Walk.

The House att Chelsey in the County of Middlesex one of th
Marquesse & Earle of Worcester Baron Herbert of Chepstow Raglan

L. Knyff. D.

Kingsinton House

of the Most Noble & Potent Prince Henry Duke of Beaufort
and Knight of the Most Noble order of the Garter.

J. Kip Scu.

MUTARE VEL TIMERE SPERNO

In the early Tudor period ... Chelsea found itself in the centre of royal, political and merchant power.

Shrewsbury House

The first significant house in the village, according to Lysons, had been built in the late fourteenth century by Thomas Beauchamp, the 12th Earl of Warwick – the nemesis of Richard II – and was later occupied by 'George Earl of Shrewsbury, an eminent military character in the reign of Henry VIII' who appears to have been residing in Chelsea as early as 1519 (*Survey of London: Volume 2*, Chelsea, Part I, ed. Walter H. Godfrey, LCC, London, 1909, pp. 76–81). The house was also occupied by his grandson, the 6th Earl and also named George, who inherited the title and house in 1560 and who, in 1568, was appointed by Elizabeth I as the 'keeper' – in effect gaoler – of Mary, Queen of Scots. The previous year the Earl became the fourth husband of Elizabeth Hardwick, better known to history as 'Bess of Hardwick', who was a prodigious and inspired builder and later

7. Below
Shrewsbury House in c. 1795 as depicted in a wash drawing from an extra illustrated edition of Daniel Lysons' *Environs of London, Volume 2, Middlesex.*

Shrewsbury House, Chelsea.

the client for the miraculous Hardwick Hall in Derbyshire. Bess and Mary spent much time together during the years she was in the earl's charge. There is no record of her being in the house in the Chelsea but it is possible and it is tempting to imagine that Bess beautified the old house but, if so, this is now an utterly lost work.

Bess outlived the Earl by seventeen years, having inherited the house at his death in 1590. She bequeathed it to her son by her second marriage, who was later created the Earl of Devonshire. His widow lived in the house until her death in 1643, when it was purchased by Joseph Alston, seemingly a Royalist because he was created a baronet after the Restoration of 1660. The house gradually descended down the social scale, owned by far less eminent families and occupied by tenants. In the early eighteenth century Shrewsbury House was, according to an early historian of Chelsea, Thomas Faulkner, acquired by a Robert Butler and then went 'into the possession of Mr. Tate, and was occupied as a stained paper manufactory' (Thomas Faulkner, *An Historical and Topographical Account of Chelsea, and its Environs*, 2nd edition, 1829). Thomas Richardson's 1769 map of the Cadogan Estate and Manor of Chelsea is a curious affair because it excludes representation of non-estate freeholds and its large scale makes pin-point precision difficult, but it appears to show Shrewsbury House in the ownership of 'Mrs State, late Dr. Butler'. Richardson presumably means Mrs Tate, and Dr Butler was Robert Butler's son (see pages 70–1).

During the eighteenth century the mansion continued to dwindle in importance and in 1795 housed a paper manufactory (*Environs of London*, pp. 78–90). Faulkner states in the second edition of *Chelsea, and its Environs* (vol. 1, 1829, p. 282), that what remained of the mansion was demolished in 1813.

The exact location and probable appearance of this seminal Chelsea mansion is pondered at length, in most poetic manner, in the 1909 edition of the *Survey of London* dealing with this portion of Chelsea: 'The visitor to Chelsea will find no one to direct him if he asks for Shrewsbury House, the very memory of the old mansion of the Earls of Shrewsbury seems to have departed, and even those who are versed in the local history have disagreed regarding its exact site.' But, with an excitement that is still palpable, the author of the *Survey* assures his readers that the house's 'position can be identified' and that 'some actual remains of the original house are still to be seen' (*Survey of London: Volume 2*, pp. 76–81). The compelling evidence is a lease of 1711 for 46, 47 and 48 Cheyne Walk, which 'stand just east of Cheyne Row' and that describes the houses as 'adjoining Shrewsbury House upon the east' with, in 1909, the east wall of number 46 attached to 'a group of buildings that possess clear proof of having been on their present site long before the destruction of Shrewsbury House in 1813'. In the *Survey*'s opinion, 'These buildings may fairly claim, therefore, to be either part of the original house, or to have been incorporated with it at some early period,' partly because they contain 'casement windows of the same appearance as those in the early views of Shrewsbury House'.

In addition, the *Survey* discovered that the 'boundary wall between the garden of no. 46 and the land at the rear … is a fine specimen of undoubted Tudor brickwork' and 'parallel with this wall at a distance of something over 100 feet to the east is another Tudor wall of the same long and narrow red bricks bonded in the old English manner'.

As to the appearance of the building, there is little evidence beyond a wash drawing of its courtyard that appears 'in the extra illustrated edition of Lyson's [sic] *Environs* at the Guildhall Library' (*Survey of London: Volume 2*, pp. 76–81) and a poor quality

8. Above
Numbers 42 to 49 (from right to left) Cheyne
Walk in the 1890s, drawn by W.W. Burgess,
looking towards the King's Head and Eight
Bells on the corner of Cheyne Row and the
recently completed tall Carlyle Mansions,
with the tower of the Old Church in the
background. The decrepit numbers 42 to 45
were eventually demolished in the late 1920s
after a tough but futile conservation battle.
At the time it was argued that the gabled
number 45 was the surviving west wing of the
late medieval Shrewsbury House, see page 24.

engraving in the 1829 edition of Faulkner's *Chelsea, and its Environs*, which shows part of a courtyard framed by two-storey buildings asymmetrical in plan and form, and with gables of different dimensions. As was usual from the late fourteenth century to the late sixteenth century, the mansion appears – as Faulkner implies – to have been organised around a large central courtyard, and while the illustrations do not confirm the exact location of the mansion, the engraving does offer some evidence. As the *Survey* points out, in Lysons' 'engraving … on the left-hand (i.e., the west) side are shown some buildings, apparently of the 18th century, which bear a marked resemblance to part of the existing … Nos. 43 and 44 [Cheyne Walk]' that 'still contains the relics of a fine stairway, some good panelling, and a carved chimney-piece on the second floor'. Number 45, which broke south towards the river, was, speculated the *Survey*, essentially the west wing of Shrewsbury House. Faulkner evidently remembered Shrewsbury House when it still stood and recalled that it occupied three sides of a quadrangle but, argues the Survey, 'there are many reasons for supposing that there was originally a fourth side which would have fronted [the river], and from which the wings may have projected forward to form gables' (*Survey of London: Volume 2*, pp. 76–81).

The author of the *Survey of London: Volume 2* seems to have been persuaded that 'the discovery on the ground floor of the later buildings' (43 and 44 Cheyne Walk) with 'two sides of a room apparently in situ, with panelling and two doorways of the 17th century' was further evidence of the survival of part of Shrewsbury House. In 1909, however, this fascinating evidence seemed not long for this world: 'The whole block of buildings [forming 43–45 Cheyne Walk] is in a very poor condition. In most parts the brickwork is sound; but the woodwork, unless cared for, will soon perish: the 17th century

9. Above
The four houses – built c. 1695–1705 – formed a small square or court closing the north end of Lawrence Street. The pair on the right (east) were occupied by 1718 by the Duchess of Monmouth. In the early 1740s the Chelsea Porcelain Factory was located in and behind the houses on the left. This characterful group – shown here in around 1800–10 by Marianne Rush – was demolished in 1835.

10. Above right
The magnificent Jervoise monument, dated 1563 and an early example of English Renaissance design, in the north aisle of Chelsea Old Church, adjoining the Lawrence Chapel. In the 1540s or 1550s the Jervoise family occupied the nearby Old Manor House.

panelling is falling to pieces' (*Survey of London: Volume 2*). On the other hand, 46–48 Cheyne Walk – originally three houses but by 1909 two separate houses with 47 joined to 46 – 'seem to be in good condition' noted the Survey (*Survey of London: Volume 2*, pp. 82–3) The houses appear to have been built soon after the building lease of 1711, and were somewhat altered. Numbers 43 and 44 Cheyne Walk are shown in a watercolour perspective looking west, produced in 1858 by Henry and Walter Greaves. The view extends past the turning into Cheyne Row as far as the east end of Chelsea Old Church. The watercolour shows numbers 43 to 45 breaking far forward of 47 and 48, indeed to the extent that 46 is masked. The houses are shown as two storeys in height, modest in scale, rendered, and the house adjoining number 46 to the east – number 45 – was furnished with a tall gable. Another Greaves view, dated 1861 and looking east from the corner of Cheyne Row, also shows 45 Cheyne Walk

breaking forward and gabled. Undoubtedly this building looks pre-eighteenth century. As predicted by the *Survey*, 43 and 44 (and 45) were demolished, but not until the late 1920s to be replaced first by a house deigned by Sir Edwin Lutyens and ultimately in 1937 by a tall apartment block named Shrewsbury House (see page 296). Numbers 46, 47, 48 – a mixed group with eighteenth-century façades of different dates – survive, but significantly altered, since 1858. Number 47 is shown on the Greaves watercolour with a very early eighteenth-century brick front. This front is now painted. Number 48 remains much the same but number 49, a modest two-storey building in 1858 (of indeterminate eighteenth-century date), was replaced before 1900 by a four-storey house designed in the manner of the 1830s or 1840s.

The building of the late 1930s apartment block has left the party wall of 46 Cheyne Walk painfully exposed, but it also opened up a view of the long east garden wall, described in the *Survey*. Much of it is indeed composed of Tudor brickwork, and it is very impressive. Other remnants of the buildings and boundaries of Tudor Chelsea can be seen in garden walls behind the 1830s houses on the east side of Paultons Square and in what Thea Holme described in the early 1970s as a builder's yard on the east side of Danvers Street (Thea Holme, *Chelsea*, London: Hamish Hamilton, 1972, p. 51). All are presumably remnants of structures on Sir Thomas More's estate.

Chelsea Old Manor House

A most significant early mansion in the village was the Old Manor House that, with its gardens and outbuildings, lay to the east of Church Lane (now Old Church Street), stretching around the north and east sides of the parish church. The Old Manor House dated from the late fourteenth century, if not earlier (*Victoria County History*, pp. 108–15), and in 1795 Lysons wrote that Henry VIII, in possession of the manor, had 'parted' with it 'to the ancestors of Sir Thomas Lawrence, having built a new house upon another site (*The Environs of London*, p. 77). The Sir Thomas that Lysons is referring to is the eminent portrait painter, active in the late eighteenth and early nineteenth centuries, but if indeed related to the family he did not live or work in its Chelsea house because, as Lysons observed in 1795, it had been 'pulled down many years ago', with 'a row of houses' now supplying 'the place of the old mansion'. (*Environs of London*, pp. 77–8). The 'row of houses' that Lysons is referring to form part of Lawrence Street with, by tradition, the site of the Old Manor at its north end. But this location is contested. The *Victoria County History* (*VCH*) states unequivocally that 'the belief that the manor house lay on the site of the houses known in the eighteenth century as Monmouth House, at the north end of the later Lawrence Street, is unfounded'. The *VCH* suggests that it was likely that the manor lay just north of the Old Church (*Victoria County History*, p. 14).

The history of the Old Manor is brief but a trifle complex. It had perhaps been rebuilt between 1485 and 1503 when Sir Reginald Bray was Lord of the Manor and which he, along with the manor estate, surrendered in 1510 to Lord Sandys. In 1536 Sandys conveyed the manor to Henry VIII as part of an exchange. However, the king did not occupy the Old Manor House, instead occupying a new and larger manor house on a nearby site to the east, and he soon rid himself of the overlordship of Westminster Abbey (see *Survey of London: Volume 4, Chelsea, Part II*, ed. Walter H. Godfrey, LCC, 1913, pp. 58–9; *Victoria County History*, pp. 108–15). In fact, the king did not 'part' with the Old Manor to the Lawrence family as Lysons states. He seems to have immediately lost interest in the house, which in the 1540s or 1550s was leased to Richard Jervoise. A spectacular Jervoise monument, in the form of a large triumphal arch, survives in Chelsea Old Church. It is dated 1563

although Faulkner suggests Jervoise died in 1557 because in that year the house was granted to a John Caryll and in 1583, purchased by Thomas Lawrence, a goldsmith (see *Survey of London: Volume 4*, pp. 58–9; *Survey of London: Volume 7, Chelsea, Part III (the Old Church)*, ed. Walter H. Godfrey, LCC, London, 1921, pp. 14–28).

Interestingly, the manor's or 'Lord's' chapel in the church remained in the possession of the occupants of the old manor house – presumably Henry had no interest in a chapel in a modest village church – and from the 1580s became, and remains, the Lawrence Chapel.

Confusion now sets in. Faulkner (*Chelsea, and its Environs*, p. 266) states that in 1714 Ann, Duchess of Monmouth, wife of the Duke of Monmouth who was executed in 1685 for leading a Protestant uprising, 'resided in the great house in Lawrence-street'. For long it was assumed that the 'great house' or old manor house stood on what became the north end of Lawrence Street. However, the consensus now is that this is not the case. Additionally, the duchess could hardly have occupied the 'great house' in 1714 because, according to Dr King, it had been demolished before 1704 (see his *Transcript*), with the *Victoria County History* suggesting demolition took place soon after 1687 (*Victoria County History*, pp. 31–40).

In fact, in 1714 the site at the north end of Lawrence Street was occupied by a group of four houses, organised rather charmingly around a small three-sided court or square, two on the north side and one each on the west and east sides. These houses were built as a speculation on Lawrence-owned land between c. 1695 and 1705, when they were included by Dr King in his description of Chelsea, written in, or soon after, 1705. King's manuscript includes a survey plan on which 'Laurence [sic] street' is shown and named (see page 85). These houses, forming a court at the north end of the street, are clearly shown. Placed in the centre of the composition, between the two houses on the north side of the court, was an arched-over passage, served by two doors, leading to the rear gardens and no doubt to a set of cesspits. Above these two doors was a shared pedimented hood, a most happy design that surely gave the occasional clearing of the cesspits by night soil men some dignity.

Dr King's plan also shows a group of houses on the east side of the street, closing the vista east along Justice Walk from Church Lane. This group includes what are now numbers 23 and 24 Lawrence Street. These were built in 1705–06, at just about the time of Dr King's survey. Additional houses were soon built to create a complex but intriguing building history for this small street, the southern part of which was probably complete by 1689 (see page 86). Its story is told in great detail in the 1913 edition of the *Survey of London*, which observes that the existing 23 and 24 Lawrence Street – now notable for their adjoining front doors sharing a pedimented hood – 'have the appearance of originally being one house'. The *Survey* also speculates that the pedimented hood is 'quite possibly the same hood' as that which formerly adorned the house occupied by the Duchess of Monmouth (*Survey of London: Volume 4*, pp. 58–9). However, in recent years the possible relationship between the duchess and these houses has been ruled out. For example, *the Victoria County History* volume on the County of Middlesex, published in 2004, confirms unreservedly that the duchess occupied the houses, with the paired and pedimented doors, at the north end of Lawrence Street. Sadly, this most interesting group was demolished in 1835 for the creation of the west arm of Upper Cheyne Row. But there is something strange about this story. The pedimented double doors are of an unusual design, but presumably merely reflect the taste of

a speculating builder active on Lawrence land. The odd thing is that 23 and 24 Lawrence Street are named Duke's House and Monmouth House (*Victoria County History*, pp. 31–40). It must be assumed these names dates from the time when it was assumed the duchess and these houses had a connection.

The western houses in the lost group at the north end of Lawrence Street were occupied from 1742 by Nicholas Sprimont, the Huguenot entrepreneur behind the establishment of the nearby Chelsea porcelain manufactory (see *Survey of London: Volume 2*, p. 86), and from 1750 to 1762 by the novelist Tobias Smollett. Rocque's map of 1744–6, too large in scale and lacking in detail, does not make things absolutely clear. Church Lane (now Old Church Street), the main north–south thoroughfare, is easy to see, striking north to the King's Road and beyond. To its east and parallel is Lawrence Street, the south and central portions framed with buildings, and the street does terminate with a small court or square at its north end, making it a cul-de-sac. However, the court is not shown fully built up, although this must be where Monmouth House stood. Presumably this is a slight error on the part of the cartographer, but it does little to help clarify a confusing building history. North of the court, built upon or not, was mostly open ground – including the Rectory and its large garden – as far as the line of the King's Road.

Sir Thomas More's estate and Beaufort House

From the Old Church and Church Lane (Old Church Street), stretching as far west as Milman's Street and north from the river to the King's Road, lay the estate that from 1524 More assembled in the delightful fields of Chelsea. By this time he had become one of the pillars of the Tudor state, being the secretary and personal advisor to the king. More had trained as a lawyer but mixed in the elevated circles of the

11. Right
Detail of Dr King's survey of c. 1705 that
corresponds closely to Kip's bird's-eye view of
c. 1700. To the left (west), is the 'E of Lindsey's
House' standing next to the 'footpath to
Little Chelsey' (now Milman's Street) which
led to 'Queen's Road' (now King's Road)
and continued north as 'Lover's Walk' (now
Park Walk). To the east of Lindsey House and
garden was the 'D of Beaufort's House', the
site of Danvers House and garden, described
as 'Ld Wharton's Gdn' with the stub of
Danvers Street marking the route of the drive
that led to the lost Danvers House. To the east
is Church Lane (now Old Church Street).

Northern Renaissance and – with his enquiring mind, shrewd wisdom, piety and probity – had forged a lasting friendship with Desiderius Erasmus, one of the sharpest intellects of the age. They had met in 1499 when More was twenty-one and studying law at Lincoln's Inn, and Erasmus was on his first journey to London. Both men were humanists, with a deep belief in the almost divine and certainly elevating attributes of education and scholarship, and both were questioning the established Roman Catholic church and open to aspects of the coming religious revolution that was to be termed the Protestant Reformation. However, both, after much inner thought and rational debate, remained true to their Roman Catholic convictions and belief in the Pope as head of the Christian church. Indeed, More, in an almost irrational manner, developed an intense distaste for Christians who deviated from the Catholic path and lapsed into what he regarded as heresy.

By the early 1520s Thomas More had achieved much. He had navigated with morals and principles unsullied and intact through a political and diplomatic career, having been a member of parliament, an undersheriff of the City of London, since 1514 a Privy Counsellor and since 1521 an under-treasurer of the Exchequer,

which brought with it a knighthood. And he was still in the ascendency. In 1523 he was elected Speaker of the House of Commons, in 1525 Chancellor of the Duchy of Lancaster and in 1529 he won one of the great and glittering prizes of state when he was appointed Lord Chancellor. He was well on the way to being one of the most brilliant – and powerful – courtiers of the Tudor age. So his time at Chelsea should have been sweet – and at first it was.

From 1524 More started to acquire farmland, meadows and gardens, along with modest buildings, from various freeholders to assemble his Chelsea estate. He even secured a house and a wharf – called Butts Close – so that he could be sure of access to the river and ease of loading and unloading goods. (*Victoria County History*, pp. 115–18). Life was good. As the *Survey of London* observed in 1913, More 'loved to escape from London and from the Court, and to give himself up to his family and his own literary pursuits in his Chelsea home, and here he entertained many friends, among whom were Erasmus and Holbein' (*Survey of London: Volume 4*, pp. 18–27). In fact no one now believes Erasmus visited More in Chelsea (Holme, p. 3).

The exact location of More's initial or primary home on his estate remains debated. It is generally agreed that he

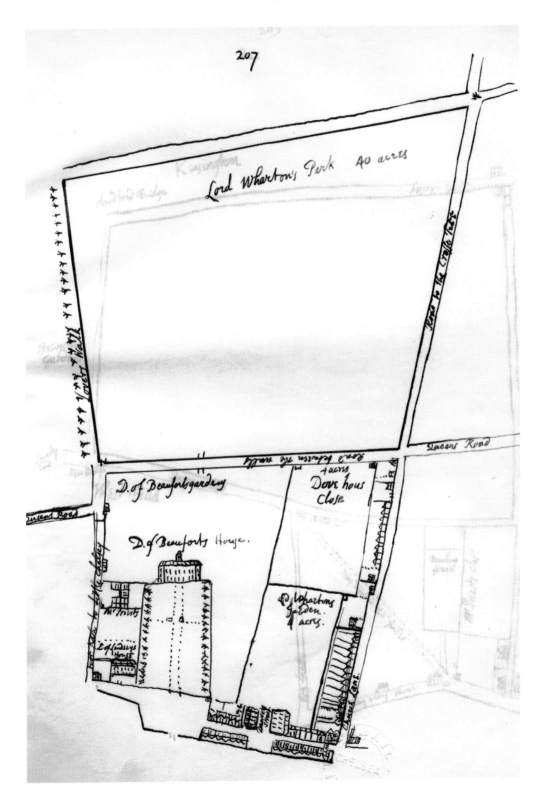

207

Lord Wharton's Park   40 acres

D. of Beauforts garden

D. of Beauforts House.

Dove hous Close

4 acres

L? Whartons garden. 4 acres.

Queens Road

12. Above
Sir Thomas More and his family in their Chelsea home,
painted by Rowland Lockey in c. 1593, copying a now lost
original of c. 1527 by Hans Holbein. More sits in the centre,
the figure in front of him – staring out of the painting and
who in his looks and pose is strangely reminiscent of Henry
VIII – is Henry Patenson, the man More employed as his
'fool' or jester.

did build the mansion that became known as Beaufort House, containing a chapel, library and gallery, however it seems likely that he initially occupied and possibly extended an existing building. This might well have been a medieval house, close to the riverside. (*Victoria County History*, pp. 115–18).

However, what is known with a degree of accuracy is where More's 'new building' stood and what it looked like, or at least how it was planned. This is because between 1592 and 1597 an accurate drawn survey of More's 'new building' – as it then existed – was made for its new owner, Lord Burghley or his son Sir Robert Cecil, from 1605 the 1st Earl of Salisbury. Cecil was a courtier with great and enduring political power during the latter reign of Queen Elizabeth and during the reign of James I, and who in 1611 was the client for the prodigious Hatfield House in Hertfordshire. It must, however, be pointed out that the authority of these drawings as a survey of the house as More knew it is contested. No one doubts that it was carried out for Burghley or Cecil but, as the *Victoria County History* points out, by that time More's house could have been substantially altered by subsequent owners, in particular the Marquess of Winchester who is documented as having put up 'new buildings' on the estate before his death in 1572. As it explains, 'the design of the house itself', as shown in Kip's view of c. 1700, is a good indication 'that the house shown in the Cecil survey plan of c. 1595, and later known as Beaufort House, was built by Winchester and not by Sir Thomas More' (*Victoria County History*, pp. 14–26 and 115–18).

The 1590s survey plans, along with some tentative plans for altering and enlarging the house, survive in the archives of Hatfield House. The plans show the ground and first floors. They are remarkably interesting and, if in fact of More's house, make it possible to imagine the world he and his family occupied, along with their

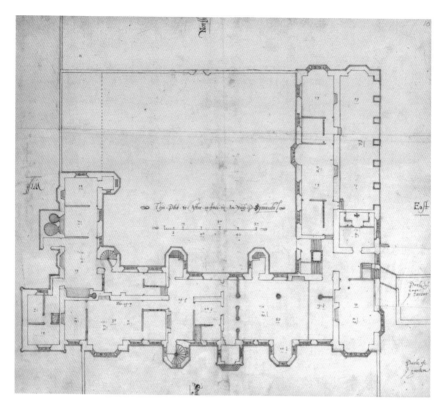

13 and 14. Above
Survey plans showing ground floor (left) and first floor (right) of Sir Thomas More's house, that became known as Beaufort House. These plans were made by John Symonds, between c. 1592 and 1597 for William Cecil, Lord Burghley and his son Sir William Cecil. These record the house occupied by Sir Thomas, although almost certainly with significant later sixteenth-century alterations and additions.

guests such as Hans Holbein. They also offer an insight into sixteenth-century Chelsea domestic architecture.

The south, main front of the house was remarkably symmetrical with a central two-storey porch that was flanked by canted bays, one containing a newel staircase, the other an oriel window. The porch led to a screens passage with the great hall to the east and buttery, pantry, servants' hall, kitchen and service quarters to the west. These were extended to the north in a short wing.

At the east end of the great hall was a dais where family and guests could eat in state on ceremonial occasions. East and north of the dais were, as tradition dictated, family rooms. These included a parlour, probably for more informal and private dining, lit by large but shallow oriel windows on its east and south walls – the latter matched for symmetry's sake by an oriel at the west

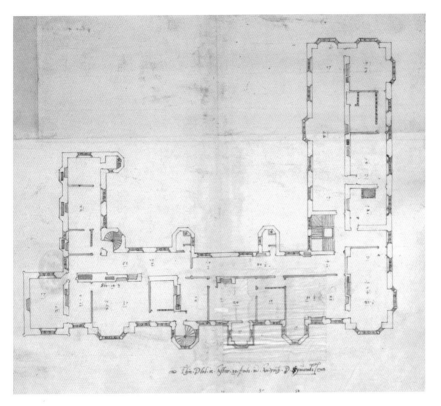

end of the south front that lit what was the servants' hall or kitchen. Northwest of the parlour was a grand ceremonial staircase that the family would have used to reach the great chamber and bedroom apartments on the first floor. Opposite the staircase, set against the east wall of the house, was a chapel, seemingly double height, with those on the first-floor portion being able to see the altar, located at ground level, during mass by means of a shaft cut into the floor. North of the chapel and staircase was a wing – with an open, east-facing loggia that must have been a delight on sunny summer mornings – which the Survey concluded was largely an addition to the house after More's ownership. Set against the north wall of the main range was a pair of garderobe towers containing privies, one off the hall and so presumably for family and guests, and the other off the wide corridor leading to the kitchen and so presumably for servants. The first floor is remarkable

for a plan offering comfort, privacy and convenience. Rooms here were not entered by passing one through another, which was usual in the sixteenth century, but by means of a generous gallery forming a corridor set along the north front and turning north into the east wing. The gallery was reached not only by the main staircase but also by a wide newel staircase at its west end, giving direct access to the kitchen and service quarters below.

To the south of the corridor, and grouped in the centre of the house, appear to have been two adjoining three-room apartments, each presumably comprising a bed chamber, private parlour and closet. The apartment to the west had contact with the newel staircase in the canted bay and so had direct and speedy connection with the ground floor. The apartment to the east had the upper portion of the well-glazed oriel that also helped light the great hall below. By the late sixteenth century, when it was common to have a single-storey great hall, the large room above it generally served as the great chamber, which became the family's more intimate and private gathering place. A similar three-room apartment is shown contrived in the east wing, which also contained, on its west side, a long gallery. Was More's house ahead of its time or does this plan show, as the *Victoria County History* suspects, a late sixteenth-century remodelling or proposal?

The room in the southeast corner of the main range, set above the ground-floor parlour could, alternatively, have been the great chamber or, more likely, the high parlour or solar. This must certainly have been a most handsome room with its two well glazed shallow oriels on its south and east walls allowing light to flood inside from the morning onwards.

Off the gallery were the two garderobe towers and, interestingly, a screen is suggested just to the east of the west garderobe tower. This suggests the gallery was divided into two portions – to the east for family and guests, and to the west largely for servants, although the occupants of the west apartment would no doubt have made use of this perhaps lower status part of the gallery. Or perhaps not, because the plan shows that a lobby was contrived at the junction of the two apartments so that those occupying the west apartment could in fact enter it from the higher status east portion of the gallery. All most subtle, and suggesting an insight into the hierarchies that governed the occupation of Tudor great houses.

Information about the appearance of More's Chelsea home, and some feel for its atmosphere, is provided by Erasmus, who observed that More 'hath built near London upon the Thames a commodious house, neither mean nor subject to envy, yet magnificent enough'. Of family life,

it is evident that the City household that Erasmus had earlier admired still thrived, as one might expect, when transported to the idyllic setting of rural, riverside Chelsea. Here Erasmus noted, More 'converseth with his family, his wife, his son and daughter-in-law, his three daughters and their husbands, with eleven grandchildren'. It was Erasmus who furnished Hans Holbein with an introduction to More. So one day in 1526, the twenty-nine-year old artist arrived in Chelsea and, as far as any one now knows, lived in More's house for much of his two-year sojourn in England. More's Chelsea house became a popular resort with many, including the king. He would have himself rowed up or down river, from Westminster or Hampton Court, or dropped in on the way between the two, invited or not, for discourse or amusement with More in his pretty Chelsea garden.

It also became a place of trial – indeed of inquisition – for those whose religion did not please More, particularly Christians persuaded to support Martin Luther's protests against, and proposed reforms of, the Catholic Church. When Lord Chancellor More used his powers to suppress, punish or attempt to return a Protestant meanderer to the true Catholic path, his house at Chelsea became one of his centres of operations.

More's pursuit of heretics, and all that went with his offices of State came to an end in 1532. Henry VIII's determination to marry Anne Boleyn and his seemingly insatiable lust for wealth and uncontrolled power promised – for More – national catastrophe. His whole world – monastic life, scholarship, and Roman Catholic hierarchies admittedly in need of reform – now faced obliteration in England. More's philosophic dialogues in his Chelsea garden with Henry were over. This was to be a battle of wills. More must have realised that there could be only one victor if it came to mortal struggle with the king. More saw, with clarity, what was coming. He had given part of his Chelsea estate to his daughter and son-in-law and now he dispersed the rest to his family because if he were found guilty of treason his possessions would be forfeit to the Crown.

As Henry became more autocratic and grabbed more power for himself and more possessions from the Catholic Church, he wanted his actions vindicated and legitimised in the eyes of his peers and his subjects. Consequently, he demanded oaths of allegiance and, more specifically, from key characters an oath acknowledging his supremacy in points of law and faith. As he feared, More could not avoid the demand for his oath to the king and events took their unavoidable course. More refused to swear the oath of Supremacy that would have contradicted not only his faith in the Catholic Church but also, he argued, the terms of the Magna Carta and the laws of England. He was tried, condemned and in 1535 executed for treason. On the scaffold he declared his basic position in simple terms. He was, he stated 'the king's good servant' but 'God's first'. The same year Holbein accepted the post of 'King's Painter' from the man who had done most to drive More to his death. More was correct in his concern for his estate. Despite his precautions, his land and buildings in Chelsea were seized by the Crown, apart from the Butts Close portion that he had conveyed to his daughter and son-in-law. After More's death his house and the bulk of his estate was granted to Sir William Paulet, later the first Marquess of Winchester whose son relinquished both in 1575 to Lord Dacre and his wife. Lady Dacre perhaps added the wing to the northeast corner of More's former house, as recorded in 1597. Lady Dacre died in 1595, leaving More's former estate to Lord Burghley, who in 1597 passed it to his youngest son, Sir Robert Cecil. Cecil might have undertaken some works to the house, but cannot have done much, because in 1599 he sold the house and land to the Earl of Lincoln.

The Earl settled the house and land on his son-in-law Sir Arthur Gorges, who, after the earl's death in 1616, built on part of the estate, notably Gorges House, which stood to the southwest of More's house. During the following decades Gorges sold, leased or settled on family members various portions of the estate. At an early point, before 1620, More's house – more or less altered and extended – was sold to Lionel Cranfield, the Earl of Middlesex. Cranfield added to the portion of the estate he had purchased by acquiring land north of the King's Road on which he created a deer park, as shown on Kip's view of c. 1700. Cranfield also commissioned new buildings for the estate, most importantly a fine gate set on the drive leading south from the King's Road. The gate incorporated engaged Doric columns supporting a pediment and set against a screen formed with vermiculated rustication. The architect for the gate, designed in 1621, was Inigo Jones. This was a relatively early work for Jones and of intense interest because he had already established himself as the preferred architect of the Stuart court and was the first man to introduce – in significant and coherent manner – north Italian late Renaissance architecture, particularly the work of Andrea Palladio, into the British Isles. This architecture became the house style of the Stuart dynasty and of its courtiers to the outbreak of the Civil War. And it is fascinating that an early and particularly exquisite outrider of this style was built in Chelsea village.

Cranfield fell out of favour with the king and the Crown seized his land, which in 1627 Charles I granted to his hapless and incompetent favourite, the 1st Duke of Buckingham. After the duke's assassination in 1628, his family continued to live in the house until the Civil War when it was seized by Parliament. The 2nd Duke of Buckingham regained the house and estate following the Restoration but did not hold them long. They passed through the hands of the Earl of Bristol and were acquired

The most evocative physical memorial to More's time in Chelsea is formed by the fragments that survive in the old parish church.

15. Above
This pedimented gate was designed in 1621 by Inigo Jones to grace the King's Road entry to Beaufort House. In 1738 the gate was moved to Chiswick House, where it still stands.

16. Right
Details of the capitals in Sir Thomas More's chapel in Chelsea Old Church. They were carved in 1528, perhaps to the design of Hans Holbein, and show numerous emblems related to More's offices of state.

in 1682 by the Marquess of Worcester, who subsequently was made the Duke of Beaufort. Now known as Beaufort House, it was the focus of Kip's c. 1700 view over the western part of Chelsea. The house as shown bears clear connections to the house on the site surveyed in 1597, but there are also clear alterations and the north wing appears to have been removed. Inigo Jones's gate on the King's Road can just be made out. Beaufort's family retained the house until 1720, then, having fallen into some decline, it and its lands were purchased in 1724 to be turned into a school but, this venture failing, all was sold in 1737 to Sir Hans Sloane.

Sloane did not then live in Chelsea, although he already owned the New Manor House, and he did not buy Beaufort House so that he could repair and occupy what was almost certainly then the best house in Chelsea. Instead it was demolished by Sloane within three years, with the Inigo Jones gate dismantled in 1738 and sold by Sloane to his friend Lord Burlington, who re-erected it at Chiswick House, where it remains. The subsequent history of the grounds and the site of the house is strange. Beaufort Ground, as the site became known, was leased for ninety-one years to the Protestant Moravian community that was to soon acquire and occupy the nearby Lindsey House. A chapel was built and a burying ground laid out on the site of the former stable yard of Beaufort House (some graves can still be seen, along with a few ancient fig trees) but funds were not secured for the construction of a Moravian settlement – to be called Sharon – on the rest of Beaufort Ground. The Moravians pulled out of Chelsea in the mid-1770s, during which time building plots were granted on Beaufort Ground with, in 1781, Beaufort Street being laid out, crossing north–south through the site of More's house.

Chelsea Old Church

The most evocative physical memorial to More's time in Chelsea is formed by the fragments that survive in the old parish church. The origin of the church is ancient, certainly no later than the twelfth century, but its central and west portions – including the tower – were rebuilt c. 1670 (for details see Randall Davies, *Chelsea Old Church*, London: Duckworth & Co., 1904). The chancel, built of brick with stone quoins and window tracery, survived from a thirteenth-century rebuilding of the church, and is thus an early instance of the use of brick in post-Roman London. Immediately west of the chancel, on the north and south sides of the church, two large chantry chapels were added in about 1345. The one to the north was for the use of the lords of Chelsea Manor, and it was here that beadsmen were employed to pray for the dead of the manorial family. Placed around the interior of the church and in its burial ground were numerous monuments to leading local families. The church was a precious record of life in Chelsea over centuries past. (For more on the church, see pages 153-7). However, this world was blown apart in April 1941 when a large German mine, dropped by parachute, landed on or near the west end

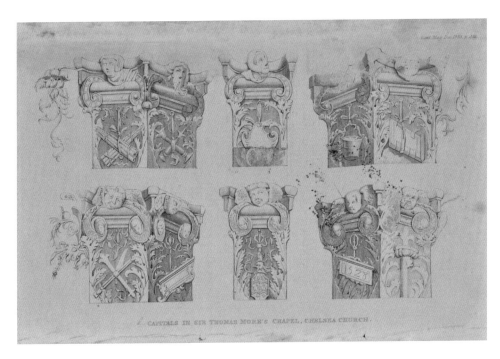

CAPITALS IN SIR THOMAS MORE'S CHAPEL, CHELSEA CHURCH.

of the church, toppling the tower on to the west and central part of the church. The destruction was appalling but what survived was remarkable. When the dust cleared there were portions of the north chapel and chancel still standing, as well as most of the walls of the south chapel. The north chapel had long been called the Lawrence Chapel, after the family that had acquired the Manor of Chelsea in 1583 and still held it when the old Manor House was demolished c. 1687. The south chapel was the More Chapel. This chapel had been acquired by Sir Thomas More in 1528 and was largely rebuilt by him. The date is on one of the capitals on a pier at the junction between chapel and chancel. The capitals are certainly unusual and personal because they take a most idiosyncratic and mannered Ionic form. They are topped with a type of Ionic volute with representations of cherubs' heads that are probably references to More's heraldic emblem of a Moor's head. In addition, there are symbols of his offices of State. The capitals are said to be have designed by Hans Holbein who, in 1528, was living at More's Chelsea home.

Within the chancel adjoinging the chapel is a four-centred arch beneath which is placed a low altar tomb, and on the wall above the tomb is a marble slab that bears a long epitaph. This was written in Latin by More himself and explains much about his life and the motifs for his actions. The tomb and slab are dated 1532, so More wrote his own epitaph as he saw his end approach, rapidly and remorselessly.

The tomb has probably been rebuilt since 1532 and the inscription has been restored, recut, even replaced. John Evelyn in his *Lives of Eminent Men* stated in the late seventeenth century that More's monument, 'being worn by time, about 1644 Sir John Lawrence of Chelsey erected to his memory a handsome inscription in marble' (*Lives of Eminent Men (Brief Lives)*, volume II, p. 463). A brass plate fixed to the marble states that the slab was 'restored' once again – probably recut – in 1833 (*Survey of London: Volume 7*, pp. 14–28). What of More's mortal remains? Having died a traitor's death by decapitation, the disposal of More's body and head was a troubling issue in 1535. His body was not carried back to his prepared Chelsea tomb but buried in St Peter ad Vincula in the Tower of London. His head was put on public display on London Bridge, at least for while, until it was obtained by his daughter Margaret. It was claimed that she interred the head in the Roper's ancestral vault beneath the chapel of St Nicholas in St Dunstan's Church, Canterbury. So the tomb in Chelsea is no tomb at all but a cenotaph, merely a monument to a person whose body lies elsewhere. More's supposed head was last seen in 1835 when the ceiling of the vault in St Dunstan's Church was broken into by accident and a head was revealed, placed behind a grill in a niche in a wall and housed in a leaden box (see *The Gentleman's Magazine*, May 1835, pp. 494–5). When Margaret died in 1544 she was interred in Chelsea Old Church. However, when years later her husband died and was placed in the Roper vault, she was moved to St Dunstan's to lie with him – and with the head of her father. So Margaret was laid with the man she had loved, and with the man that she adored. St Dunstan's Church survives and so – presumably – does St Thomas's head rest in its leaden box in the long-sealed Roper vault. Certainly that is what the pilgrims believe when they make their way to this small eleventh-century church.

The New Manor House: Chelsea Place
Henry VIII remains many things to many people, and perceptions of the man are often disconcertingly conflictive. However, most might agree that his behaviour was at times most odd and sinister in its seemingly uncontrolled narcissism. And in few places and times was his behaviour more odd than in Chelsea in the 1530s.

Henry made demands on Sir Thomas More – a man at one time he admired greatly – that he knew would, more likely than not, lead to More's 1535 death by execution. So what did Henry do? He brazenly moved into Chelsea by acquiring the house and estate next door to the home of the man he had entrapped and driven to his death. Charitably, it can be argued that Henry had fallen in love with the beautiful riverside village during his many visits there during the 1520s to talk with More. It would be reasonable to assume that More's violent death, and the circumstances surrounding it, would, for Henry, have dampened the delights of Chelsea. Instead, it seems he wanted to acquire what More had possessed and enjoyed, much as he had earlier acquired and enjoyed Cardinal Wolsey's delightful Hampton Court Palace and the palace of York Place, Whitehall. So in 1536, a year after More's execution, Henry got his hands on the manor house and manor of Chelsea, standing immediately to the east of More's former estate. However, he did not keep the house long. Indeed, he seems never to have stayed there. As we have seen, from 1536 Henry occupied the New Manor House, a fifth of a mile to the east of the Old Manor House and fronting south on to the river. This is one of the more intriguing lost buildings of London.

Until recent times the assumption is that the New Manor House was purpose-designed for Henry, seemingly being completed around 1543, and one of the sixty or so palaces or mansions he built or acquired during his long reign. However, the Victoria County History volume on Chelsea paints a different picture: 'there is no contemporary evidence', it points out, to show the manor was built for Henry, instead suggesting that it was 'probably' built by Sir Reginald Bray or Lord Sandys just before, and certainly by, 1519 when Sandys is known to have let the Old Manor House. Improvements and repairs are recorded in 1536 or 1537 when prefabricated timber frame components were transported from Whitehall for the construction of closets for the king and the queen, and in November 1537 plants, including bay and rosemary, were sent from Charterhouse to the king's gardener for use at Chelsea.

There are virtually no early representations of the New Manor House – often referred to as Chelsea Place – but, as already mentioned, Dr King in his plan of the central portion of Chelsea village suggests that the New Manor House had a conventional plan with ranges disposed around a quadrangular court. Presumably there was a great hall, high chamber and parlours in the main range shown facing the river. We can assume that state bedrooms, lodgings, kitchen, buttery and pantry were in the east and west ranges, with offices and porters' lodges and guardrooms in the north range that contained the main, towered, entrance gate. Dr King's Manuscript Account of Chelsea was no doubt composed over a period of time but internal evidence suggests a start date of around 1705, which it also a reasonable date to ascribe to his survey plan.

A poor quality image of this 'North Front' of the New Manor House was published in 1810 by Thomas Faulkner and shows a two-storey battlemented entrance block with a Tudor Gothic door and four chimney breasts breaking forward like buttresses and topped by pairs of tall chimneys that read as towers. In a sense it was a reduced version of the standard Tudor entrance gate of the type built in the 1530s at St James's Palace. To the west of this gate is shown a three-storey and a two-storey range, of simple design but with large mullioned and transomed windows (Faulkner, Chelsea, and its Environs, plate bound opposite page 311).

Faulkner's elevation appears to be based on a perspective included on James Hamilton's Chelsea map of 1717, an update of a survey of 1664 that was also published by Faulkner in volume I of the 1829 edition of his *Historical and Topographical Account of Chelsea, and its Environs*. Dr King explains that the original of this 'actual survey of the parish of Chelsea' by Hamilton was in the 'possession of the late Mr. Cadogan', suggesting that he had been commissioned by the Cadogan family. Henry VIII first occupied the manor during the aftermath of his brief and deadly marriage to Anne Boleyn, who was executed in May 1536, and during his ill-fated and equally fatal marriage to Jane Seymour, who died in October 1537 soon after giving birth to the future Edward VI. It is perhaps little wonder, given his personal tribulations and the enormity of the implications of the break with Rome and of the Reformation, that there is no evidence that Henry showed 'interest' in, or enjoyment of, Chelsea. He probably enjoyed precious little at the time and perhaps gloomy associations with Sir Thomas could not be shaken off.

A subtle indication of Henry's attitude towards New Manor House is the fact that in 1544 he gave it as part of her dowry to his sixth and final wife, Katharine Parr. It is hard to know what, if anything, is to be read into this but certainly the building must, for the king, have had some sombre associations. Perhaps giving it to his new wife was in a sense an exorcism, a break with past ill fortune. Whatever the meaning, three years later Henry was dead and the 'Queen-Dowager', at just thirty-five years of age, took up permanent residence in the manor, accompanied by the royal jewellery and court gowns that she was permitted to retain. Her life was far from quiet. First she was given charge of her fourteen-year old stepdaughter, Princess Elizabeth, whose mother was the ill-fated Anne Boleyn. Elizabeth was close in line to the throne but she had powerful enemies, so Katharine's position was most political. Secondly, as if all this was not enough, Katharine resolved to marry her old flame, Thomas Seymour. This would be

her fourth marriage and his first. Seymour was the brother of Jane Seymour and thus uncle to the underage King Edward VI. This marriage to his brother-in-law's former wife and his nephew's stepmother was legal, although more than a little odd. After Katharine's death following complications in childbirth in September 1548 and Thomas's inglorious traitor's death after having been caught, in most curious and suspicious circumstances with a loaded pistol outside King Edward VI's apartment in Hampton Court, the New Manor House was forfeit to the Crown. In 1551, Edward VI granted the manor to John Dudley, the 1st Earl of Warwick and later the Duke of Northumberland. However, the manor continued to be stalked by violent death.

After Edward VI's death in 1553, Northumberland promoted the claim to the throne of his daughter-in-law Lady Jane Grey. This was unwise and led to the deaths of both of them in 1554, victims of the wrath of Queen Mary I. Interestingly, Mary's vengeance did know bounds and Northumberland's widow was permitted to remain in the manor until her death in 1555. By all accounts the death, although speedy, was natural. From 1560 to 1638 the Crown leased the manor to various grandees, including the widow of Lord Protector Somerset and in 1591 to the wife of Lord Howard of Effingham, later Earl of Nottingham and the commander in 1588 of the English forces that defeated the Spanish Armada. In 1638 James Hamilton, later the Duke of Hamilton, bought the lease and soon was granted the manor by Charles I. Soon after this date Hamilton appears to have added a large wing to the west side of the Tudor manor house.

Hamilton fought for Charles during the Civil War and, remaining active in the king's cause after his defeat, was deemed a traitor by Parliament and executed in March 1649, adding another name to the manor's grisly roll call of executed

Henry VIII ... was at times most odd ... and in few places ... was his behaviour more odd than in Chelsea in the 1530s.

17. Below
The 'north front' of the New Manor House, which was the landward elevation looking towards the King's Road – as illustrated by Thomas Faulkner in his *Chelsea, and its Environs*. The plate is dated 1810. The New Manor house was occupied by or built by Henry VIII in 1536 and Faulkner's elevation shows a mix of what appear to be early Tudor and seventeenth-century buildings.

incumbents. In his will the duke had left the manor to his brother William, but he died in 1651 while fighting for the Royalist cause in the forlorn Battle of Worcester. The manor house and manor passed to Parliament, which did little with it beyond seemingly deciding, in about 1655, that the Tudor manor house and its 1630s wing should be considered as two separate dwellings. In 1657 negotiations started for the sale of the manor and the Tudor manor house to Charles Cheyne, a gentleman from Buckinghamshire who had acquired considerable wealth by his marriage in 1654 to the daughter of William Cavendish, Duke of Newcastle. The deal survived the collapse of the Commonwealth and the Restoration of Charles II and by 1661 Cheyne was in possession. Cheyne was in favour with the new regime and was created Viscount Newhaven in 1681. At his death in 1698 Cheyne left his estates to his former and current wives and to his son William, who did not reside in Chelsea but in 1708 made a significant contribution towards the already growing urbanisation

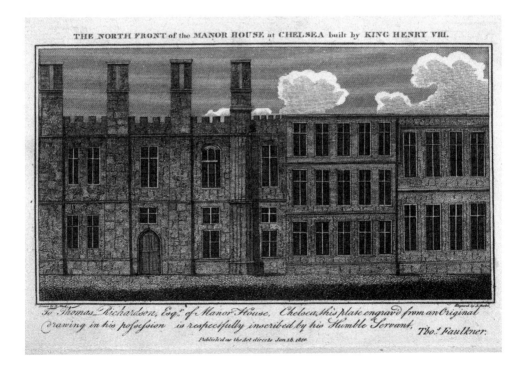

THE NORTH FRONT of the MANOR HOUSE at CHELSEA built by KING HENRY VIII.

To Thomas Richardson, Esq.ʳ of Manor House, Chelsea, this plate engraved from an Original Drawing in his possession is respectfully inscribed by his Humble Servant, Thoˢ Faulkner.

Publish'd as the Act directs Jan.16. 1810.

of the village by letting building leases for houses in Cheyne Row (see page 92).
In 1712/13 William Cheyne, Viscount Newhaven, sold the manor of Chelsea, advowson of Chelsea Parish church, the New Manor House and numerous other 'great houses' to Hans Sloane, a eminent physician and obsessive collector of specimens of natural history. At the same time Charles Cheyne's second wife, the former Countess of Radnor, who had inherited property in Chelsea at her husband's death and who herself was to die in 1714, also sold her interests in Chelsea to Sloane (see Danvers House, p. 49).

In 1716 Sloane, an eminent figure in the Enlightenment, was created a baronet; his wealth and fame increased and he continued the Cheyne interest in property speculation. This had, after all, become an ever-increasing occupation of London landlords and builders since the miraculously speedy and profitable rebuilding of the City after the Great Fire of 1666, largely through the mechanism of speculative house building. Cheyne and several of his contemporaries in Chelsea had seen the great potential of the exercise, notably the Lawrence family (see page 84). Although he had a great interest in the economic and medical benefits of plant collecting and horticulture, and supported the Apothecaries' Physic Garden (see page 244), Sloane did not maintain the 'Great Garden', the garden of the Tudor New Manor House. Instead he made over much of the garden ground to the east of the manor house for the construction of houses (see page 96). So Lord Cheyne's charming orchard and the 'ingenious waterworks' admired by the diarist John Evelyn succumbed to development. The house plots fronted Cheyne Walk and construction got under way in 1717. Some of houses were built by Sloane himself, working with his builder John Witt (Holme, p. 113). Ever the visionary, Sloane chose some of the finest building land; it offered pleasing views of the river to the south

and was also easily accessible, not only by water but also because the ground adjoined the ancient path or carriageway that connected Paradise Row and the City to the east with the parish church and the village's palatial riverfront houses. Thanks to Sloane, the making of modern Chelsea got under way, first as a residential suburban adjunct to London and then as a quarter within the city.

The 'Great Garden' just before its demise is shown on Dr King's map of Cheyne Walk of c. 1705 (see page 85) and on James Hamilton's map of 1664 that was revised in 1717 (see page 62). On Hamilton's map, the 'Great Garden' is shown packed with apple trees, and the west part of Cheyne Walk is lined with terraces from just east of Lawrence Street as far as the south end of Danvers Street.

When Sir Hans Sloane retired to Chelsea in 1742, he occupied the New Manor House, or Chelsea Place, and it was here that Sloane housed his library and museum. A description of the New Manor House in 1748 makes it clear that the house was square in plan, with four ranges each 100-feet long arranged around a court, with one range containing a first-floor long gallery. Sloane wanted the house preserved after his death as a vast cabinet of curiosities with his collection – which he gave to the nation – on display to the public in perpetuity. The model, to a degree, was the old Ashmolean Museum in Oxford, but Sloane's project was far greater in scale. So for a moment Chelsea seemed set to become London's new museum quarter. However, other forces intervened. Sloane died in 1753 and with his death came a change of plan.

His collection was accepted by the nation but rather than housing it in distant Chelsea the government purchased Montagu House – a late seventeenth-century mansion on the northwest edge of central London in Bloomsbury – as the home of Sloane's bequest, which became the core of the British Museum. So instead of becoming the nation's new national museum, the New Manor House was demolished in 1753 soon after Sloane's death, excluding its seventeenth-century wing, which by then was known as Winchester House or Palace and was in separate ownership. However, clues to the Tudor building still survive, built into the basement vaults of 24 Cheyne Walk. (*Survey of London: Volume 2*, pp. 65–75)

Much of the Cheyne Walk portion of the site of the New Manor House was soon covered with speculatively built houses and their gardens, currently numbered 19 to 26 Cheyne Walk, built between 1759 and 1765 (see page 48). Oddly, John Rocque's large-scale London map of 1746 shows the New Manor House demolished and with is frontage to Cheyne Walk still open. All that is now left above ground of the New Manor House is part of its garden, beyond the wall of Cheyne Mews. After Sloane's death and the demolition of the New Manor House, the land remained in the possession of his family and heirs. By his will, Sloane left the manor jointly to his daughters, Elizabeth, the wife since 1717 of Charles, 2nd Baron Cadogan, and to Sarah, the widow of Sir George Stanley.

This marked the origin of the Cadogan Estate in Chelsea. The portion of the manor Sarah had inherited was in 1821 largely reunited with the portion Elizabeth had inherited due to a series of childless marriages. However part of Sarah's land did not pass to the Cadogans and is still known as the Sloane Stanley Estate. This estate has its own history, derived from the land purchases made in Chelsea by Sir Hans Sloane's brother William Sloane. Ultimately, in 1821, William Sloane's grandson was offered the estate of his Stanley cousins – by then based in Paultons, Hampshire – providing he adopted the surname Sloane Stanley. This he duly did. Elizabeth, Lady Cadogan (who died in

1768) and Charles (who died in 1778) were succeeded by their son Charles Sloane Cadogan, created Earl Cadogan in 1800 and dying in 1807. His heir, Charles Henry Sloane Cadogan, the 2nd Earl, was insane for the last twenty-five years of his life – he died in 1832 – so the estate was administered through Trustees. The 2nd Earl was succeeded by his half-brother George, who was the 3rd Earl and also, from 1831, Baron Oakley. After his death in 1864 the estate passed in direct male line with the earldom and the Cadogan Estate had become synonymous with the Manor of Chelsea.

The 5th Earl, George Henry Cadogan, the man who masterminded much building on the estate, inherited in 1873 and in 1875 launched the Cadogan and Hans Place Improvements, a limited liability development company that created the estate's residential and architectural jewel, Cadogan Square.

In the early twentieth century death duties took their toll (with the deaths of the 5th and 6th earls occurring only eighteen years apart), and the estate became encumbered with heavy mortgages in the 1930s as the only means of preserving its Chelsea landholdings. In 1961, to avoid further crippling death duties, Cadogan Estates Limited was created to hold most of the estate. Subsequently, this enabled planned payments to be made to the exchequer at regular intervals to avoid jeopardising the Chelsea landholdings in the event of an unexpected death when a large amount might suddenly becoming due.

Winchester House
The west wing of the New Manor House – added around 1638 by the Duke of Hamilton – has its own distinct story. In 1663 the wing, physically separated from the main house in 1655, caught the eye of the Bishop of Winchester who was house hunting. His medieval palace in Southwark,

18. *Top*
Detail of the 1799–1819 edition of Richard Horwood's London map. Winchester House is shown bottom left. Terraces, constructed from 1717 and fronting on to Cheyne Walk, occupy the sit of the New Manor House and its 'Great Garden'.

19. Above
Winchester House, constructed in c. 1638 as a west wing of the New Manor House, was acquired in 1664 for the Bishop of Winchester and soon extensively remodelled. This view shows the house soon before its demolition in 1825. Oakley Street now runs through its site.

damaged during the Reformation and virtually destroyed during the Civil War, was abandoned and its site sold off and, instead, something more salubrious was acquired for the Diocese, whose boundary stretched to the south bank of the Thames. In 1664 the Diocese bought the wing from the Cheyne family, who had just finally and fully acquired Chelsea Manor and the New Manor House – so perhaps an exercise in asset stripping on the Cheynes' part. A crucial part of the purchase was the successful negotiation by the Bishop to have his house and grounds exempted from the jurisdiction of the Bishop of London – in whose domain it stood – and instead be regarded as legally part of the Diocese of Winchester. So Winchester House became, ecclesiastically, something of a miniature island state. During the following couple of decades the Diocese spent considerable sums embellishing the house, particularly the interior, and constructing a chapel, so that by 1781 it was described as an 'incomparable mansion' (*Victoria County History*, pp. 108–15). However, this was the high point of the mansion's reputation. As architectural tastes changed, the status of the mansion declined, presumably hastened on its way by the demolition in 1753 of the adjoining New Manor House and its replacement with a terrace of speculative houses. By 1821 the mansion was in poor shape and in 1823 the then bishop sold it and the two-and-a-half acres of garden to the trustees of Lord Cadogan. Winchester House appears on Richard Horwood's London map of 1799–1819, set well back from Cheyne Walk, with gardens behind it stretching as far as the King's Road. The Cadogan Trustees had bought the house and grounds for real estate value and in 1825 the dilapidated mansion was demolished and an Act of Parliament was acquired, allowing the Cadogan family to grant building leases for its site and grounds. Oakley Street, started in the early 1850s, was eventually built through the site of the house.

By 1998 the Cadogan Estate had sold, largely due to the influence of Leasehold Reform, the freehold of the ground once occupied by Winchester House and its garden to various house builders and occupants (*Victoria County History*, pp. 108–15). Richard Horwood's inclusion of the mansion on his London map of 1799–1819 offers a glimpse of the last days of this once 'incomparable mansion'. It is shown as an oblong building, set back some distance in a garden that stretched down to Cheyne Walk and the river. All trace of the Tudor New Manor House to its east had gone, replaced by terraced houses on Cheyne Walk and their long gardens stretching to the north, many of which led to yet wider and deeper walled gardens. To the north of Winchester House was open ground – seemingly in use as various market gardens – stretching as far as the King's Road, the south side of which was most mostly lined at this time with semi-detached houses.

Danvers House

The land forming the east portion of Sir Thomas More's estate, that in 1534 he conveyed to his daughter Margaret and her husband Thomas Roper, also has its own story. The land was not forfeited to the Crown after More's execution but was reunited with More's former estate in the early seventeenth century when its then owner – the Earl of Lincoln – purchased the Roper land. His son-in-law, Sir George Gorges, might have taken an interest in it, but this was for a relatively short period because in 1622 the 3rd Earl of Lincoln sold the Roper's former ground to Sir John Danvers. What happened next is the start of an architectural detective story that has yet to be fully resolved.

Danvers soon built a house on the ground – probably in 1623 – that in its design was, for Chelsea in the early 1620s, most extraordinary. It was in fact a late Renaissance-style villa, inspired primarily by the sixteenth-century architecture of Andrea Palladio, of the sort being pioneered in England by Inigo Jones, notably with his Queen's House in Greenwich commissioned in 1616 by James I for his wife Anne of Denmark. The Queen's House is now regarded as an epoch-forging work. Yet at Chelsea, before Jones's Greenwich project was complete (in the early 1630s), another Renaissance-inspired riverside villa had been built. This architectural pioneer is now all but forgotten because Danvers' thought-provoking house was tragically short-lived, being demolished between 1696 and 1716. As David Le Lay observed in 2001, the house was 'one of the earliest examples of Italian Renaissance design to be carried out in England', and was, together with its garden, of 'seminal importance' because both 'had an enormous influence upon the future of both architecture and garden design in this country' (David Le Lay, 'Danvers House', *Chelsea Society Report*, 2001, pp. 35–8).

It is now possible to visualise Danvers House because its plan and appearance are recorded in a number of early surveys. These form part of a folio of drawings in the Sir John Soane Museum, associated with the somewhat mysterious English architect John Thorpe, who was born around 1565 and might have lived until 1655, although some authorities speculate he died as early as 1618. The status of many of the drawings in the folio is uncertain. Whether they are buildings Thorpe designed, with which he was involved with the design, or simply buildings he surveyed, is often unclear. What is now generally accepted is that he was involved in significant manner with the design in 1605 of Holland House, London; in 1607 of Charlton House, Kent; and in 1597 for an unidentified house in Chelsea where he seems to have introduced the novel idea of a corridor that allowed independent access to individual rooms in place of the then generally followed 'enfilade' arrangement in which rooms were entered one through

another. This is an intriguing story, given the 1590s Cecil survey of Sir Thomas More's house (see pages 36–37) that includes a gallery-like corridor. However, in the absence of firm evidence no connection can be established between this plan and Thorpe. What seems more certain is Thorpe's connection with the design of Danvers House. The drawings of the house in the Thorpe folio in the Soane museum (published in J.A. Gotch, *Early Renaissance Architecture in England*, part II, 1891) is remarkable for its Italian Renaissance villa appearance, which makes it very unlike the other houses with which Thorpe is associated. These, by contrast, are solidly and conventionally Jacobean in appearance, with towers, heavily mullioned windows and a lingering flavour of Tudor Gothic. If Thorpe was involved, then the difference is probably due to the client, Sir John Danvers. It is likely that he was not only the client but also the inspiration behind the design – essentially the architect – using Thorpe to detail the building in a workmanlike manner and supervise execution. The evidence is tangential but compelling. David Le Lay, in his brilliant analysis of the house, points out that its plan 'closely resembles' those of Palladio's villas and suggest that 'most likely the design was largely the work of Sir John Danvers himself'.

John Aubrey, in his *Natural History of Wiltshire*, compiled between 1656 and 1691, observed that Danvers' houses and gardens in Lavington, Wiltshire and in Chelsea 'remain monuments of his ingenuity'. Aubrey also reveals something about the man. Danvers, he records, had travelled much in France and Italy, where he had 'made good observations' and that he had 'a very fine fancy, which lay chiefly for gardens and architecture'.

So it can be assumed that Danvers had seen, first hand, late Renaissance villas of the sort he emulated at Chelsea. In addition, there is circumstantial evidence to suggest that Danvers knew Inigo Jones, because when Jones retuned to Italy in the summer of 1613 – a trip that took him to Vicenza to see Palladio's work – he took with him a charge from Lord Danvers to purchase works of art. Lord Danvers – more correctly Henry Danvers, and from 1626 the 1st Earl of Danby – was Sir John's elder brother (see the *Dictionary of National Biography, 1885–1900*, volume 30, entry for Inigo Jones).

In 1622 Lord Danvers gave the University of Oxford land to create a botanic garden and in 1632 commissioned a monumental classical gate for the garden designed by Nicholas Stone, a mason who moved in Jones's circle. No doubt Henry Danvers played a significant role in the creation of Danvers House in Chelsea, as perhaps did Jones who was working next door for the Earl of Middlesex as Danvers' House started to rise on site. The cultural hinterland within which Danvers House was created was most fertile and rich in possibilities. Henry Danvers, Nicholas Stone and Inigo Jones could all have been involved, but there are also others. Sir John Danvers' first wife, whom he married in 1609 when only twenty years old, was Magdalen, the widow of Richard Herbert. She was twice Danvers' age and the mother of ten children. One of these was George Herbert, aged about sixteen at the time of the marriage and who was to become a Church of England priest and a poet of great and enduring distinction. Magdalen was also a close friend of the poet John Donne, who preached a commemorative sermon in Chelsea Parish Church where she was interred in 1627. So Donne and the thirty-year old George Herbert could also have had roles, to a now unknown degree, in the making of this extraordinary Chelsea house. They could also, of course, have been influenced by it.

The house, when completed, would have been both novel and a compelling example of the visual power of Palladio-derived Renaissance design. For Renaissance artists proportion was of fundamental importance, with classical architecture of the ancient world offering a path to exemplary proportional systems. Palladio's architecture is characterised by the application of a series of harmoniously related proportions that – determining plan, elevations and details such as doors and windows – unifies the whole into a coherent work of art. He based his system on principles established by earlier Renaissance architects and on the study of antique buildings.

The rational beauty of Palladio's buildings, seemingly based on the very laws of nature, led many in early seventeenth-century Britain to regard them as virtually divine in inspiration. The proportional system they enshrined was thought to reflect the building blocks of God's creation and to be the very cornerstones of beauty, whether in architecture, gardening, painting or music.

The Renaissance proportional system refined and codified by Palladio was derived from the primary forms of the cube and the sphere, and permutations such as the cube and a third, the cube and a half and the double cube. Danvers House, as the drawings in the Thorpe folio make clear, was an essay in squares and cubes. The basic plan of the villa was a square, with small square-plan additions to east and west elevations for the service staircases. The ground-floor entrance hall, raised above a basement storey, was probably of cubic volume – it was certainly square in plan – while the staircase hall to its north was a square and a half in plan. Both these halls together, including their central staircase area, took the form of a triple square in plan. Main rooms in the flanking apartments were also square in plan or simple permutations.

The rational arrangement of the plan and its strict symmetry was also

Danvers House is undoubtedly a lost masterpiece of English seventeenth-century architecture and garden design.

20. Below
The ground floor plan and south elevation of Danvers House, built in about 1623, to the east of Beaufort House, for Sir John Danvers. The architect of this most inventive and idiosyncratic jewel of a Renaissance villa remains unknown, but the architect John Thorpe probably produced this drawing.

quintessentially Palladian with its central axis formed by cubical halls, reminiscent of a few of the designs published by Palladio in his *l'Quattro Libri dell'architettura* of 1570, for example the Villa Mocenigo at Marocco. However, the presence of a centrally placed staircase does not chime with Palladio's villa designs where such an arrangement, although present at Mocenigo, is rare. In his villas the main rooms are generally on a raised ground level, so a space-consuming ornamental staircase was usually not deemed necessary. However, evidently Danvers wanted to get his guests to the first floor in style from where, in the tradition of the Elizabethan prospect tower, they could enjoy the villa's fine views. This planning was much appreciated by visitors. Samuel Pepys, who explored the house in September 1661 (Pepys, Diary entry for 30 September 1661) described it as 'the prettiest contrived house that I ever saw in my life'. This was largely the case because,

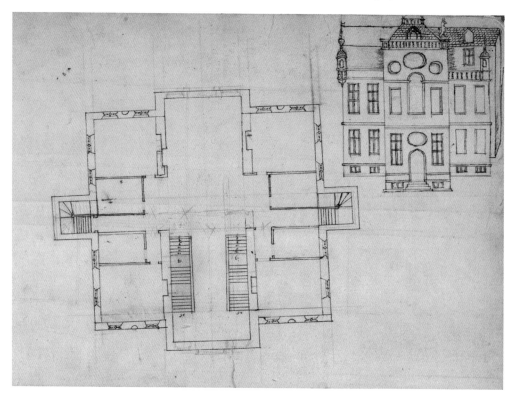

as Le Lay pointed out, 'the main hall was raised well above the surrounding ground level and extended the full depth of the building, allowing for a view of the river and the distant Surrey hills to the south and the garden to the north'.

The elevation of Danvers House, as presented in the Soane museum folio, is as striking as the plan and garden. The centre, which breaks forward and marks the presence of the cubical halls, combines elements of pure and radical Palladian classical design with curious traditional motifs. The first floor of the centre break-front is most individual. It has an elemental Venetian or tripartite window formed by a central arched window flanked by a pair of narrower and lower flat-topped windows. Above are two circular openings and a single oval oculi, seemingly inspired by the architecture of Roman baths. The direct source could be Palladio's Villa Poiana, of 1548, near Vicenza and published in his I'Quattro Libri. However, below this pioneering Palladian first floor is a front door with a Tudor Gothic pointed arch and, on the parapet, diminutive Tudor-style corner tower-like pinnacles with ogee roofs. These somewhat quirky traditional details, perhaps an attempt to give the Italian architecture of Palladio an English character, suggest that a provincial designer like Thorpe might have been involved with detailing the house. Or perhaps Danvers involved a far from provincial designer with a feel for wilful and idiosyncratic north European Renaissance architecture. We know that Henry Danvers – the Earl of Danby – was to employ Nicholas Stone in Oxford and that Sir John Danvers commissioned Stone to carve a sundial and two statues for his Chelsea garden. Stone was a sculptor and an architect who had trained and worked in Amsterdam and who had supervised the construction of the Inigo Jones-designed Banqueting House in Whitehall for James I. Stone's best known architectural works of his own design are the Botanic Garden Gate in Oxford and the York Water Gate off the Strand of 1623–6. Both works are most Mannered in style, with the latter seemingly influenced by the published mid-sixteenth-century designs of Sebastiano Serlio. This is all much in the style of the architecture of Danvers House, and indeed the type of tripartite window featured on the house was often called a Serliana because it was included by Serlio in many of his published designs. So it is possible that Stone had a hand in the creation of the house, perhaps no more than making drawings for Danvers and supplying designs for details.

However, the house, jewel-like as it was, formed only part of the world Danvers created in Chelsea. Its setting was all important. Aubrey observed that 'Twas Sir John Danvers, of Chelsey, who first taught us the way of Italian gardens.' David Le Lay, who explored evidence about the design of the garden (including Kip's bird-eye view of Beaufort House c. 1700) has offered an explanation of its meaning and significance. The 'most remarkable' aspect of the design, points out Le Lay, 'is the way in which the house and garden were conceived as a single design, a notion then unknown in England'. In this, and in several details, Le Lay gave it as his opinion that the relationship between Danvers House and its garden 'was most closely related to the Villa Giulia in Rome', built from 1551–2 to the design of Giacomo Barozzi da Vignola.

The garden at Danvers House was, in Renaissance manner, conceived as an allegory with its key features visible from, and relating to, the house. Viewed from its north windows the garden 'represented', explains Le Lay, 'in a stylised way a progression from a wilderness with shades of the garden of Eden, to an elysian arcady with its perfect lawn and happy shepherds'. Furthest from the house, at the north edge of the garden, was a towered banqueting room, perched over a grotto and with a raised terrace beside it.

In Le Lay's interpretation, the banqueting room hovered – symbolically – 'between the hell of the grotto and the elevated heavenly towers above'.

Danvers House is undoubtedly a lost masterpiece of English seventeenth-century architecture and garden design, and a reminder that architectural history is generally defined by the buildings that happen to survive and not by those that happen to be destroyed. If Sir John Danvers' villa had survived beyond 1716, not only would Chelsea's architectural character be richer but also the general perception of seventeenth-century English architecture would be a little different. Danvers died in 1655, in debt, with his daughter Anne (who had married Sir Henry Lee) receiving his Chelsea estate. Anne died soon after, in 1659, with the estate passing to her daughters Eleanor and Anne Lee. In 1661 the house and lands were seized by the Crown because Danvers had been a regicide and it was at this time that the house was visited by Pepys, when occupied by the Lord Privy Seal, who between 1661 and 1673 was John, Lord Robartes, the future 1st Earl of Radnor. He was a former Parliamentarian but seems to have developed a good relationship with Charles II who in 1673 was, with his court and the French ambassador, entertained at a brilliant assembly in the villa. On occasions such as this, Danvers House, cubical, upright and well-windowed, must have sparkled on the riverbank like a rare and exotic jewel.

In 1675 ownership of the house was regained by Danvers' granddaughters, Eleanor and Anne, who by then had evidently established congenial links with the ascendant aristocracy, into which both had married. In 1672 Eleanor married the 5th Baron Norreys, a son of the 2nd Earl of Lindsey and who later became the 1st Earl of Abingdon, while in 1673 Anne married Lord Wharton (son of Philip, 4th Baron

21. Above
Danvers House, in the setting of its complex allegorical Thames-side garden, as reconstructed in c. 2001 by David Le Lay. The house was demolished between 1696 and 1716. Danvers Street now runs through its site.

Wharton) who in 1706 was created the Earl of Wharton and in 1715 Marquess. Norreys was related to Wharton through marriage because in the late 1650s Norreys' brother – the future 3rd Earl of Lindsey – had married Wharton's sister Elizabeth. So sisters had married brothers-in-law, and all with claims of various sorts on Danvers property that evidently raised thorny issues over rights on inheritance.

The year 1685 seems to have been something of a watershed. The Earl of Radnor – seemingly still in occupation of Danvers House – died, his wife Letitia inheriting his interests in Chelsea. Three years later, in 1688, she married her Chelsea neighbour Lord Cheyne. In the same year, perhaps in consequence of regaining possession of Danvers House, long-running litigation between Eleanor and Anne and their husbands over property was finally resolved by legally dividing their shared assets, with Anne and Wharton getting Danvers House, among other things (*Victoria County History*, pp. 123–45). But the house's great days were over. The pair appears to have had little interest in it or its garden, which they evidently viewed merely as potentially valuable real estate. Between 1696 and 1716 the house was demolished, with, in c. 1696, the south end of Danvers Street laid out on the route of the drive that had led from Cheyne Walk to the lost house's front door (Holme, p. 53 and *Victoria County History*, pp. 31–40). It was during this period that James Hamilton produced his map of Chelsea, based on a survey of 1664 but revised in 1717, which shows Beaufort House but not Danvers House, with its site and garden simply styled 'Lord Wharton's Garden'. Lord Wharton died in 1715 and in 1717 the estate was sold to Sir Hans Sloane or his brother William Sloane (accounts differ), but what is generally agreed is that in 1719 the land was conveyed to William's son, William Sloane junior. In this lies the origin of what became the Sloane Stanley Estate (see page 47).

To the north of 'Lord Wharton's Garden', stretching as far as the King's Road, Hamilton's map shows 'Dove House Close', also owned by Wharton. North of the King's Road, reaching west to 'Lover's Walk' and north to what is now Fulham Road was the lavish 40-acre wooded enclosure here termed 'Lord Wharton's Park'.

Soon after William Sloane junior gained control, 'Lord Wharton's Garden' was let to speculators for house building. These included William Clarkson, who was to become a significant operator in the area. Work had already started on the construction of Danvers Street, because a stone, inscribed 'This is Danvers Street, begun in ye year 1696 by Benjamin Stallwood' (see page 87) was salvaged in 1941 from a bombed house and once stored in the garden of adjoining Crosby Hall (Holme, p. 53). However, not much seems to have happened in the 1690s or the very early years of the eighteenth century because Danvers Street is shown as no more than a small court leading north off Cheyne Walk on one of Dr King's landownership maps in his account of Chelsea written between c. 1705 and 1717 (see *Dr King's Account of Chelsea*, p. 48). The houses in Danvers Street that were eventually numbered 5 to 17, completed in around 1720, are described in detail in the 1913 edition of the *Survey of London*, shortly before all were demolished. Nothing from the early eighteenth century survives in Danvers Street. Development of the land did not acquire momentum until the late 1820s, by which time it was part of the Sloane Stanley Estate (see page 47). The most significant development was Paultons Square – named after the Stanley's Hampshire seat – the west side of which continues the line of Danvers Street to the King's Road. Construction of the square started in the 1830s but was not completed until the 1850s. There is no trace of it on F.P. Thompson's Chelsea map of 1836, which still shows the ground as gardens as far north as the King's Road (see page 109).

Lindsey House

The sole survivor among Chelsea's ancient and great riverside mansions is Lindsey House. It lies towards the west end of Cheyne Walk, west of the modern Tudor-style fantasy mansion that incorporates the transplanted fifteenth-century Crosby Hall, and immediately west of Battersea Bridge. However, if you plan to stroll to see this sole survivor, be warned. Traffic thunders along Chelsea Embankment, which in front of Lindsey House is still named Cheyne Walk. Consequently, Lindsey House is now screened by multiple attempts to protect it from noise, fumes and glaring lights. It is set some way back, behind gardens and a high wall that has been made into an even more effective screen by lengths of trellis and lush and lofty planting. So visiting the house can be rather unrewarding. To more than just glimpse portions of its front you now have to penetrate the wall and the planting, or study old photographs and prints.

The house was almost certainly built in 1674. Faulkner in 1810 mentions a stone bearing that date on the house, and there appears to be a modern copy above the entrance to number 100. It stands on land that was once part of Sir Thomas More's estate and that in his time was occupied by a substantial farmhouse. It has long been suggested – because of the thickness of some internal walls – that this house might in part be incorporated within the existing building. What is known with more certainty is that the client for the house was Robert Bertie, 3rd Earl of Lindsey and Lord Great Chamberlain of England, who bought the site in 1671 along with the still existing farmhouse from the heirs of Sir Theodore de Mayerne. A Swiss-born Huguenot, Mayerne moved to London in 1610 and the following year was appointed physician to James I and his wife Anne of Denmark. He also treated Sir Robert Cecil, and perhaps through him got to know Chelsea. He purchased the old farm in 1635, where he lived until his death in 1655.

What is not known is who designed Lindsey House. This is of some considerable interest because the house is very carefully composed, most sophisticated and fashionable in form and detail. If the old farm was retained, it can only have been for the sake of its structure because no obvious trace of it can be seen on the existing elevation. All the *Survey of London* has to say is that the house 'represents a fair sample of the design which we should expect for the year 1674' (*Survey of London: Volume 4*, pp. 35–41). What this means is that the house has a general French feel about it but – more in particular – in its composition it makes reference to the great English model of the day for the design of town mansions or country houses, which is represented by Clarendon House, built in Piccadilly in 1664–7 by the brilliant amateur architect Roger Pratt.

Lindsey House is two storeys high and had a central three-window wide pediment, removed in around 1775, at which time the house was much altered. Kip's view of c. 1700 shows the central pediment and records that the centre block as a whole was originally nine windows wide, similar to Clarendon House in Piccadilly. Its centre block is now only seven windows wide but Lindsey House does retain its full-height, two window-wide end bays that break forward, although not as far as those on Clarendon House. Also, as at Clarendon House, corners at Lindsey House are emphasised by stone quoins. Even if the source of inspiration for the design of Lindsey House is agreed, the question still remains: who was the architect who executed this elegant permutation of Clarendon House? A clue is offered by Peter Kroyer in his detailed history of Lindsey House, published by *Country Life* in 1956. He notes that the Lindsey family seat was Uffington House, near Stamford, Lincolnshire where the 3rd Earl built a house of 'similar style and date to Lindsey House' (Peter Kroyer, 'The Story of Lindsey House', *Country Life*, London, 1956, p. 23).

22. Right
Lindsey House, built in 1674 and shown here, by Marianne Rush, as it appeared in the very early nineteenth century. Compare with Kip's view of the house in 1700 as shown on pages 22 and 23. In the mid-1770s the mansion was divided into five independently occupied terrace houses, which probably explains when and why the ranges each side of the centre block were rebuilt, as each is only two windows wide as opposed to three as shown in the Kip view.

Uffington House was a glorious design, built between 1681 and 1688 and, with its two-storey high and nine-window wide pedimented entrance front, was essentially Clarendon House without the wings. The house was destroyed by fire in 1904. It is usually pointed out that Uffington was inspired by nearby Belton House but although precise dating of design (as opposed to construction) can be tricky, it seems fairly certain that Uffington House was started before Belton. While the current consensus is that William Winde designed Belton House (he went on to design the Clarendon House-inspired Buckingham House in London in 1702), the only name attached to Uffington is that of Mr Grant, probably a local surveyor.

Additional contemporary documents throw up the names of other men who might have had a role in the design of Lindsey House. An indenture of 1716 between the Countess Dowager Lindsey (her husband, the 3rd Earl, had died in 1701) and her son Robert Bertie includes signatures from two most interesting men, Roger North and Edward Chute. North was the executor of the 'Countess Dowager's' brother Lord Guilford, and 'Edward Chute of the Vyne' (Kroyer, p. 23). North was a lawyer and amateur architect of distinction, now best known for the exquisite pedimented gatehouse he designed for Middle Temple that was built on Fleet Street in 1684. Chute was the brother of Chaloner Chute, who in 1654 added a spectacular pedimented portico of antique perfection to the Tudor country house he had purchased in Hampshire. This is famed as the first such large-scale portico designed for a British county house. The architect was John Webb, the pupil of Inigo Jones. Chute inherited the Vyne in 1685.

North and Chute's names on the indenture suggests that the Lindseys moved in most elevated artistic company and that the designer of their London mansion would have been a leading architect. It is also possible that the same architect would have supplied designs for Uffington House, executed by the surveyor Mr Grant. John Webb died in 1672, but Roger Pratt did not die until 1684 so must be a contender, as is gentleman architect William Winde, who was twenty-nine in 1674 and did not die until 1722. And then of course there is Lindsey himself. He had travelled in Italy and France during the early years of the Commonwealth, attending university in Padua in the early 1650s. He must certainly have seen enough inspirational architecture to make a strong impression and might have had an unusually direct and creative hand in the design of his house.

When the dowager countess died in about 1717, Lindsey House was bequeathed to her son Robert Bertie, by then elevated in the peerage to the Duke of Ancaster and Kesteven. He let it to his cousin, the Dowager Countess of Rutland. She died in 1733 and the house stood empty or was let on short tenancies until 1753. In the same year it was bought by the Protestant Moravian church that aimed to establish a community in Chelsea, with the house as its headquarters. The moving force behind the Moravian's mission was Count Zinzendorf, but when he died in 1760 the project faltered. In 1775 the house was sold and converted into five separate houses, which is no doubt why the centre was rebuilt as seven bays wide as opposed to the original nine. Subsequent divisions and additions took place and Lindsey House is now numbered 96 to 101 Cheyne Walk. Later works include the addition in 1890 of a canted bay to the west wing of the house (number 100) by architect George Devey, and major repairs of 1909, at which time Edwin Lutyens made additions to the northeast portion of the house.

Chelsea beyond the village
The story of the early years of the village of Chelsea is not just a story of the great houses clustered along the river and near

the ancient village church. There were more distant houses and buildings, some along the river to the west near Chelsea Creek, such as the long-lost Cremorne House, the site of which became a popular pleasure garden from the mid-nineteenth century until the late 1870s. And then there were the great houses and estates further inland, along or just north of the King's Road, notably from the late seventeenth-century Stanley House (see page 102), Argyll House (211 King's Road) that was built in 1723 for John Pierene to the designs of the eminent Venetian architect Giacomo Leoni (see page 102), and to the northeast of the King's Road Blacklands House on Blacklands Lane, that ran from King's Road to Fulham Road. This house is shown on James Hamilton's map of 1717 and on one of Dr John King's early eighteenth-century sketch maps of this portion of Chelsea. The house is said to have been occupied by Charles Cheyne in around 1665 and, with more certainly, in 1684 by Count Montefeltro. By 1702 it was occupied by Mrs Judith Nezerauw until 1720, who used it for a French-style exclusive boarding school for young ladies. By 1724 Sir Hans Sloane was leasing land on the King's Road frontage south of the house for speculative building operations. Blacklands House survived into the mid-nineteenth century – it was used as an insane asylum in 1829 (*Victoria County History*, pp. 51–60).

Among the late arrivals was yet another manor house, but this one set well north of the river and perched opposite the northwest corner of what is now Burton Court, at the junction with Smith Street and looking northeast along what is now St Leonard's Terrace. The detached house was built by Thomas Richardson. The land was leased from the Cadogan Estate, and Richardson – who had produced the 1769 map of the estate's freeholds in the Manor of Chelsea and was Lord Cadogan's 'steward' – must have been given permission to call his home the manor. The house was large and handsome, but

was not in any practical or administrative sense a manor house. As a speculation, in 1790 Richardson built Durham Place to the south of his manor house and perhaps houses at the south end of Smith Street. The manor house and Durham Place are shown clearly on Horwood's map of 1799–1819 and on F.P. Thompson's Chelsea map of 1836. Until 2020, Durham Place survived intact, although much altered, but the manor house and its large garden were swept away in 1870 to make a connection to Tedworth Square, then being laid out by the Cadogan Estate and lined with architecturally unadventurous brick and stucco speculatively built houses of standard classical design (see Le Lay, pp. 57–61). To the east of Chelsea village were other houses – such as the very early eighteenth-century Gough House (see page 184) – and from 1682 the Royal Hospital, large in size, majestic in design and of vast importance in the development of Chelsea (see page 122). When the hospital, designed by Sir Christopher Wren and commissioned by Charles II, was completed and occupied by 1692, it initiated the speedy expansion of Chelsea by speculative house builders. The hospital brought architectural style, royal connections, improved communications and security to Chelsea, all of which attracted residents and fuelled investment in property and construction (see page 121). The improvement of communications in Chelsea, primarily the construction of new roads, but also their paving and lighting, is a significant part of the story of the growth of the area. Roads not only made travel quicker, easier and safer but they opened up the fields and meadows of Chelsea for construction by creating plots and frontages on which to build. This story, told in detail in Chapter Three, can be grasped in broad terms by the contemplation of early maps, notably James Hamilton's map of 1717 (see page 62), and surveys of probably a few years earlier by Dr King. Hamilton's map shows the King's Road as the east–west spine of Chelsea.

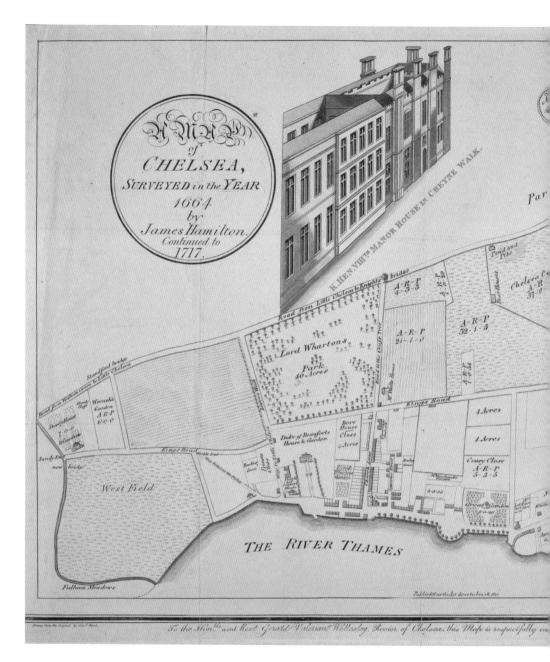

23. Above
Chelsea in 1664, surveyed by James Hamilton, 'continued in 1717' by the Chelsea Rector Dr King and published in this form in the early nineteenth century by Thomas Faulkner. From the left (west), the map shows – along the river frontage – Lindsey House, Beaufort House, Church Lane (now Old Church Street), the Old Church and Lawrence Street. Strangely, Cheyne Row is not shown, although built in 1708 on the site of the 'Bowling Green'. To the east are the remains of Shrewsbury House, Winchester House and the New Manor House with its 'Great Garden' and orchards shown before houses were built along its south edge from 1717 facing on to Cheyne Walk. At the west end of 'Kings Road' is Stanley House. The perspective of 'King Henry VIII Manor House' is, rather bafflingly, the mirror image of the elevation offered by Faulkner in the text of his book.

This was a road of great strategic importance. From the early sixteenth century an east–west route – on or near the site of the existing King's Road – became the main land connection between Henry VIII's collection of palaces in St James's – notably Whitehall Palace – and Hampton Court Palace. This important route was sustained by the Stuart monarchs and it seems that the existing line of the King's Road was established during the reign of Charles II. At this point it remained a 'private' royal road, although it was no doubt used as something of a 'back route' through Chelsea by local residents. The road's strategic and political importance waned a little in the reign of William and Mary who retained an interest in Hampton Court and St James's Palace, but who had given up Whitehall for Kensington. By 1720 the nature of this road changed significantly because royal and court interests had shifted more extensively, if not absolutely, from St James's in the west to Kensington in the north. This reduction in the royal significance of the King's Road led to it being opened in 1719 more widely to 'Gentleman Landowners' and those who had business along its length on the purchase of a token. In 1830 it was fully opened as a public thoroughfare, a change that accelerated speculative house building that had already started on land flanking the road.

Hamilton's map shows that to the north of, and roughly parallel with, the King's Road is 'the road from Little Chelsea to Knightsbridge', now the Fulham Road. To the south of the east portion of the King's Road is Paradise Row. This led, via Cheyne Walk, to the heart of Chelsea village and so Paradise Row formed a crucial link in the land route from Chelsea village to the City to the east. However, by 1717 its direct route had been interrupted by the laying-out of the 'College Court' (now Burton Court) to the north of the Royal Hospital. The main north–south route from Chelsea village to the King's Road and beyond was

Church Lane (now Old Church Street) that by 1717 was still not fully lined with buildings. The interruption of the line followed by Paradise Row was not the only influence of the Royal Hospital upon the established pattern of principal roads and streets in Chelsea. Wren's design for the Royal Hospital is strictly symmetrical around a strong central axis. The axis determined the arrangement of planting and paths in the garden to the south of the hospital buildings, it runs through the hospital's south court, through the building itself – being marked by the north and south porticoes and by the passage dividing the hall from the chapel – and then continues to the north, expressed by the path and planting of the 'College Court' (now Burton Court). However, as Hamilton's map reveals, that was not the end of it. To the north of Burton Court the axis continues north, as far as the King's Road, in the form of the Royal Avenue. A survey by Dr King of the 'Glebe Land in East Field' that lay to the northwest of the hospital's 'College Court' shows the route of the Royal Avenue, with its two rows of trees, most clearly. King calls the King's Road the 'Queens Road', so the survey must date from the reign of Queen Anne, and therefore is not earlier than 1702 or later than 1714, with other evidence suggesting a date nearer to 1705. King also states that the Royal Hospital paid the parish £3 a year for the use of this portion of the Glebe land (*Dr. King's Manuscript Account of Chelsea*, p. 22).

History offers slightly different interpretations for why the axis was continued. If you go to the south end of Royal Avenue today you will see, on its west side, a metal plate erected in recent years by the Royal Borough of Kensington and Chelsea. It informs curious passers-by that the Royal Avenue 'was laid out by Sir Christopher Wren in 1682 as a direct route from the Royal Hospital to Kensington Palace', but that construction north of King's Road was stopped after Charles

II – the road's royal 'sponsor' – died in 1685. The curious thing about this statement is that there was not a Kensington Palace in 1682. What became Kensington Palace was, in 1682, Nottingham House, and William and Mary did not purchase it until the summer of 1689, after which, remodelled by Wren to serve as the king and queen's London home, the house became known as Kensington Palace. So, with no royal presence in Kensington, there was no reason why, in 1682, Charles would have driven a wide avenue nearly a mile and a half long through the countryside to Kensington, beyond the desire to manipulate the landscape with a startlingly ambitious piece of Baroque garden design and make his mark in a most expensive manner. Charles was not this kind of king or man, and in any case he did not have the money. The *Victoria County History* offers a more plausible explanation, based on documentary research. It states that 'in 1693 the Crown made a payment towards building a road between Kensington and Chelsea, presumably for Royal Avenue from the Royal Hospital to King's Road, thought to be the only section built of a grand route planned by William III to run between the Royal Hospital and Kensington Palace' (*Victoria County History*, pp. 26–31).

It seems clear and logical – the origin is post-1690 and money was probably the problem – yet there remains a problem. The Royal Avenue is a continuation of the axis around which, from 1682, the Royal Hospital was designed. And for whatever reason – coincidence or by design – this axis is focused on distant Nottingham House. But why? There really is no easy answer. Perhaps William and Mary did not, as the story now goes, shop around for a London home after 1688 and eventually chose Nottingham House. Perhaps it had long been on a shopping list for royal or state acquisition if and when circumstances permitted or demanded. So, knowing this, Wren chose to aim his axis at Nottingham

House. Admittedly this reasoning in not compelling, but it could explain why the palatial and very urban Kensington Square was laid out in the fields immediately to the south of Nottingham House in 1685 by an ambitious speculator named Thomas Young. If Nottingham House was to become a palace, courtiers' houses would be needed close at hand and Young wanted to be ahead of the game and in a position to supply that demand. Perhaps by chance, or perhaps not, the line of the east side of Kensington Square – in fact orientated north–east – is parallel to, and quite near, the route the Royal Avenue could have taken. All most curious.

There is yet another twist. Wren might not have determined the axis around which the Royal Hospital is organised but inherited it from the previous and substantial building on the site. In 1609 construction started on 'King James's College at Chelsey', which was a royal project intended to assist in the formulation and co-ordination of arguments against Roman Catholicism. The college was to consist of two symmetrically designed courts organised around a central axis. Intriguingly, the house that in 1619 became Nottingham House had been built in 1605 for a rich City merchant named Sir George Coppin. So if the axial relation between the Royal Hospital and Kensington Palace is not coincidental, then its original intention was not to link them but to link Coppin's house with the college. Exactly why, if this is the case, is I fear a riddle we may never answer. Whatever the origin of the axial relationship between the Royal Hospital and Kensington Palace, there was a practical reason why Wren and the monarch – be it Charles or William – would want to construct it.

Charles's father had been ousted and executed following an armed uprising. William, with Mary, had gained the Crown of England through military action. True, they had been invited to invade by a large number of influential English Protestants and fighting had been minimal, but William had landed with an armed force. Both men understood the potential of military action in contemporary politics. The Royal Hospital was founded as an almshouse for veteran soldiers, aged, injured or infirm. However, these men were well trained, many had combat experience, were still able-bodied, relatively young and – most important – loyal to their 'Founder' and benefactor. And small arms and ordnance were kept on site with a powder magazine in Burton Court. Clearly, among its several attributes, the Royal Hospital was a depot for a militia that could come to the aid of the monarch if necessary, and guard crucial routes of communication. The King's Road, kept open by this militia, would allow speedy communication, of forces if necessary, between Whitehall and Hampton Court Palace. And the Royal Avenue – if completed – would have allowed equally speedy communication between the militia's depot in the Royal Hospital and Kensington Palace. Consequently, it is reasonable to conclude that the Royal Avenue was not primarily intended to be merely a vast and ornamental Baroque gesture but – like the King's Road – a military road and part of a plan to defend the monarchy in times of trouble.

There is circumstantial evidence to support this. Charles II retained the site of King James's College for some years after his Restoration in the hope of using it for the construction of a barracks for the standing army that he desired to create as a means of protecting himself. However, his policy was political dynamite and much opposed by many who remembered the attempted military-backed tyranny of Charles I, and who remained deeply suspicious about the true intentions of their new Parliamentary monarch. Charles was not strong enough to force the issue and so in 1682 decided to use the site for the next best thing to a barracks for loyal and lusty young soldiers – a hospital for loyal veteran soldiers.

Life on the edge

Riverside Chelsea to the east of the village had a very distinct, bucolic character. East of the junction of Cheyne Walk with Paradise Row there was – until the construction of the Chelsea Embankment in the 1870s – no continuous road or path along the river's edge until Mill Bank was reached. So this part of Chelsea was a most picturesque place where long gardens ran down to the river, often marked by Venetian-style water gates. The jewel in the string of Thames-side retreats was the Apothecaries' Physic Garden, established in 1673 (see page 244).

The Royal Hospital also enjoyed a very intimate relationship with the river but to its east things changed dramatically after 1723. In that year the Chelsea Waterworks Company was established by Royal Charter to supply water to households in west London and the West End. The process was basic. The company gathered water from the Thames at high tide and stored it in an extensive collection of riverside ponds that were shaped like stunted canals. From these ponds the water was pumped into towers to gain some pressure and then fed into elm pipes, at limited hours, to supply those households who paid for connections to the company's water mains.

This portion of riverside Chelsea, with its canal-shaped ponds, windmill-like water pumps and market gardens, had the distinct feel of a Dutch water-land. This water landscape is captured by numerous contemporary prints, which tend to show an extensive waterscape in the foreground with Westminster and the towers of the Abbey in the distance. It is reminiscent of contemporary Dutch views of Delft or Amsterdam. The presence and visual character of this water-land is made clear on John Rocque's map of 1744–6 that shows a large collection of waterworks and ponds immediately east of the Royal Hospital and the Ranelagh pleasure grounds. Horwood's map of

1799–1819 gives an even better impression of the huge scale of the water company's works (see page 120). The story of the Chelsea Waterworks Company is part of the larger story of the life that evolved on the water's edge in Chelsea. Kip's aerial perspective of c. 1700 depicts a terrace of two-storey houses with tall gables set along the water's edge in front of the east portion of Sir Thomas More's estate. For a period this section of what is now Cheyne Walk was called Duke Street, with Lombard Street immediately to its east. The terrace is of regular design, looks well built and far from an ad hoc assemblage of waterside hovels. Most houses appear to be set back slightly from the river's edge, which is apparently embanked, and possess small closets or outbuildings of irregular design that seem to extend to the very water's edge. It is unclear what functions these buildings fulfilled beyond being homes or work places. No vessels are shown moored beside them but it is reasonable to assume that they were occupied by people following river trades, and that this was the working heart of riverside Chelsea, with wharfs and landing stages continuing as tradition stretching back to Roman times. Rocque's map of 1744–6 confirms that these river-edge buildings, or buildings on their site, still existed. It shows they extended as far to the east as the church and records that one of them related to a 'Horse Ferry' across the Thames. According to Rocque, what had been Duke Street was by this time known as Beaufort Street.

East of the church Cheyne Walk was open to the river, with no buildings along its water's edge as far as the junction with Paradise Row, with the exception of one structure. This was located immediately to the east of the junction with Cheyne Row, and described by Rocque as 'Feather Stairs' and 'Magpye Stairs', so evidently landing places. Richardson's 1769 estate map shows buildings still clustered along the river's edge at the west end of Cheyne Walk, west of the church.

Chelsea, with its canal-shaped ponds, windmill-like water pumps and market gardens, had the distinct feel of a Dutch water-land.

24. *Above*
Chelsea's water landscape, looking east in 1752. In the foreground is part of Chelsea Waterworks – with sheds containing steam-powered pumps and canal-like storage ponds – and in the distance, left to right, are St John's, Smith Square, St Paul's Cathedral and Westminster Abbey.

It also shows their plan-forms in greater detail. For example, the block of buildings between the church and Danvers Street was U-shape in plan, offering a court to the river. This presumably was a wharf. The 1769 map also records the great change then taking place on Chelsea's waterfront. Battersea Bridge is shown and named, although it was not to open to pedestrian traffic until late 1771 and to wheeled traffic until 1772. Earl Spencer had recently acquired the right to operate the busy ferry that functioned from this site. The demolition of Beaufort House in 1740 and the construction through its site of a new street (now called Beaufort Street) connecting Cheyne Walk to the King's Road provided – or indeed created – the opportunity for a new bridge. Earl Spencer commissioned the work but the new bridge, which charged a toll, was something of a sorry, cut-price affair. It was constructed largely of timber, with narrow spans and numerous piers that made it a hazard to shipping. It also seems to have alarmed people driving vehicles. The designer was the architect

A View of CHELSEA.

London Printed for Robert Sayer, Map & Printseller, near Serjea

25. Above
The east portion of Chelsea village from the
south bank of the Thames in c. 1745, after a
view made by John Maurer. From the right
(east), is the west wing of the Royal Hospital,
then the 1704 Gough House, pedimented and
set back from the river, Turret House – with
cupola and roof-top walk, built in the late
seventeenth century, and demolished in 1816,
the Swan Inn, with a diminutive attic, located
at the south end of Swan Walk and, on the
left, the Physic Garden.

26. Overleaf
Detail of Thomas Richardson's 1769 'Plan of the
Estate and Manor of Chelsea in the County of
Middlesex' produced for the Cadogan Estate.
The map is a trifle confusing because in general
it shows only Cadogan Estate property in
any detail.

du Village de CHELSEA *.*
Fleet Street.

Henry Holland, who was soon to undertake a significant expansion of Chelsea with the construction of Hans Town (see page 111). The bridge, with its central piers removed and the widened span strengthened by the addition of iron girders, survived until 1885.

During the first half of the nineteenth century the river's edge at Cheyne Walk – ancient-looking, picturesque and seemingly authentic in its portrayal of London's riverside community of working people – was haunted by early photographers and artists, many living in Chelsea. One of the most curious and important of these artists, certainly in terms of the quantity of depictions of Chelsea, was Walter Greaves. He was born at 31 Cheyne Walk in 1846, the son of a boat-builder named Charles William Greaves who was also the boatman used by J.M.W. Turner, who lived the last years of his life at 119 Cheyne Walk, dying there of cholera in December 1851. So as a child Greaves no doubt observed Turner, which might have kindled within him the desire to draw and paint. From the mid-1850s, if not before, Walter, sometimes collaborating with his brother Henry, started to produce watercolour perspectives, drawings and etchings of Cheyne Walk, depicting its buildings and its life in changing moods and seasons from both land and water. In the process the brothers compiled a precious record of a soon to be lost world.

These watercolours appear closely observed, are at times somewhat sketchy but are nevertheless detailed and charmingly naïve when it comes to figures, and they have about them an air of great authenticity and apparently topographical accuracy – although no doubt with a touch of poetic licence. Trees are just right, dirt, grime, drays and heavy traffic are generally absent (part of Cheyne Walk was, after all, a working wharf with coal merchants in operation), and instead children dance in the road as a hurdy-gurdy man plays the barrel organ.

27. Above
The west portion of Cheyne Walk in 1857, as painted by Walter Greaves, showing the long-lost Cricketers' Tavern and Thames Coffee House looking to Prospect Place and the Old Church. This view gives a good idea of the intimate and picturesque character of river-edge Chelsea village before the construction of the Embankment in the early 1870s.

28. Above right
Lindsey House, left, looking east towards Duke Street and Cheyne Walk before the construction of Chelsea Embankment in the early 1870s. The central block of late eighteenth-century houses survive. 'Greaves Boat Builder' was a business owned by Walter Greaves' father, who had been Turner's ferryman.

So perhaps a slightly idealised rendering of a true world. Some of Greaves' drawings and watercolours are dated to the mid-1850s and, if this is correct, confirm that he was a precocious talent. At this time Greaves was also being trained in the family trade – as a shipwright and boatman – so opportunities for drawing must have been limited, but he seems to have frequented Chelsea's riverside in his spare time and it was here in 1863 that the Greaves brothers met James McNeill Whistler who had arrived in London in the late 1850s and was soon drawn to the river's edge in Chelsea. The boys showed Whistler the river and he made them his studio assistants and showed them how to paint. As Greaves is quoted as saying, 'he taught us to paint and we taught him the waterman's jerk' (see E. Robins Pennell and J. Pennell, *The Life of James McNeill Whistler*, 2 vols, 1908; 5th edition in 1 vol., 1911). The relationship that developed between Walter and Whistler in the late 1860s was most odd, if the

atmosphere of Walter's portraits of Whistler are to be taken at face value. One set which show Whistler strutting along the balcony of Lindsey House are positively alarming. Attired as the ultimate dandy, Whistler looks imperious, arrogant, cruel – almost satanic as he disports himself before his adoring acolyte.

The views the brothers produced during the 1860s show that they, and Walter in particular, developed an obsession with the small stretch of London's riverfront, particularly around the Adam and Eve pub on the river near the west end of Cheyne Walk. The river-edge is shown in different lights and angles, at high tide and at low when the river embankments rose from a muddy foreshore. And Cheyne Walk and Duke Street are shown as part of a working riverside, with wharfs, coal merchants, boat houses, breweries, stables, a lime wharf and with rows of moored barges. However, it was also a place of

festivity, with regattas and numerous inns, including not only the Adam and Eve but also the Old Swan, and the Waterman's Arms beer house (see page 232). There were also, among these working and commercial buildings, a smattering of cottages (*Victoria County History,* pp. 31–40). The palette of building materials the Greaves brothers recorded was rich and varied – brick, stone, timber frame and timber weatherboarding (pitch or tar covered in nautical manner), lime render and lime wash and red pantile roofs. The brothers' drawings make it clear that the sixteenth- or seventeenth-century gable-topped terrace shown on Kip's view mostly survived into the 1860s, with the Adam and Eve pub attached to its east end. Whistler also depicted the Adam and Eve and adjoining buildings, looking west from the river towards the church. He made the scene look more rambling, more like a working wharf, with barges and various craft moored on the muddy foreshore.

29. Above
The artist James McNeill Whistler, dressed as
the quintessential Bohemian dandy, painted
in 1872 by Walter Greaves. Whistler is depicted
disporting himself on the balcony fronting
his apartment in Lindsey House, with in the
distance Battersea Church spire and chimneys
on the south bank of the Thames.

However, his etching is dated 1889, so must
to a degree have been based on memory
because by then this world was over.

The watercolours and drawings produced
by the Greaves brothers are wonderfully
evocative, particularly those by Walter.
However, a perhaps better-known image
of Chelsea's water-edge is Whistler's
*Nocturne: Blue and Gold – Old Battersea
Bridge*, painted c. 1872–5. It shows one
pier of the bridge, its height exaggerated,
supporting a vertiginous carriageway
with, in the background, the tower of the
Chelsea Old Church rising above a huddle
of water-edge structures on Cheyne Walk,
just discernible in the gathering gloom and
utterly romantic.

The painting marks a defining moment
in the history of Chelsea's riverfront and
in the history of the community of artists
who gathered around that waterfront.
When first exhibited, the painting led to
an extraordinary legal action in which
most of the protagonists were, in one way
or another, Chelsea men. It started when
the influential pundit and art critic John
Ruskin (a regular visitor to the Cheyne
Row home of his mentor Thomas Carlyle)
called Whistler (who until 1878 lived in part
of Lindsey House and whose new home
and studio was the White House at the
Chelsea Embankment end of Tite Street –
see pages 185–6), an impudent 'coxcomb'
because exhibiting the *Nocturne* series
(which focused on Thames-side scenes and
Chelsea in particular, including Cremorne
Gardens) was tantamount to 'flinging a
pot of paint in the public's face'.

Whistler – ever vociferous and combative –
sued Ruskin for libel because he claimed his
reputation had been sullied, and his ability
to sell his work or gain new commissions
compromised. The case, tried in November
1878, focused on what limits there might
be on the freedom of expression on such
subjective issues as aesthetics and taste.
The case was the talk of artistic Chelsea.

30. Above
Nocturne: Blue and Gold – Old Battersea Bridge painted
by Whistler between 1872–5 and showing, in exaggerated
form, a pier of Battersea Bridge with, in the background,
the tower of Chelsea Old Church. This is one of the series
of atmospheric Chelsea views that prompted John Ruskin
to declare Whistler a 'coxcombe'.

It of course divided opinion but most who supported progressive or experimental art were – like sometime-Chelsea resident Henry James – delighted that Ruskin's increasingly dictatorial and conservative statements about art had at last been challenged. Whistler won the trial but was awarded the derisory damages of a nominal one farthing. Humiliated and bankrupted by the ruling that he had to pay half the trial costs, Whistler was obliged to give up the White House, having lived in it for less than a year. However, he did not give up Chelsea. Its water's edge remained his artistic inspiration. After the trial Whistler escaped to Venice, commissioned to make a series of etchings. There was an irony about this because Ruskin had made Venice his own with his seminal The Stones of Venice, published from 1851 to 1853, and the works that had inspired Ruskin Whistler was now to draw. And when the project was complete Whistler returned to Tite Street, but into a far more modest home than the nearby White House. And there was another irony. To build the White House Whistler had been obliged to assume Ruskin's stance and defend the rights of freedom of expression in the matter of art. The design for the house that he had commissioned in 1877 from the avant-garde architect Edward W. Godwin was so radically simple that the landlords – the Metropolitan Board of Works (MBW) – had attempted to apply aesthetic control and prevent its construction. The MBW, which had leased the site to Whistler because it was land 'surplus' to its requirements for the construction of the Embankment, argued that the minimalism of the design made the house look mean and cheap and would lower the tone of the street. In this case, Whistler won, but of course did not have long to enjoy his triumph.

The abrupt and brutal end of the water-edge life along Cheyne Walk came at the very moment that Whistler was painting his Battersea Bridge Nocturne.

In 1865 the MBW had started to build the Victoria Embankment between Blackfriars Bridge and Westminster Bridge. This was part of a radical plan to clean up the muddy Thames foreshore to reduce stench and disease. The water-borne cholera epidemics of 1848 and early 1850s (that had carried away Turner) demanded dramatic action, as did the 'Great Stink' in the summer of 1858, when rotting sewage in the Thames made life in central London almost unbearable. The action, formulated by engineer Joseph Bazalgette, involved pushing the north bank of the river south into the Thames to create a space for the insertion of a sewer system – designed to interrupt the flow of raw waste into the Thames and carry it off for treatment. At the same time, the ground won from the river would be used to lay track for the new underground railway, gas mains and telegraph cables. And when roofed over, this below-ground level space, protected from the Thames by a retaining wall or embankment, would be used to support a major new road, tree-lined like a Parisian boulevard. Also, wherever possible, riverside gardens were to be created between the old water's edge and the new riverside road.

The Blackfriars to Westminster Embankment was completed by 1870 and a few years later the MBW started work on the section from Chelsea Bridge to just west of Battersea Bridge, with completion in May 1874. Chelsea Embankment was similar in many respects to Victoria Embankment, although not as broad since it did not have to accommodate a railway. The arrival of the Embankment prompted other works. Some had taken place before the completion of the Chelsea Embankment, such as the laying out of Oakley Street from c.1851 to connect Cadogan Pier on Cheyne Walk with the King's Road, and the construction of the cable-stayed Albert Bridge on the line of Oakley Street. It opened in 1873, but was strengthened by Bazalgette in 1884 and

The Chelsea Embankment ... improved road communication across London.... However, it also transformed the nature of the village of Chelsea.

again in 1973 when unsightly concrete piers were added below its central span. Clearly the bridge's delicate construction was struggling to deal with modern heavy traffic. After the opening of the Embankment, Battersea Bridge was rebuilt by the MBW in 1885, again to Bazalgette's designs. The Chelsea Embankment of course improved road communication across London and no doubt did its bit to reduce water-borne disease. However, it also transformed the nature of the village of Chelsea. Rather than being a quiet refuge and backwater, it became a fleeting location of a thundering thoroughfare. Houses and institutions like the Royal Hospital lost their direct communication with the river, gardens were truncated and, of course, the wonderful array of river-edge structures – long sustaining the life and soul of Chelsea's working river-side community – were simply swept away. Chelsea was now effectively cut off from its life-giving river, the river that was the reason for its being, and long the cause of its wealth and growth. However, Chelsea – transformed as it was – endured. By the 1870s it had long

32. *Top*
Walter Greaves' self-portrait of c.1880 showing him
sitting, with his sister Alice, on the newly built Chelsea
Embankment. This desolate looking road destroyed much
of the water world that had inspired him during the
previous decades.

33. *Above*
Looking east to Cheyne Walk from Battersea Bridge.
This view by Walter Greaves, showing a regatta in
progress, was painted in the 1860s and shows characterful
riverside buildings, including the Adam & Eve tavern, that
were soon to be swept away for the construction of the
Chelsea Embankment.

grown inland from its old riverside heart, so it was possible to retreat from the new road into Chelsea's new heartland, and many artists did. Many also did not. For example, Dante Gabriel Rossetti, the poet, painter, illustrator and co-founder of the Pre-Raphaelite Brotherhood, had been happily ensconced since 1862 in the large early eighteenth-century 16 Cheyne Walk, and evidently saw no reason to move when the construction of the Embankment, noisy and disturbing, turned his accustomed world upside down. He remained stolidly in the house until his death in 1882.

Generally speaking, the grand early eighteenth-century houses at the east end of Cheyne Walk stood firm, sheltered to a degree by new planting. However, to the west, terraces of Georgian houses on Cheyne Walk fell victim, one after another, to the type of high-rise, late nineteenth-century mansion blocks that had sprung up along the Embankment east of Cheyne Walk.

The Embankment was a social success, and certainly did not drag down Chelsea. This is made clear by Charles Booth's 'Poverty Maps' of London compiled in the late 1880s and late 1890s. Booth, a most active philanthropist and battler against urban poverty, worked with a small team of assistants (and, where necessary, with police guidance and protection) to survey the streets of the capital. One consequence of this labour was a colour-coded map of the metropolis. It shows the economic status of the occupants of privately owned domestic buildings, and by implication the state of the structure of the buildings and the nature of the life lived in them and in the streets or courts of which they were part. Booth specified seven degrees of wealth and poverty. The buildings in best occupation are shown in gold: 'Upper-middle and Upper Classes. Wealthy'. The worst are shown in black: 'Lowest Class. Vicious, semi-criminal'. In between, after gold, were red, pink,

purple, light blue and dark blue, described as 'Very poor, casual. Chronic want' (see pages 282–3).

The buildings on Cheyne Walk – from Flood Street and Paradise Row (by the 1880s named Queen's Road) to Oakley Street – are all colour-coded gold. From Oakley Street to Danvers Street they are red, with Lindsey House gold. Then red along the Embankment as far as Cremorne Road, and then pink. There are only small patches of dark colour – a court shown dark blue and black west of Milman's Street, black in Paradise Walk immediately east of the gold-coloured houses in Swan Walk, purple along the south end of Church Street and in Justice Walk, but dark blue for an alley west of Church Street and – apparently – for 23 and 24 Lawrence Street.

Another artist who did not move away while the Chelsea waterside was being transformed was the one artist that must have found the change most unsettling. Walter Greaves remained in his home – 104 Cheyne Walk – where he had lived since 1855, presumably surveying the changing scene. The fact that he did not feel moved to draw or paint the new Cheyne Walk in a sustained manner probably says it all. There is one oil painting entitled *Walter and Alice Greaves on the Embankment*, dated to c. 1880 (now at Tate Britain), that shows them sitting on a bench, next to newly planted trees, with a wide road behind them and a collection of old Chelsea houses in the distant background. But the life seems sucked out of the scene and of Greaves, which is unsurprising since his muse had been destroyed before his eyes.

Greaves lived in Cheyne Walk until 1897, then ill, poor and alone he moved, ending his days as a 'Poor Brother' in Charterhouse in Smithfield. He lived until 1930, when the Chelsea riverside village he had known so intimately and drawn so lovingly, was nothing but a distant memory.

TERRACES
AND
SQUARES

Sloane Street

34. *Above*
David Wilkie's painting of Chelsea Pensioners
receiving news of the victory of Waterloo,
and painted in c. 1821, offers a splendid view
of the Royal Hospital in the urban context
it did so much to create. On the right are the
humble houses and taverns of Jew's Row.

The construction of the Royal Hospital that started in 1682 (see page 122) changed Chelsea in several most significant ways. It was a royal project and carried with it status but, more significantly, it was large in scale, with its architecture and its planning monumental. The hospital's architect, Sir Christopher Wren, worked in his more economic manner – brick and timber with only a little expensive stone – but the concept remained heroic. Giant porticoes formed the focus of views from the river and from inland Chelsea, and the manipulation of the land around the hospital – to the north Burton Court and the wide Royal Avenue (see page 120) and to the south formal gardens and avenue running down to the river's edge – meant that the hospital's physical impact on Chelsea was enormous. Key to this was its location immediately to the east of the Physic Garden and of the great houses that stood near Chelsea Church. This meant that the Royal Hospital not only reinforced the importance of the old riverside heart of Chelsea but also formed a bridge, through meadows and gardens, to link the village more closely to the metropolis.

The use of the building also had a profound effect on Chelsea. As a hospital for veteran soldiers capable of functioning as a loyal militia if required meant that the security of riverside Chelsea was improved and its roads better lit, paved and watched. Its presence also stimulated demand for commercial or domestic buildings to be constructed to serve this new Chelsea institution. Further, because many former soldiers took lodgings nearby, as they were obliged to draw their pensions in person from the hospital, the area around Jew's Row (now Royal Hospital Road) and Turk's Row immediately to the north became something of a netherworld, with cheap lodging houses, taverns and bawdy-houses (see page 241). The hospital's final completion in about 1691 therefore marked an increase in speculative house building, as various landowners and estates sought to capitalise on the area's improved development prospects.

The Rector of Chelsea parish, Dr John King, in his *Account of Chelsea*, compiled mostly in Queen Anne's reign, probably around 1705, observed that Chelsea was swelling in size but also noted that it retained its superior social character. 'The number of houses,' he wrote, 'are mightily increased of late years, for there are 350 houses in the Parish, and a great many more families at this present time, by the great concourse of lodgers to the place....' And he made it clear that these 'divers [new] houses' were – like the surviving great houses of Chelsea – of 'good reception [and] inhabited by gentlemen of good estates and quality' (*Dr. King's Manuscript Account of Chelsea*, p. 4). This makes it clear that the first post-1692 wave of expansion had gone well, with speculators aiming high and able to find prosperous occupants for their new buildings.

The Lawrence initiative: building on the site of the Old Manor House
According to the *Victoria County History*, 'serious speculative building in Chelsea village began ... on the 4-acre site of the old manor house belonging to the Lawrence family'. The first leases were granted in 1687, as the construction of the Royal Hospital was nearing completion (*Victoria County History*, pp. 31-40). Sir Thomas Lawrence clearly saw the opportunity and leased the manor house, its grounds, outbuildings and an adjoining close to a Southwark merchant named Cadogan Thomas (not related to the Chelsea Cadogans), who in the mid 1670s was also speculating in Golden Square, Soho (*Survey of London: vol. 31*, p. 41). The late 1680s were the time of a building boom – almost a building madness, following the speedy, successful and profitable building of the City of London after the Great Fire. The speculative building process had been refined by

such businessmen as Nicholas Barbon. It seemed all could win: the landlord, the speculative builder and his financial backers, and the house's first occupant, providing the markets were buoyant, politics and lending rates were stable, and the demand for houses kept just ahead of supply. Thomas demolished the ancient manor in or just after 1687.

The consortium of speculators was to operate with the landlord's approval because the lease was for only sixty-two years, after which the land and building upon it were to revert to the family. This reveals one of the potential problems with the speculative system. Speculators generally had a short-term interest, so they wanted to build as quickly and cheaply as possible, sell the leases on, and move on. The estate had a long-term interest. It received little ground rent during the term of the lease and so wanted to ensure – as far as was possible – that the buildings the estate gained at the end of the lease remained valuable. Therefore estates wanted sound and solid and, by definition, reasonably expensive buildings that enhanced the value of the land. In an attempt to ensure this, estates tried to impose conditions on the speculators and builders working on its land. This generally worked if demand was high and profits assured, but if markets fell then landlords tended to make concessions to coax builders to complete speculations that, short term at least, appeared unprofitable.

In standard manner the Lawrence family agreed the basic form and scale of the proposed houses with its lessees, which of course confirms that the Lawrence family, putting profits before sentiment or sense of history, were agreeable to the demolition of the ancient manor house. There were to be four ranges – or terraces – of houses numbering thirty 'substantial' brick-built houses in total. They were to be two storeys high with cellars and garrets, each with at least two rooms per floor and a minimum

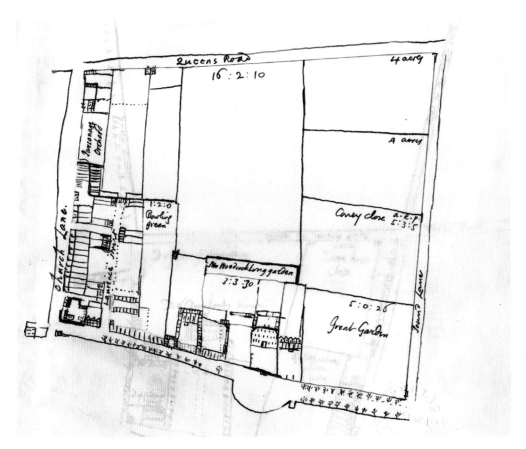

35. *Above*
Detail from Dr King's survey of Chelsea, dating from c. 1705. From the left (west), is 'Church Lane' (now Old Church Street) and the Old Church; 'Laurence Street', with a group of houses forming a court closing the north end of the street; the 'Bowling Green' on the east edge of which Cheyne Row was built in 1708; Shrewsbury House; Winchester House set back and attached on its east end to the New Manor House, which appears to be of quadrangular form with a show front set in a deep court and facing the Thames. To the east of the show front is a range of buildings and then the manor house's large 'Great Garden'. To the north is the 'Queens Road', named in honour of Queen Anne and now the King's Road.

36. *Above*
The southeast corner of Lawrence Street with Cheyne Walk, drawn in 1882 by John Crowther. This ad hoc group of modest buildings dated from the late 1680s. All was soon to be cleared away for the high-rise Carlyle Mansions, the 'writers' block', completed in 1886.

37. *Above right*
Most delightful and very characterful houses of the late 1690s stood on the corner of Danvers Street at its junction with Duke Street and of Lombard Street, both westward extensions of Cheyne Walk. The drawing was made in the late nineteenth century by W.W. Burgess.

38. *Overleaf*
Paradise Row, built in 1691 opposite the stables of the newly completed Royal Hospital, was the epitome of cosy but architecturally stylish domestic charm. It was a thing of 'immediate and surprising beauty' but this did not save it from demolition in 1906. This view by W.W. Burgess dates from c. 1900.

frontage of 16 feet. The arrangement of the four ranges is not specified in the agreement but the *Victoria County History* suggests that nine houses fronted Church Lane (now Old Church Street) between Justice Walk and the parish church, with about seven north of Justice Walk. The remaining two ranges were located on each side of the newly formed Lawrence Street (*Victoria County History*, pp. 31-40). James Hamilton's survey of Chelsea, updated in 1717, shows two groups of nine houses on the east side of Church Lane, each side of Justice Walk, but only a scattering of individual houses on the west side of Lawrence Street and no long terrace on the east side.

However, Hamilton could have been wrong. Church Lane was linked to the new Lawrence Street by a new narrow street called Johns Street, which survives as Justice Walk. This less imposing street presumably offered the opportunity to build smaller houses for less wealthy lessees or tenants, or even shops. This would have

increased the speculation's chance of success by widening the range of buildings on offer and – if shops were created – perhaps increased the value of the houses by making the new development more self-contained. However, this would have been a double-edged sword because the wrong type of shops or trades in Johns Street could have reduced the value of the neighbouring terraces.

Thomas worked with a consortium of speculating builders and by 1689, when he died, the terraces fronting on to Church Lane and Lawrence Street had been built. New houses on the Lawrence land included a row of five houses that faced the river and ran from the east end of the church to Lawrence Street. Completed in 1689, the houses were originally called Prospect Place, and later numbered 59 to 63 Cheyne Walk. The pair at the west end of the row survives, now stucco-fronted and altered externally, but still clearly late seventeenth century in origin. Number 63 is particularly fine (although rebuilt after war damage)

with its façade framed by quoins – as are the pavilions on the Royal Hospital and portions of nearby Lindsey House – and with a large carriage arch occupying most of its ground floor (*Victoria County History*, pp. 31-40).

Lord Wharton speculates

Lord Wharton was not long master of the early seventeenth-century jewel-like Danvers House, but in his ownership the house was demolished and most of its grounds, including Dove House Close, were let off for speculative house building. In 1696 Wharton leased part or all of the ground to Benjamin Stallwood, a bricklayer, who sub-let sites to other builders. The leases granted included sites on the south end of the newly laid out Danvers Street – in fact no more than a short court off Cheyne Walk, where three or four houses were built on each side. There were also houses built either side of the street facing the river. There was a plaque on 77 Cheyne Walk recording that Danvers Street had been started in 1696 by Stallwood.

Walter W. Burgess.

Paradise Row.
Pattern proof. Coll. v. Goulding

Mr. Carlyle's House   *Great Cheyne Row*

Cheyne Row ... built in 1708 ... broadly uniform ... and setting the benchmark for future speculative houses in Chelsea village.

39. Above
Cheyne Row, built in 1708, photographed
in the late nineteenth century. Many of the
later additions, such as the veranda balconies,
have been long removed.

It is probable that Danvers House was demolished around this time (see page 56 and *Victoria County History*, pp. 31–40).

The Cheynes become house builders
Soon after the Lawrence initiate and contemporary with Wharton's activities, Charles Cheyne, the 1st Viscount Newhaven, moved to exploit his land through speculative house building. Cheyne owned Chelsea Manor and the New Manor House that once belonged to Henry VIII (see page 42), and in 1691 – just after the Royal Hospital was completed – he granted building leases for land to the north of the highway leading from the hospital to Chelsea village. The site was immediately to the west of the hospital, opposite its stables, and so was visually most intimately connected with Wren's new buildings. The leases were granted to a

builder named George Norris who erected a row of ten most delightful houses, all two storeys high but of varied widths, set behind generous front gardens or courts. They were called Paradise Row, and gave their name to the entire thoroughfare until it was later named Queen's Road (*Victoria County History*, pp. 42-3). The 1909 *Survey of London* described the row in loving and lingering manner: 'Built of the warm-coloured brickwork which is so characteristic of the time of Wren, they possessed fine roomy panelled interiors, and the outside presented all the charm of a continuous tiled roof and beautiful wood cornice' with the most striking detail 'after the cornice' being 'the beautiful doorways and the wrought-iron gates and railings which were placed between square brick piers surmounted by stone balls'. The 'effect of the row', with its 'warm-coloured brickwork and standing orderly and dignified', was, mused the *Survey*, to impress, 'the beholder with its immediate and surprising beauty' (*Survey of London: Volume 2*, pp. 23-8). The houses are shown on Richardson's 1769 map and had became part of the Cadogan Estate. By this time Paradise Row had been joined by another terrace to the west, also on the north side of the road. To the east of the row stood Ormonde House, erected in the late seventeenth century by Thomas Hill – the principal mason of the Royal Hospital – also on land leased from Charles Cheyne. In 1906 Paradise Row was demolished to make way for modern flats and houses. Having tested the water with Paradise Row, Cheyne moved his speculative operations to the heart of the village and in 1695 let the Magpie Inn and its stables on Cheyne Walk for forty-one years to Chelsea builder John Clarkson. He demolished the old buildings and built two houses facing the Thames. These are among the first river-frontage buildings constructed on Cheyne land. When Charles Cheyne died in 1698, his son William, the 2nd Viscount Newhaven, inherited the manor lands and house. However, he had little interest in

Chelsea and in 1712, when he became Lord Lieutenant of Buckinghamshire, sold all of Chelsea Manor to Sir Hans Sloane (Holme, p. 32). However, he did leave one memorial to his ownership – Cheyne Row, which was built in 1708, as is recorded on a date stone on number 16, and runs at right angles to the river, set some way north of Cheyne Walk, and facing west. The land the row occupies was a bowling green, as shown on one of Dr King's surveys of Chelsea, dating from c. 1705, and set north of the Three Tuns tavern on Cheyne Walk. The east edge of the site was marked by one of the ancient boundary walls of Shrewsbury House. Curiously, the row is not shown on Hamilton's survey of 1717.

When built, the houses forming the row were not only large and handsome but also broadly uniform – and must have made a most striking group, upping the stakes after the relatively modest houses on the Lawrence land, and setting the benchmark for future speculative houses in Chelsea village. Although the row – now ten houses long – has been altered, with one house rebuilt, one at its north end demolished and others mutilated, it remains visually striking, and still more than hints at its once commanding presence. The houses at each end make the original design clear. Numbers 16 and 18 are each three storeys high above basements, and three windows wide but with a blank half window set near their party walls. Half windows like these were a common detail of London terrace houses built between c. 1690 and 1712, and invariably were placed next to the party wall that incorporated the chimney stack. This means these narrow windows, now mostly bricked-up, could have lit a small closet formed between the front wall, party wall and the side of the stack as it projects into the room. The windows in these houses, like those in the rest of the row, have straight brick arches, as was standard in London until 1716 or so when segmental arches became the prevailing fashion. Most revealing is the fact that the first-floor windows in both houses are slightly taller than those on the second floor. This soon became standard practice, reflecting the Renaissance idea of the first-floor *piano nobile* and the fact the first floor had a higher status than the second floor because it was the location of parlours or the main bed chamber. In the first decades of the eighteenth century it was common in London for the ground floor to be the most important floor – with a higher floor-to-ceiling height and richer decoration – because it was the location of the more 'public' rooms of the house, such as the dining parlour. The ground floors of numbers 16 and 18 were radically altered in the nineteenth century, so their original status is, from external examination, hard to determine. Internally these houses, like the houses in the rest of the row, have simple two-room deep plans, with closets off the rear rooms and a dog-leg staircase set in a rear corner of each house.

A most striking external detail is the bold, timber-made modillioned eaves cornice that unites both houses. Such cornices were a standard detail of London houses until 1710 or so, following an Act of Parliament of 1707 that banned timber eaves cornices to help prevent the spread of fire. This act initially applied only to the City of London and the City of Westminster but its influence spread rapidly as various landlords invoked its clauses as part of their building conditions and agreements with developers. Similarly, an act of 1709 required timber sash boxes to be set back 4 inches (one-brick width) from the face of a building to better prevent the spread of fire. The sash boxes in these houses are set back slightly, although this might be the result of later alterations.

Numbers 30, 32 and 34 – at the north end of the row – are of the same architectural language and design, except on numbers 30 and 32 a later parapet replaces the original timber eaves cornice. However, the ground floors of all three houses retain

their original design. They make it clear that ground-floor windows were originally the same height as those on the first floor, suggesting each floor was of similar status, and it seems the sash boxes were initially set almost flush with the brick façades, as remained usual in London – despite the 1709 Act – into the early 1730s. Furthermore, all three houses in this group retain doorcases that appear to be original and which are generally monuments to the wood carver's skills. The doorcases on 32 and 34 are late seventeenth century in manner, with projecting hoods incorporating half domes, supported on console brackets that are well and deeply carved and that feature – as was usual – acanthus leaves licking over the bracket's serpentine form. In fact, as the 1913 *Survey of London* makes clear, the doorcase on 34 is a modern copy (*Survey of London: Volume 4*, pp. 61-8). The doorcase was added at some time after 1949.

Numbers 24 and 26 are also largely intact and of the same uniform design, although number 24 has lost its original eaves cornice and both ground floors have been altered. A small but interesting detail is that the half windows in number 34 are open, and presumably light a closet or recess next to the chimney breast. Other half windows in the row are blind, as is usually the case, although those in number 32 are furnished by sash boxes, suggesting they were once open.

In 1709, as Cheyne Row was nearing completion, William Cheyne rounded off the development by granting building leases at the north end of the Bowling Green to various builders, including John Clarkson and Oliver Maddox, both of whom were involved in the construction of Cheyne Row. Upper Cheyne Row was laid out on a strip of land that was originally earmarked for the construction of stables and coach houses to serve the occupants of Cheyne Row. No doubt this was an attempt to make houses in the row more

Sloane's development was no mean affair.... What he planned for the Cheyne Walk site ... was a row of eighteen urban palaces.

attractive to potential tenants, but when work got under way in 1716 five houses were built, more modest than those in Cheyne Row but handsome enough. Presumably during the intervening years it became clear that Cheyne Row could be let without the incentive of stabling. But houses with gardens required more land than did stables, so Cheyne had to do a deal with Dr King to acquire some glebe land for this development. King was not only a chronicler of history and change in early eighteenth-century Chelsea; he was also an active participant in the local world of speculative building. He claimed to have started playing the housing market in 1704 and seems to have been the first Chelsea clergyman to set about augmenting the value and income of the living by granting building leases on glebe land (*Dr. King's Manuscript Account of Chelsea*, p. 164; Faulkner, *Chelsea, and its Environs*, p. 182; *Victoria County History*, pp. 238-50).

40. Below
Number 34 Cheyne Row, built in 1708 but the handsome semi-spherical and bracketed door surround dates from the mid-twentieth century, based on an original of the neighbouring house.

41. *Above*
Numbers 3 to 6 Cheyne Walk, a group of palatial terrace
houses built in 1717/18 under the control of Sir Hans Sloane.
Number 4, centre, has Doric pilasters.

Additional houses were added to Upper Cheyne Row later in the eighteenth century. Most of these survive in the group numbered 16 to 28a. Number 16 has a large first-floor Venetian window and is dated 1767. Ground- and second-floor windows are also arranged, most awkwardly, as tripartite compositions. Number 20 has the best preserved façade of c. 1716, still with flat-headed windows, while 24 and 28 (an oddly numbered pair) have one wide window per floor and share a handsome timber eaves cornice similar to those on Cheyne Row. In addition, number 28 has a very fine doorcase, incorporating large serpentine brackets supporting a cornice.

Sir Hans Sloane's first developments in Chelsea

In 1712 Sir Hans Sloane bought the New Manor House – Chelsea Place – and its grounds with an eye to developing it into something more than it was. First, he divided the garden to the east of the New Manor House and fronting on to Cheyne Walk into building plots. Although this divided the manor house from the garden and meant forgoing the orchard and 'ingenious waterworks', it meant that other newer buildings and gardens could bloom in their stead. Like many visionaries of the time, Sloane was a complex man who embodied many of the conflicts and contradictions of his age, characterised by the juxtaposition of the new insights and knowledge of the Enlightenment with an almost mystic clinging to past beliefs. This complexity included benefitting from the labour of enslaved people in Jamaica. Sloane, President of the Royal Society, displayed a fascination for the scientific study of the beauties of nature, and became a great supporter of Chelsea's Physic Garden where he had studied apothecary in his youth. Yet he built on his own 'Great Garden', presumably because the sacrifice of a large mature garden meant that many smaller gardens could themselves mature in time.

Indeed, Sloane's development was no mean affair. To maximise the potential for architectural beauty and profit – as well as increase the real estate value of Chelsea village – what he planned for the Cheyne Walk site between Robinson's Lane (now Flood Street) and the existing New Manor House was a row of eighteen urban palaces, with the number of plots increased by the creation on a new road – Manor Street (now Cheyne Gardens) – set at right angles to Cheyne Walk. The general arrangement is shown on Richardson's estate map of 1769 (see pages 70–1). The houses were all to be set within front courts, in the French manner, and separated from the public carriageway by ornate wrought iron railings and gates interspersed with massive gate piers. It is evident that the aim was to let plots to rich individuals who desired to build their own sumptuous homes but, when necessary, to build some houses, of more standard and simple design, as speculations. This strategy meant that rather than aiming for the architectural uniformity displayed in Cheyne Row, Cheyne Walk was to display variety, movement and individual Baroque exuberance.

The building plots created were generally very wide and the rear gardens generous, with some gardens to the west of Manor Street running as far as the old north wall of the Tudor 'Great Garden'. John Rocque's smaller-scale London map of 1744–6 makes clear the generous size of the gardens and suggests their formal design, with larger gardens organised so that visually separate areas lie to the north of the gardens immediately behind the house (see 'Exact Survey of City's of London, Westminster ye Borough of Southwark and the Country near London ten miles round'). More detail is added by Richard Horwood's map of 1799–1819. It indicates the designs of the gardens – although these could be generic – and that the garden area behind the Cheyne Walk houses east of Manor Street had been apportioned to be shared by houses on Robinson's Lane and Manor Street. However, the gardens behind the Cheyne Walk houses west of Manor Street remain deep with some houses – such as number 16 – retaining gardens that extend as far north as the Tudor wall of the former 'Great Garden' and that extend behind the shorter gardens of neighbouring houses.

The first building leases were granted in 1717, many to John Witt, with Sloane speculating on some of the plots himself (Holme, p. 113). Enough of the houses survive to give the initial feel of this architecturally diverse and overwhelmingly palatial terrace. 3 Cheyne Walk, built in 1717, is relatively modest and much like the earlier houses in Cheyne Row, but only bigger. Presumably it was built as a speculation rather than specifically for the first occupier. It has a doorcase with robustly carved brackets supporting a hood and has been extended in height so there is no timber cornice. Almost certainly there never was one, but there was instead a parapet, as was then the fashion. The most noticeable difference between this house and those in Cheyne Row is that here the windows have segmental arches, as was becoming the fashion.

Number 4 is a much more ambitious affair. It dates from 1718, is four windows wide with the ground and first floor embraced by giant Doric pilasters wrought out of fine rubbed red brick. This use of the Orders – as pure ornaments rather than as part of a precise and proportionally governed system – is typical of the Baroque. The pilasters support a cornice, above which rises a third floor, like an attic of a Roman triumphal arch. The upper floors are additions. All windows have segmental arches and all are furnished with large keystones, again a Baroque touch. The doorcase is particularly fine, with the door opening framed by fluted Corinthian pilasters supporting an architrave that ramps-up through the centre of the frieze. The architrave also supports a pair of boldly carved brackets. These in turn support a hood, which is detailed as a cornice to make the entablature above

the door complete. It really is a lovely and clever piece of vernacular classical design. Inside, the house is grand, although much altered. It is two rooms deep with an open-well staircase, rising to the first floor only, occupying half the front volume of the house. At the rear is a pair of closets, one at each end of the house but now almost lost in later alterations. These suggest that the rear rooms of the house were designed for comfort and convenience, with all rooms served by closets.

Number 5 is a three-bay house framed by rusticated piers, that read as pilasters, very much in the contemporary French Baroque taste, while number 6 – again built in about 1717/18 – is breath-taking in its sense of massive scale, majestic simplicity and subtle sense of proportion. It has the feel of big, bold, raw and beautiful Irish houses of similar or slightly later date, such as those in Henrietta Street, Dublin. The house is five windows wide and three storeys high above a basement, with ground-floor windows slightly taller than first-floor windows, and the first floor slightly taller than second floor. So the ground floor was the main floor. The façade is wrought of beautiful quality brickwork, with unusually generous red brick dressings to the windows and walling of pale yellow, almost amber coloured stock bricks, well laid in Flemish bond. Windows arches are still flat, in the slightly earlier manner. Floors are divided by bold stringcourses formed of red brick, with the one above the second-floor windows made of moulded bricks so it reads as a cornice. There are two breaks in the cornice and stringcourses to allow for the symmetrical placing of lead rainwater heads and down pipes. A very nice detail. The house was built for his own occupation by Joseph Danvers, whose name appears in the rate book from 1718 to 1753. It would appear that Danvers used an architect of some considerable ability to design his home but, sadly, his identity is currently unknown. Danvers – seemingly with no direct connection to the Danvers family

42. Above
Number 6 Cheyne Walk, built in 1717/8 and
impressive for is massive and sophisticated
simplicity, characterised by erudite detail,
strict symmetry and subtle and harmonically
related proportion. Note the way in which
visually satisfying central emphasis is given
to the façade in a most minimal manner by
framing the central windows with piers slightly
wider than those neighbouring. The house was
built for Joseph Danvers, an MP and Fellow of
the Royal Society.

who in the 1620s built Danvers House on a nearby site (see page 49) – was a Leicestershire gentleman, who from 1722 was an MP, from 1724 a Fellow of the Royal Society and from 1746 a baronet (*Survey of London: Volume 2*, pp. 45-9). The two lead rainwater heads on the entrance front date from the construction of the house because they bear the Danvers coat of arms. Also observe the curious arrangement above the front door – a pair of small square windows with glazing bars rather than a more conventional fanlight. In 1718 fanlights – with shaped panes of glass set into radiating lead or timber cames – were still an unusual option so this was an alternative method of getting light into the entrance hall.

Next, moving west, numbers 7 to 11 are a group of late nineteenth-century houses rebuilt on original plots, all red brick and most in the Queen Anne Revival style, number 9 with charming oriels and another with a niche topped by a shell motif, and most with tall facetted bays. These rebuildings were presumably stimulated by the construction of Chelsea Embankment and improved communications between Chelsea village and Westminster and the City to the east. The design of the houses must have been inspired by the work of Norman Shaw and the development of Pont Street and Cadogan Square (see page 212).

Number 15 Cheyne Walk is another house of 1717–18, four windows wide with segmental arches and restrained in design, although its façade is flanked by a pier of striking width, visually duplicating the role of the Doric pilasters on number 4. The ironwork in front of the house is particularly fine. Elements are from c. 1718 but much has been renewed in sympathetic manner. The gilded dolphin perched on the overthrow above the gate is the crest of Lord Courtney, a one-time occupant of the house. Above the first-floor windows is a sundial that proclaims 'Lead Kindly Light' and a pair of now much weathered terracotta panels. That to the west shows the heads of Erasmus and More, that to the east Mazinni and Carlyle (see *Chelsea Society Tenth Annual Report*, 1937, p. 180). The house immediately to the west, number 16, is far more architecturally assertive and a rich and rather original repository of Baroque mannerisms. The house was built in 1717–18 by John Witt, who speculated much on Sloane's estate, but it seems so ornate and individual that it must surely have been designed with the collaboration of the first lessee. The excellent early ironwork in front of the house includes the monogram 'RC', which refers to Richard Chapman, the first occupant and for whom the house was probably built.

The design of the main façade is extraordinary. It is five windows wide and three storeys high above a basement, with ground and first floors framed by brick-built pilaster strips embellished with rustic blocks. This is broadly similar to the design of number 4 Cheyne Walk (both houses also have two rear closet wings, suggesting the same builder or architect was responsible), but in the case of number 16 the pilasters terminate with a brick fascia topped by a stone ogee moulding rather than Doric capitals. This detail is continued across the façade to form a rudimentary cornice. Above this cornice the central three bays of the façade break forward and are topped by a pediment, with stone carved mouldings and dentil course, which is partly supported on stone brackets. Above the apex of the pediment there now sits a large and ornate stone urn. It is all most distinctive and it is typical of the individualistic and diverse nature of Baroque Cheyne Walk that this pediment does not mark the centre of the Walk or the centre of a palatial uniform group, but simply draws attention to the house on which it sits. Also Baroque are the large keystones set in the segmental window arches. However, despite these notable features, the most visually striking aspect of the house is the two-storey canted bay, set in the centre of the façade, above the front door. This bay is made of timber and plaster, and was probably added around 1760 to make the most of the prospects offered by the house's delightful riverside location. It was this house that Dante Gabriel Rossetti occupied from 1862 (see page 178).

Numbers 17 and 18 Cheyne Walk date from 1717–18 and occupy the most westerly building plots marked out by Sloane on the Manor House's Great Garden. Indeed, number 18 abutted the boundary of the Manor House. Much of the original external fabric survives but the houses were greatly altered in 1867, when cast iron balconies with verandas were added to their first floors and the ground floors were rendered. In the early eighteenth century, number 18 was the location of Don Saltero's famed coffee house (see page 234). To the west, numbers 19 to 26 Cheyne Walk were built from 1759 to 1765 on the frontage occupied by the Tudor Manor House, soon after its demolition. They form a loosely uniform, plain but imposing terrace, four storeys high with square 'attic' windows set above a masonry cornice. Most have pedimented Doric doorcases. In 1906, number 23 was embellished with a late seventeenth-century door surround with carved brackets salvaged from nearby Paradise Row (*Survey of London: Volume 2*, pp. 65–75). Interestingly, Rocque's smaller-scale London map captures the moment of change. It shows the Manor House demolished but its site not built upon so there is a wide gap in the Cheyne Walk frontage, with gardens over the ground on which the house stood. Rocque's map was, in theory, issued between 1744 and 1746, but was evidently revised after 1753, when the New Manor House was demolished.

West beyond these the next significant group of early buildings on Cheyne Walk are numbers 46, 47 and 48, that adjoin the site of Shrewsbury House (see pages 26-7). This is now a rather mixed and altered group that probably dates from 1711. On the site of number 49, now rebuilt, was the Feathers tavern, while numbers 46 to 48 stand on the site of the Three Tuns tavern, demolished by 1711, soon after Cheyne Row was built on its bowling green. Of the existing group, the façade of number 46 appears to date from the mid-eighteenth century but its interior is earlier, with, according to the *Survey of London*, an archway between entrance passage and stairwell that is ornamented with 'beautifully carved Ionic capitals' (*Survey of London: Volume 2*, pp. 82–3).

The façades of numbers 47 and 48 appear to date from 1711, but with number 48 now rendered and the brickwork of number 47 unfortunately painted white in recent years. Number 47 retains half windows, like the houses in Cheyne Row, with those on the ground and first floor being fitted with narrow sashes. On the corner of Cheyne Walk and Lawrence Street is the towering Carlyle Mansions of 1886–8, designed in a red brick Queen Anne Revival style that was the usual urban manifestation of the Arts and Crafts movement. When designed, the block displayed little sympathy for the established architectural character or scale of Cheyne Walk, but then it was part of the new riverside Chelsea being ushered-in by the construction of the Embankment (see page 76). However, the block does have some beguiling details, notably the white painted relief panels on its Lawrence Street façade that offer a fine display of favoured Arts and Crafts motifs, including a wide variety of birds and vases of sunflowers. The mansion block was evidently comfortable and its lofty prospect of the Thames inspiring, because it has accommodated, over the years, an extraordinary number of writers including Henry James, T.S. Eliot, Somerset Maugham and Ian Fleming. West of Lawrence Street are the streets and houses laid out on the site of Beaufort House and its gardens after the house had been demolished in c. 1740 (see page 40). Beaufort Row was started in the 1760s on the line of what became Beaufort Street. This development was presumably conceived in anticipation of the construction of Battersea Bridge – planned in 1766 and opened in 1771 – that is aligned with Beaufort Street. Houses were built in the 1770s on Beaufort Ground facing the river, the best surviving group is numbers 91 to 94 that date from 1771 to 1777. Number 91, on the corner with Beaufort Street is very fine – as is number 92 – forming a boldly designed composition with a central full-height canted bay and an array of Venetian windows facing the river, and a door with a wide semi-circular fan light.

Chelsea's growth after 1750

The growth of Chelsea during the one hundred years after the demolition in 1753 of the New Manor House is essentially the story of the creation of a series of squares and streets of more or less uniform terraces, although often of greatly differing ambition and scale, on different estates and the work of varied builders or architects. Most were located inland from the river and on, or just off, the King's Road. Much of the building took place from 1810, particularly around 1830 when the King's Road was finally and fully opened to the public. *The Victoria County History* offers some statistics to illustrate the rate of Chelsea's growth. In 1674 it contained around 172 houses and in 1777 there were 741 houses. By 1795 Daniel Lysons calculated that Chelsea – still defined as shown on Hamilton's 1717 survey (Fulham Road to the north, the Thames to the south, Knightsbridge to the east and Chelsea Creek to the west) – contained 1,350 houses. Lysons observed that 'within the last two centuries ... few parishes in the Kingdom have increased in population to so great a degree at that of Chelsea', with 'in the last ten or twelve years, about 600 new houses' having been built (Lysons, p. 116–71). For the following fifty years after 1795 Chelsea grew at the rate of nearly one

hundred new houses per year, at least in part due to Acts of Parliament receiving royal assent in 1825 permitting the Cadogan Estate to grant building leases for the site of Winchester House (see page 49) and the rector to grant building leases for glebe land (*Victoria County History*, pp. 26–31). Between 1720 and 1810 building in Chelsea, inland of the river, tended to be located on ancient thoroughfares such as Church Lane (now Old Church Street) and the King's Road. There were numerous relatively small estates in Chelsea that, like the Lawrence Estate, related to sites of lost houses and their gardens and grounds. However, there was also glebe land, which belonged to the parish and that was in one way or another to produce income or capital to support the incumbent and the parish. There was also the ever dwindling Chelsea Common, north of the King's Road – once 30 acres in extent – that was for the use of specific landowners and owners or tenants of specific houses (such as the Manor House and Shrewsbury House) for specific purposes, such as the pasturing of cattle and horses. It was also a place of gravel pits and small ponds. Dr King gives some detail in about 1705: 'This is a Common belonging to some Ancient Houses ... for the Depasturage of 40 cows & 20 Heiffers. To keep these there was always a Cow-keeper, whose business it was to mark the Cattle, to drive home the Cows at night to Several Owners, and to impound all Cattle ummarkt or any Horse wch broke into the sd Common, or be found there. He was usually put in by the Lord of the Manor's Bayliff, and allowed by the Commoners and paid by them' (*Dr. King's Manuscript Account of Chelsea*, p. 216).

Much of the east side of Church Lane (now Old Church Street) south of the King's Road was glebe land, parts of which had been let to the Lawrence Estate and to the Cheyne family for developments north of Cheyne Row. In 1719 the rector, Dr John King, let 2½ acres of glebe land, fronting on to the south side of the King's Road and which formed part of Great Conduit Field, to John Narbonne. In 1722 Narbonne sublet a portion – stretching 50 feet along the south side of the King's Road and 130 feet deep – to John Pierene. What are now 213 and 215 King's Road had just been built (probably in 1720, also on Narbonne land), each set within a small front garden or court that looked on to a rural road that was still essentially private. Number 217 is slightly smaller in size, and is somewhat later, perhaps c. 1735.

These houses are modest and self-effacing exercises in vernacular classical design. However, their neighbour to the east – built on the land let to Pierene – is none of these things. Number 211 King's Road is not greater in height than its neighbours, although admittedly much greater in width. But its extra width is not what makes it so different. This lies in its vaulting architectural ambition. Now known as Argyll House, number 211 was designed in 1723 by the eminent Venetian architect Giacomo Leoni, who arrived in Britain in about 1714 and stayed and worked in the country until his death in 1746. Despite, or perhaps because of, his Italian origin, Leoni became a key figure in the early eighteenth-century development of the Anglo-Palladian style, not least because between 1715 and 1720 he published the first English translation of Andrea Palladio's seminal l'Quattro Libri dell'architettura.

Number 211 King's Road was built by Pierene for his own occupation and he lived in the house until about 1740. What he created was a small county house, essentially a villa inspired by those designed and published by Palladio, but rather oddly positioned – set beside a road and as part of a terrace of modest houses. Contemplation of Pierene's houses is most rewarding. The details are sober and exquisite, particularly the stone doorcase with its engaged Doric columns united as a single and most elegant composition

with the pedimented window above. The brickwork – if somewhat gaunt – is beautifully executed and has, no doubt as Leoni intended, something of a Roman feel. What is curious, of course, is that this Venetian architect produced a classical building that is quintessentially English and a prime example of what became known as Georgian Palladian architecture. It is solemn externally, with beauty coming from studied simplicity and harmonically related proportions. The interior is less reserved – as is the way with English Palladian architecture – but is also most precisely detailed and carefully organised to make the best use of the site and its orientation (*Victoria County History*, pp. 31–40).

Stanley House
Stanley House, set in its own grounds, north of the King's Road, towards its west end, is a remarkable survival. It was started in 1691 – seemingly the rebuilding of an earlier house on or near the site – for the Stanley family. The house does not appear to have been completed for some years and was probably not occupied until 1701 when Thomas White was in residence. When complete, the house took the form of a charming brick box, five windows wide and two storeys high, with a centrally placed pedimented doorcase and a timber eaves cornice. Names of occupants changed fairly regularly during the eighteenth and early nineteenth centuries but the most significant is Sir William Hamilton, the antiquary, British Envoy at the Court of Naples and husband to Lord Nelson's mistress and one-time London harlot Emma, Lady Hamilton. Sir William was Secretary to Lord Elgin and helped to superintend the transportation of the marble metopes and fragments of sculpture and frieze Elgin acquired from the ruins of the Parthenon in Athens. Most of the 'marbles' had arrived in London by 1812 and at some point near this date Hamilton added a large hall to Stanley House and installed within it casts

43. *Above*
The central portion of Argyll House, numbered
211 King's Road, designed in 1723 by the
Venetian-born architect Giacomo Leoni.
The house possesses a solemn, almost gloomy,
external grandeur, with its bold simplicity
relived by fine detail and noble proportion.

44. Above
The entrance hall and staircase within Argyll House looking through the open front door towards the King's Road. Painted by John Lavery on a summer's day in the 1930s, the view features interior decorators Sybil Colefax, then owner of the house, and Syrie Maugham. All joinery is painted in shades of white, a fashion promoted a few years earlier by Maugham.

45. Overleaf
Part of the central portion of the terrace forming the east side of Paultons Square. Designed in simple uniform manner, with the central part of the terrace emphasised by extra height and extra decoration, the square was built during the 1830s and into the 1850s.

of some of the marbles. They were copied many times after, but this room at Stanley House marks the marbles first appearance in a London building (*Survey of London: Volume 4*, pp. 43–4).

Paultons Square

To explore Chelsea squares and terraces built after 1810 it is convenient to move from west to east along the King's Road. The first major event is Paultons Square that was laid out on the 4-acre Dove House Close as a continuation of Danvers Street. In the early sixteenth century the close had been part of Sir Thomas More's estate and in the early seventeenth century had been owned by Sir John Danvers (see page 53). By the time construction of the square started in the early 1830s the land was owned by the Sloane Stanley family, which was descended from the 1717 marriage between Sir Hans Sloane's daughter Sarah and George Stanley (see page 47). Named after the family's Paultons Park estate in Hampshire, the square was not completed and fully inhabited until the 1850s and significantly not shown on Thompson's map of 1836 (see page 109). It is a visually impressive affair, designed and executed in the late Georgian tradition with architectural presence coming from the ruthless repetition of the same simple basic and uniform unit – a two-window wide house, three storeys high above basement with white painted stucco ground floors and a masonry eaves cornice. The potential monotony of long elevations formed by identical houses of such simple design is reduced by the subtle and harmoniously related proportions of the façades, and by giving the two long north–south vistas central emphasis. This is achieved by raising the central groups of houses in height by means of an attic storey set above the cornice and a bit more detail around the windows. This really is a case where the whole is worth far more than the sum of the parts. It works, with the sustained rhythm of the very long terrace

that is the direct continuation of Danvers Street possessing a really most sublime quality. These terraces are the epitome of late Georgian urban domestic design, which gives their almost mechanical elevations a pleasing charm when viewed across the picturesque planting of the garden square. It is an outstanding exercise in the late Georgian planning ideal of *rus in urbe*.

Carlyle Square

Carlyle Square lies north of the King's Road and was until 1872 named Oakley Square. The majority of its houses date from the mid-nineteenth century, designed as detached villas, but the pair of pavilions at the square's south end, forming the junction with the King's Road, reveal its slightly earlier origin. Both pavilions present seven-window wide, four-storey frontages to the square with the centre three bays framed with Grecian Ionic pilasters sitting on a stucco ground-floor podium. Above the second-floor entablature are square attic windows. All is late Georgian in character, and dates from when the King's Road was fully opened to the public in 1830. As with Paultons Square, the garden is richly planted in picturesque fashion, creating a pleasant contrast with the regularity of the classical architecture that frames it. The square is shown, unbuilt, on Thompson's 1836 map (see page 109).

Chelsea Square and Sydney Street

Manresa Road runs north off the King's Road and off its west side is the remains of Chelsea Common, now no more than a garden at the centre of Chelsea Square. This started life in 1812 as Trafalgar Square but the name was changed in the twentieth century. All the original villas and terraces have gone, with, in their place, a diverse collection of mostly twentieth-century domestic architecture, most of it undistinguished but there is a pair of 1930s houses by Oliver Hill (see page 258).

The creation of Trafalgar Square was part of a larger building operation in the early nineteenth century to develop the fields north of the King's Road. For example, building started in 1808 in Jubilee Place, with Burnsall Street and Godfrey Street somewhat later. The aspirations of the builders were limited, with the houses generally small and architectural ambitions modest. These were streets and houses aimed at the more hum-drum residents of London – City clerks perhaps, scriveners, petty shopkeepers, minor merchants, craftsmen and tradesmen; essentially the population that was swelling as London expanded into the world city of commerce and manufacturing. It was these modest streets, particularly the narrow Manor Buildings, reached off King's Road and running between Chelsea Manor Street and Blenheim Street (now a combination of Burnsall Street and Astell Street), that by the 1880s were among the worst of Chelsea's slums (see page 291).

The Victoria County History records that of the one hundred of so houses built by speculators in Chelsea per year from 1831 to 1842, well over half were classed as fourth 'Rate'. Since the London Building Act of 1774, terraced houses were divided into four different 'Rates' according to their volume and expense of construction. The object was to control construction to improve solidity and ensure houses were as fire-resistant as possible.

The largest and most expensive houses were classed as first 'Rate', while the fourth 'Rate' were the smallest and most economic, generally only one or two storeys above ground level and worth no more than £150 (Victoria County History, pp. 26-31). The uniform two-storey high terrace that survives on the south side of Coulson Street, parallel with King's Road, that looks like it dates from around 1830 or just before, is a good example of fourth 'Rate' housing. Another example are the two-storey terraces houses on the east

side of Burnsall Street that were once part of the fearsome late nineteenth-century Blenheim Street/Manor Buildings slum, lying in the shadow of the Anchor Brewery.

So late Georgian and early Victorian Chelsea, taking form on the fields and gardens around King's Road, was a place of trade and commerce with a population made up of the humble and industrious rather than the rich and fashionable. Even its squares, which were of course the top-end residential locations, were formed with relatively simple terrace houses rather than monumental mansions. Sydney Street is a good example of early nineteenth-century enterprise. It was created in phases to connect the King's Road to Fulham Road, so providing a strategic north–south link through Chelsea. The street also provided the opportunity to create numerous plots on which to build speculative houses and gave direct access from the King's Road to the site proposed for the new parish Church of St Luke. Eventually built from 1819–24, the church was instigated by the then Rector of Chelsea, the Rev. Gerald Wellesley, a brother of the Duke of Wellington and husband of Lady Emily Cadogan (sister of 3rd Earl Cadogan) (see page 158). The street has been much rebuilt but numbers 117 to 123 on the west side, near the King's Road, is a small but very good and representative early group. They were part of a long terrace formed by houses of matching size, if not absolutely matching design, built between 1810–36. The southern portion of the terrace was demolished in recent years but what survives is outstanding. All houses appear to be fourth 'Rate' – each only one window wide – and three retain the substantial remains of beautifully designed and splendidly detailed timber shop fronts of c. 1810–20. Evidently, from its origin, this portion of Sydney Street was intended to be a commercial and retailing thoroughfare serving neighbouring Chelsea households. Of these shop fronts, number 119 is outstanding, indeed one of the best

46. Above
A portion of F.P. Thompson's map of
Chelsea, published in 1836 and dedicated
to the Earl Cadogan. This is a most detailed
and seemingly authoritative map, full of
fascinating information. Significantly, there is
no sign of Paultons Square between Danvers
Street and the King's Road and, off the King's
Road, Trafalgar (now Chelsea) Square is
shown laid out but only partly surrounded
by buildings. Oakley (now Carlyle) Square
is shown laid out but seemingly not framed
by houses. The location of Markham Square
is named but no layout is shown and what
was to be Wellington Square is marked by a
slight recess or court named Johnsons Square.
Curiously, the site of the New Manor House
on Cheyne Walk, that was demolished in 1753
with terrace houses soon built along its south
edge, is shown as a blank space.

Sydney Street ... retains ... beautifully designed ... timber shop fronts.... Number 119 is outstanding ... one of the best late Georgian shop fronts surviving in situ in London.

late Georgian shop fronts surviving in situ in London, with a full panoply of favourite Regency neo-classic details. It has Gothic fanlights above the two doors – one to the house and the other to the shop; there is a frieze with lozenge motifs; gesso masks and palm leaf motifs adorn the brackets framing the house door which is itself wonderful, embellished with an arcade pattern formed by reeded mouldings. The terrace opposite is formed by slightly later and very slightly larger buildings – all designed for residential use except for a corner tavern – with good ironwork, including cast iron balconies to first-floor windows and on the railings of number 86 an elegant lamp-holder that was originally fitted with a glass globe containing a lamp burning whale oil.

Markham Square and Smith Street
Markham Square and Smith Street enjoy an informal relationship, with their north–south axis loosely aligned north and south of the King's Road. Smith Street was

47. Above
Detail of a delicately and eruditely decorated shop front of c. 1810–20 on 119 Sydney Street. It is a mini-masterpiece of late Georgian retail design, and one of the best of its date and kind in London.

constructed from 1794 by Thomas Smith on land owned by the Green family, who were Chelsea-based brewers (see Faulkner, *Chelsea, and its Environs*, p. 216). Several groups of houses – for example, numbers 3, 4 and 5, and 48, 49 and 50 – date from the 1790s, with semi-circular doorways embellished with keystones and imposts made of a robust terracotta called Coade stone. Other terraces in the street, uniform but of varied design, date from the early nineteenth century. They all combine to make Smith Street one of Chelsea's most visually rewarding late Georgian thoroughfares.

Markham Square is of a slightly later date. An Act of Parliament for its construction on the site of an orchard belonging to Box Farm was obtained in 1825 by the landowner Matthew Markham. However, construction did not get underway until 1840, by which time the sophisticated simplicity of late Georgian street architecture was starting to be compromised by the addition of ornamental architraves and cornices to most windows. Nevertheless, the overall feel is still Georgian and the relationship between urban terraces and the lush planting of the square's garden – the result of a post-war design inspired by picturesque parks – is a particularly powerful evocation of the *rus in urbe* ideal. The square was not completed until 1852, by which time it was owned by Matthew Markham's heirs.

Wellington Square

Wellington Square is unlike other Chelsea squares in several respects – the fronts of all houses are entirely stucco clad, now painted white, and all are ornate and rich in an odd mix of Greek Revival and Roman Renaissance decoration. The houses are tall and narrow, rigidly uniform but with pilaster-framed doors punctuated at regular intervals by porches, all visually linked by a continuous first-floor cast iron balcony. In plan the square is also odd, as it is narrow in proportion to its width, a cul-

de-sac, with a narrow garden. The square is late, perhaps conceived soon after 1830 but not completed until the late 1840s. Unlike the other squares along the King's Road, this one was architect-designed as a coherent composition, which of course explains its somewhat overwrought visual presence. The architect was Francis Edwards, who from 1806 to 1810 worked for Sir John Soane, during which time he also attended the Royal Academy Schools. Edwards' client was Thomas Goding who, according to evidence given at the Old Bailey during a trial in May 1833, was a Knightsbridge-based 'ale-brewer', publican and speculative builder who was the victim of embezzlement by an employee (Proceedings of the Old Bailey, t18330516-54). Edwards worked for Goding on a regular basis. In the mid-1820s he designed, for Messrs Goding & Company, the Bell and Horns public house on the Alexander estate, Earls Court and in 1836 the Lion Brewhouse on the South Bank (*Survey of London: Volume 41, Brompton*, ed. F.H.W. Sheppard, LCC, London, 1983, pp. 58–86).

Sloane Square and Hans Town

The final square in this sequence is the most significant by far because it formed the centrepiece of what was essentially a new town that was to transform the nature of Chelsea and its physical relationship to the rest of the city. Sloane Square, placed at the very east end of the King's Road, was laid out in 1777, and connected to Knightsbridge and the metropolis to the northeast by the long, straight and broad Sloane Street, and to Turk's Row and the Royal Hospital by Lower Sloane Street.

Together, the square and the boulevard-like Sloane Street formed the core of the aspirational residential enclave christened Hans Town. The entrepreneur behind this enterprise was the Fulham-based master builder Henry Holland and his most able and experienced architect son, also named Henry Holland. They worked on land leased

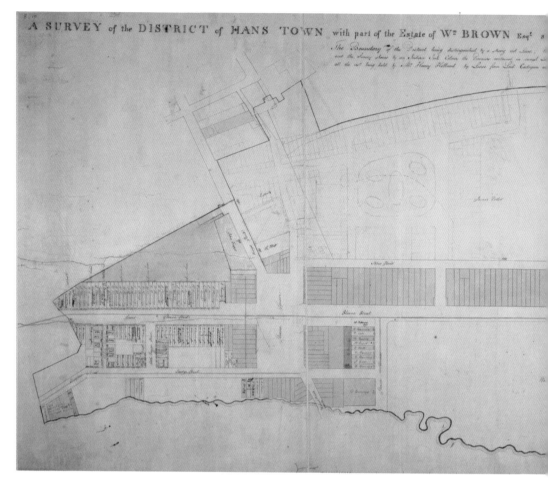

48. Above
A detailed plan, dating from the 1770s, showing the sublime proposal for Hans Town, as developed by Henry Holland and Lord Cadogan. North is to the right, with Sloane Street running north from the newly created Sloane Square. Terraces are shown lining the west side of Sloane Street but the east side – where Cadogan Place was to be built, set behind gardens – has not yet been designed. West of the north end of Sloane Street is the irregular octagon of Hans Place. The meandering red line marks the route of the River Westbourne, acting as an ownership and administrative boundary.

from the heirs of Sir Hans Sloane, primarily Lord Cadogan. Initial agreements were signed in 1771 and confirmed in 1777 with obligations to complete a certain number of houses – initially along Sloane Street – by 1785. The vision promoted by the Hollands and Lord Cadogan was extraordinary. The creation of a large square across the route of the King's Road and of a long, wide avenue connecting this square – and indeed Chelsea – to Knightsbridge and the rest of London was a great public work with city-wide implications. However, it was to be realised by a private landlord through the process of speculative house building. Thus, of course, were most of Britain's Georgian cities made. They are now much admired works of urban art, but were primarily

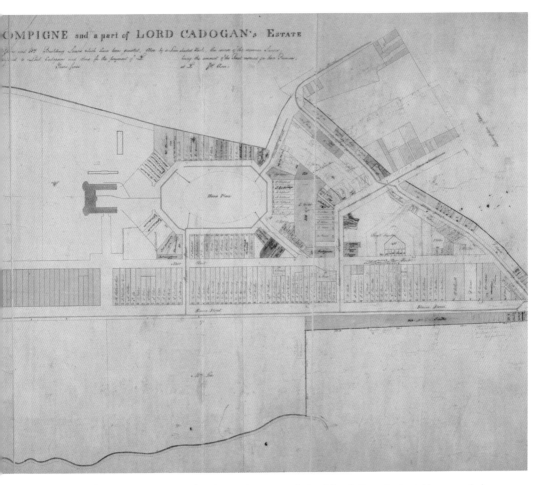

...OMPIGNE and a part of LORD CADOGAN's Estate

money-making exercises, and only works of art by accident. The name of the 'town' was, of course, to honour Sir Hans Sloane and mark the Cadogans' relationship – through marriage – with the man who had played such a key role in Chelsea's history. As well as the square and Sloane Street, Holland junior laid out the eastern part of Pont Street, Cadogan Place and the elongated octagon of Hans Place – 89 acres in extent. (Pont Street was not extended westwards to link Beauchamp Place with Belgravia until 1874.)

Richard Horwood's London map of 1799–1819 makes the scale and form of Hans Town very clear. Sloane Square, a rectangle of double-square proportion, sits diagonally across the meandering route of the King's Road, that Horwood shows continuing northwest to Pimlico. From near the centre of the north side of the square, Sloane Street heads almost due north. From the south side of the square the short Lower Sloane Street heads south, on the same axis as Sloane Street. The scale of Sloane Street is sublime, as it cut straight and true through fields and largely open ground. At its south end some subsidiary streets and terraces run off its east side – Sloane Terrace and Cadogan Terrace (now Place) – but sustained runs of terraces line only the west side of Sloane Street. The east edge of the street is treated in most generous manner. Not only is it not lined with terraces – which could have given the vista along Sloane Street a monotonous and claustrophobic appearance – but much of the east side of the street is treated as a linear garden square, with terraces set way back along the garden's east side. These terraces are now Cadogan Place, with the northern section built in around 1804, probably as a speculation by Holland's nephew Henry Rowles. The southern section – now with a mid-nineteenth-century stucco façade and Doric porches – was probably built in the 1820s. The east–west aligned south section of Cadogan Place, composed of groups of large first 'Rate' houses and slightly smaller second 'Rate' houses was mostly built just before 1819 because the terrace appears on Horwood's map. The long, narrow garden – in fact, two gardens, with the south much larger than the north – has a telling history. The northern garden – the centrepiece of what Horwood called Cadogan Square – was landscaped by Humphrey Repton between 1802 and 1806, and reserved for the use of the occupants in the surrounding terraces. The southern garden was, from the late eighteenth century, the London Botanic Garden, created by William Salisbury, and in the 1820s became a promenade for Chelsea's 'exquisites', dandies and other people of fashion. So, from the time Sloane Street was first laid out in the 1770s, these gardens were a noble work, calculated to serve as a useful public ornament and to greatly improve the setting of the houses that framed them and, of course, enhance their desirability and financial value. Horwood's map also shows most clearly the stretched octagonal form of Hans Place, with its oval central garden and the large detached villa – known as the Pavilion – set in extensive grounds. Henry Holland junior built the Pavilion for himself to the south of Hans Place that, in effect, formed the forecourt to his own secluded domain. He also built some speculations along Sloane Street – most utilising then fashionable white brick and with refined neoclassical detail – but the majority of houses were built on sub-leases granted to a variety of tradesmen and investors

who, presumably, worked to a Holland masterplan and produced houses designed in accordance with the 'Rates' specified by the 1774 London Building Act. Much of Hans Town was complete by the mid-1780s, by which date some houses around Sloane Square were already occupied. The scale of the operation was suggested by Daniel Lysons in 1795, when he pointed out that of the '600 new houses' built in Chelsea since 1780 or so 'most ... lie within the district called Hans-town'. Lysons also presented an image of industry in Hans Town, combined perhaps with a degree of uncertainty, because of 1,350 houses in Chelsea parish in 1795 he calculated that over one hundred were 'for the most part unfinished'. Presumably most, if not all of these, were in Hans Town. This, one assumes, was not predominately evidence of abandoned speculations but of work in progress on a vast scale. However, the war with the American colonies and with France in the 1770s and early 1780s caused great uncertainly and financial instability that sapped confidence, slowed down sales, undermined speculations and drove many builders to bankruptcy.

As for Sloane Street, Lysons noted that in 1795 it contained 160 houses, almost entirely on the west side of the street so rear rooms could enjoy prospects over largely open country and evening light. Of Sloane Square, Lysons observed that it was 'handsome' but 'as yet unfinished' (*Environs of London*, pp. 116–7).

Very few of the first buildings in Hans Town survive, most having been rebuilt in very different scale and architectural style soon after their initial ninety-nine year leases expired from the mid-1870s (see page 206). However, the few existing fragments of eighteenth-century Hans Town suggest much. 123 Sloane Street of c. 1780 is an almost solitary survivor of a long 1780s terrace. It is a simple and sophisticated design, with its once pale bricks now sooty black. It is three windows wide and three

49. Above
139 Sloane Street, designed in c. 1780,
probably by Henry Holland – or at least under
his control – in an exquisite and inventive neoclassical manner. The proportions are carefully
modulated and the ground floor lunettes are
embellished with boldly abstract fan or bat's
wing decoration.

50. Above
95 Sloane Street, dating from c. 1780, although now much rebuilt, retains its original door surround formed with vermiculated voussoirs and river god keystone wrought out of a patent terracotta known as Coade stone. The large urn is a most unusual motif and is almost certainly a later addition.

storeys high above a raised basement, so that the front door – with a doorcase embellished with most unusual abstract decoration – is approached up a flight of steps. The proportions of the windows are controlled – the first-floor windows are double square, the second-floor windows are square and the ground-floor windows are one-and-three-quarters deep as wide. All most sophisticated. Number 139 Sloane Street is another late eighteenth-century survivor, although more altered. However, its remarkable door design seems original, compromising a large lunette containing a stucco fan or bat's wing decoration, which at the time was a fashionable antique motif. This arrangement is echoed by the adjoining ground-floor window. Most unusual.

Holland was an architect of genius and originality, and these striking designs must be his. Other scattered survivals are good but not quite up to these. Number 120 has a door with stone or Coade stone voussoirs. Number 95, rebuilt around 1900, retains its Coade stone door surround, with vermiculated voussoirs and river god keystone, as does 91, where the Coade stone door surround, also comprising voussoirs and keystone, is very fine. Numbers 88, 89 and 90 probably date from around 1790, with on number 89 a Coade stone keystone embellished with a female head – perhaps Flora – crowned with a wreath from which dangle ribbons.

These few buildings are enough to tell you what the original Sloane Street looked like. The houses were similar in design and scale but not identical, with details generally limited to the high-quality neoclassical door embellishments offered in the Coade stone catalogue. Other significant survivals are 149 Sloane Street, which forms a group with 1, 2 and 3 Sloane Terrace. All have first-floor windows set within an arcade, as became popular in the second decade of the nineteenth century, from when the group must date. However, the most complete and sustained survival from the first manifestation of Hans Town, and which gives a true sense of its majestic scale and simple uniform architecture, are the terraces of Cadogan Place, built from about 1804 to around 1825. Particularly good are numbers 21 to 27 and 30 to 33 of c. 1804, most with good cast iron first-floor balconies and fanlights, and the slightly later stucco-clad numbers 86 to 89 with handsome trellis and pavilion-roofed first-floor balconies. Other early buildings survive around the east end of Pont Street and in Hans Place where numbers 30, 33, 34, 40 and 15 all date from the 1790s, most altered and heightened, and many with simple Coade stone imposts and keystones embellishing their doorways.

The rebuilding of Hans Town in the late nineteenth century was largely unsentimental. The basic intention was good enough: to increase the volume, convenience and value of buildings on individual plots. However, it has to be said that good intentions aside, the late Victorians did not understand or appreciate the simple repetitive nature of Georgian street architecture. They saw not its sophisticated good manners and simple majesty but mass-produced monotony: the Victorian urban and social vision of the 1870s was very different to that of one hundred years earlier (see page 205). For better or worse, the architecture of Holland's Hans Town was largely swept away to realise the new vision of transforming and extending Hans Town to reflect the then current fashions of Queen Anne Revival and early seventeenth-century Flemish Renaissance styles. So all-encompassing was the new vision that this particular historicist revival style became known as Pont Street Dutch (see page 212).

CHAPTER THREE

ON
PARADE

Chelsea is home to two monumental buildings, both of which have serious architectural ambition and both of which are connected to the military.

51. Left
Detail of Richard Horwood's London map
of 1799–1819, showing the plan of the Royal
Hospital with its axis continued northwest
as the Royal Avenue, towards the King's Road.
To the north of the Royal Hospital is the Royal
Military Asylum, facing towards the route of
the Royal Avenue. To the southeast of the
asylum is the complex pattern of closely set
gardens, alleys and courts between 'Jews
Row' and 'Turks Row'. Note: 'Chelsea Water
Works' buildings, bottom right, and canal-
likewater storage ponds, some serving as
oyster beds.

Chelsea is home to two monumental buildings, both of which have serious architectural ambition and both of which are connected to the military. The most significant by far – architecturally, historically and socially – is the Royal Hospital for the reception of aged, infirm or injured soldiers. A royal project designed by Sir Christopher Wren, the hospital provoked a fundamental change in the nature of Chelsea even before its completion in 1689 and the first reception of pensioners in 1692. It brought the riverside village architectural and royal kudos and stimulated, in fast order, the growth of Chelsea through a spurt in house construction (see page 83).

The other building is the Royal Military Asylum for the children of soldiers' widows. Opened in 1801 and located at the east end of the King's Road, on land acquired by the government from the Cadogan Estate and which – as shown on Thomas Richardson's estate map of 1769 – was occupied by a large well-planted garden and detached house, sometimes known as Chelsea House. The Military Asylum was designed by John Sanders in a solid and conventional manner with its enduring character coming from the excellence of its materials and the craftsman-like manner of construction. Perhaps the most noticeable aspect of the Military Asylum – now known as the Duke of

York's Headquarters building in the Duke of York Square – is its orientation. It does not face on to the King's Road, now the major neighbouring thoroughfare, but instead turns its side to the road and displays its pleasant but ponderous entrance portico to the west. In a sense the asylum faces a Chelsea that was not to be. It appears to address Royal Avenue, laid out in the 1690s to the northwest of the Royal Hospital and planned as a processional route to stretch all the way to Kensington Palace (see page 64). Construction of the avenue did not progress beyond the King's Road, but it seems as late as 1801 there was still a belief that it could be constructed – at least in part – and had that occurred, it would have been a major thoroughfare in Chelsea, at least as important as the King's Road.

Consequently, it would seem that the avenue provided the location that architects of ambitious buildings, such as the Royal Military Asylum, felt obliged to address. Now terraces stand between the asylum and Royal Avenue, so the initial intention is unclear but Richard Horwood's map of 1799–1819 helps clarify the position. At that date the asylum looked west across the open ground in front of it and had a clear view to the west side of Royal Avenue and to the rear elevations of houses on Smith Street. An intriguing observation was made in 1805 by Thomas Faulkner in

52. Right
A portion of the Royal Hospital's north, inland facing, elevation. The Doric pedimented frontispiece can be read as a triumphal arch sitting astride the hospital's main axis. To the west of the frontispiece is the hospital's Great Hall or dining room – visible here. To the east is the Chapel.

his *Historical and Descriptive Account of the Royal Hospital and the Royal Military Asylum in Chelsea* (T. Faulkner, 1805, p. 65). He confirms that the memory of Wren's grand avenue lived on and offers an explanation for the original failure to complete it: 'There is a tradition ... that it was the intention of Queen Anne to have extended [the] avenue through the fields to the gates of the palace at Kensington, but that this design was prevented by her majesty's death. Had the plan been carried into execution it would certainly have formed a *coup d'oeil* not to be equalled in this kingdom.'

The Royal Hospital
The project to build the Royal Hospital started in the 1670s, in large measure as a response to the lingering aftermath of the English Civil War of the 1640s and as part of Charles II's establishment in 1661 of a standing – regular – army. Coming only a year after his restoration as a Parliament-controlled monarch, this was a risky move on the king's part. It was the first time in British history that there had been a standing army and many found it extremely troubling. Why, they asked, did the monarch require such a force in peacetime unless he had a plan to overthrow Parliament and rule as a despot? Disquiet did not result in turmoil or rebellion, partly because the proposed

army was miniscule – no more than 7,000 men – but there were consequences. The veterans of the army, and those maimed or injured while serving, would have to be supported, as were veterans of the Civil War. In 1593 Parliament had approved a statute for the relief of soldiers who had 'adventured their lives or lost their limbs in the service of Her Majesty and the State'. The statute lapsed at the outbreak of the Civil War but was re-established in 1660 as part of the king's plan for raising and sustaining a standing army. The political aspect of the admirable concern for military veterans is revealed by the fact that in 1662 the statute was extended so that government money could be granted to former Royalist soldiers who were not maimed but merely destitute or in need of cash.

As well as providing pensions and support for eligible veterans, the idea grew that it might be economically more sound – and more useful – if accommodation was provided for those veterans who required it. Not only would this make financial sense in the long term, it would also provide the king with a trained militia, readily available in times of emergency, and no doubt loyal to the monarchy since Charles II was their main benefactor (see page 65). But what form should this accommodation take? There were admirable models to hand.

L'HOSTEL DE MARS DIT LES INVALIDES

Dessiné par Perelle.

53. *Above*
A bird's-eye view of 1726 of the Hôtel
des Invalides, Paris, designed by Libéral
Bruant and Jules Hardouin-Mansart and
started in 1670, on the orders of Louis XIV
to house aged, infirm or injured soldiers.
It was the primary inspiration and model
for the Chelsea Royal Hospital.

In 1672 Charles II's eldest illegitimate son, the Duke of Monmouth, had visited Paris and inspected the Hôtel des Invalides. Begun in 1670 on the orders of Louis XIV, the hospital was intended to house 5,000 old soldiers and was designed in monumental manner to celebrate France's military triumphs. Emulation of the Invalides offered tempting possibilities. A London equivalent could house veteran and maimed soldiers in a dignified manner and so help build morale within the new army and encourage enlistment. It also offered Charles II the opportunity to create a handsome architectural monument to his reign.

In 1677 Monmouth returned to the Invalides and requested a set of plans. He was not the only one intent of making a copy. In 1675 the Lord Lieutenant of Ireland, the Duke of Ormond, proposed the creation of an Irish Invalides. The project was priced and approved by the Treasury and Charles II in late 1679, and in 1680 building began on Kilmainham Hospital, just outside Dublin. It was designed in a most handsome manner by Sir William Robinson, the Surveyor-General, and in 1684 received its first pensioners.

The scene was now set for the construction of England's Invalides, by way of Kilmainham. In early September 1681 the Earl of Longford, who had laid the foundation stone for Kilmainham, had a number of discussions with the king about the application of the lessons learned in Ireland to the construction of a London establishment. The talks seem to have been a success because on 6 September Charles II referred Longford to the Treasury to hammer out the details. Less than two weeks later the king instructed Sir Stephen Fox – the man he made responsible for sorting out finance for the Royal Hospital and who would guide its growth during its early years – to get the project in motion. In 1681 Sir Christopher Wren was President of the Royal Society and Surveyor-General to the King's Works. His most important

The Porch or Entrance of the Royal Hospital of Chelsey.

54. Left
The earliest image to survive of the Royal Hospital, dating from c.1690 and engraved by J. Collins, shows the south-facing Doric Portico or porch in the Figure Court. The engraving emphasises the route through the octagonal vestibule that divides the Great Hall from the Chapel, and offers a distant vista, across Burton Court, to the Royal Avenue and the King's Road.

building – St Paul's Cathedral – was six years into construction, and he had overseen the design of most of the fifty-two City churches to be rebuilt after the Great Fire of London in 1666. It was natural that he should be appointed architect to the new hospital in Chelsea. Wren worked fast. His client was, effectively, Sir Stephen Fox, who was the pivotal figure who organised everything and was, in many ways, the true founder of the hospital. Through discussions between these two men the precise function and form of the hospital emerged. By late January 1682 Wren had produced a draft plan, to which Fox responded, adding more precise detail. He listed the numbers of 'Pensioners' organised in regimental formation, suggesting the practical and potentially military application of the hospital: '... 4 Companys consisting off, In all, 384 Private Sentinells, 8 Drummers, 12 Corporalls, 8 Serjeants, 4 Ensigns, 4 Lts, 1 Martial and Adjutant, I Governor, being 422 military persons.' Pensioners were only to be enlisted men, so the officers were to be members of the 'twenty-nine proposed staff' listed by Fox, that included an apothecary, wardrobe keeper, porter, baker and brewer, and 'thirteen women to wash the linen and clean the house'.

On 25 May 1682 Wren's revised scheme gained final approval. John Evelyn described it, that day, in his diary: '... it was a Quadrangle of 200 foote square, after the dimensions of the larger Quadrangle at Christ Church, Oxford, for the accommodation of 440 persons with governor and offices. This was agreed on.' By July the old buildings of Chelsey College had been demolished and in August the footings and foundations were underway for the construction of the hospital that, as Charles II declared, was 'for the relief of such Land soldiers as are, or shall be, old, lame, or infirme in ye Service of the Crowne'.

No single drawing from Wren's office for the Royal Hospital survives, nor any building accounts or bills. The earliest image that does survive is probably an engraving of c.1690 by J. Collins that shows the Figure Court portico, seemingly based on an original drawing. The loss of the drawings and bills remains an unexplained mystery but as there is no mention of Chelsea in the sale list of drawings following Wren's death in 1723, they probably disappeared early on.

Although these key documents are lost, a surviving memo, dating from early 1682 and almost certainly drafted by Wren himself, outlines his vision for the hospital: 'The two sides of ye Court are double building in three stories and garrets,

55. *Above*
The Figure Court looking southeast towards one of the residential ranges, with its central pediment and end pavilion framed by Portland stone quoins. The paired columns in the foreground are a French motif, probably inspired by Claude Perrault's design for the 1660s east façade of the Louvre, a work Wren much admired.

56. *Above right*
Detail of a Royal Hospital façade – well wrought brown and purple brick walling, finely detailed red brick window jambs and arches, offset by Portland stone quoins and white painted or pale stone coloured joinery.

both containing 16 galleries, in each of which are 24 cells divided off with partitions of wanscot, and two larger Cells for corporals.... The upper end or front hath an Octagonall Vestibule in the middle covered with a Cupolo and Lanthorne 130 feet high, and before it a Portico of Dorick order ... on each hand of which are lower Porticos leading to each Wing. On each side of the Vestibule are assents to the Hall on one hand and the Chappell on the other.... On the corners of the Building are 4 Pavilions.... The lesser Porticoes and principal doorways are Portland Stone. The rest of the Fabrick is brick, and the whole pile well and durably built with good materials.'

Adjoining the main building were to be 'enclosures of brickwalls for Walks, Gardens, Kitchin garden, Back Courte and Buriall place'. This describes the hospital essentially as it was built. As Evelyn suggested, Wren took his inspiration for the layout of the building from the colleges of Oxford. The collegiate building form –

with a central court or quadrangle, deriving from monastic design – incorporating a mixture of domestic and 'public' buildings was particularly appropriate for the Chelsea project. As in Oxford college buildings (notably New College and Wadham, where Wren had been an undergraduate), the Hall and the Chapel are grouped together to form a dominant central feature of the composition. However, there is a major difference from the standard collegiate form because at Chelsea the court is defined by only three ranges, with the fourth, south-side, left open. Wren had a particular reason for this arrangement because it allowed the centre block, with its giant pedimented portico, to be seen from the Thames to the south and the open south side of the court provided a good view of the river and the verdant south bank from the hospital.

A striking aspect of Wren's building is its odd relationship to the river. Rather than confronting the Thames head-on, the hospital's central court (now known as Figure Court) faces the river at a peculiar angle. Obviously Wren wanted the wards for the pensioners in the two side ranges to be well lit and the orientation he chose means that none of the ranges looks directly north. All the wards enjoy direct sunlight at some time during the day. However, Wren was also wedded to a particular axes, around which the hospital buildings and gardens are arranged in symmetrical manner, and which was continued in the 1690s to the northwest and outside hospital grounds by the construction of Royal Avenue. This axis seems to have been inherited from Chelsey College but, if continued to the northwest, would terminate at Nottingham House that, from c. 1689, became Kensington Palace (see page 64). Such a long straight avenue, slicing through the fields of west London and uniting two significant royal buildings would not only have been a grand Baroque gesture worthy of Louis XIV but

CHELSEA HOSPITAL.

London, Pub. Jan.1.st 1816 at R.Ackermann's Repository of Arts 101 Strand.

At the Royal Hospital Wren achieved grandeur, dignity and monumentality in a relatively simple manner.

57. Above
The Great Hall in 1810, as portrayed by Rowlandson and Pugin, showing in-pensioners seated at their sixteen long dining tables. The Governor, staff and guests are seated to the west at the high table, above which rises a mural featuring an equestrian portrait of Charles II painted by Antonio Verrio and Henry Cooke.

would also have served a most practical purpose as a military road allowing troops from Chelsea to be deployed with speed. It is now difficult to determine when the idea for this long, straight avenue originated or if its construction in its entirety was ever a serious proposition. It would seem so, because in 1693 Wren did approve an estimate for the construction of a new road from Kensington Palace to the Royal Hospital at Chelsea. It was to be 8,059 feet long, 11 feet wide and was to cost £870 (*Wren Society*, vol. xviii, p. 103). The only physical evidence of this great Baroque town-planning scheme is Royal Avenue.

Wren's design
In 1750 Wren's grandson published *Parentalia*, the history of the eminent members of the Wren family and Sir Christopher in particular. It includes

Wren's somewhat random 'Tracts on Architecture', gathered together by his son. One section of the 'Tracts' does, perhaps, explain one aspect of the Chelsea design: the visual accent on each range being placed in the centre – by means of columns, pilasters and pediments – while the end pavilions of each range have minimal emphasis. As Wren wrote, 'Fronts ought to be elevated in the Middle, not the Corners; because the Middle is the Place of greatest dignity, and first arrests the Eye; and rather projecting forward in the Middle, than hollow. For these Reasons, Pavilions at the Corners are naught; because they make both Faults, a hollow and depressed Front.'

One of the most attractive characteristics of the architecture of the Royal Hospital is the way in which Wren achieved grandeur, dignity and monumentality in a relatively simple manner. During his rebuilding of the City churches he had evolved an economic manner of construction combining brick – that was relatively cheap to make and use – with the judicious use of a small amount of stone, usually for corner quoins and architectural detail. This form of construction had ancient origins, used in England in the sixteenth century and made popular in France from the very early seventeenth century, but Wren made it into a very fine art. This is the language of the Royal Hospital: brick for walls (always executed with exquisite craftsmanship), more expensive stone for corner quoins, doorcases and, occasionally, for columns and pilasters, with elements such as entablatures and cornices made of timber and plaster and painted originally to look like stone. However, the main ornament of the façades are the handsome and well-laid brown/purple bricks from which they are built, with the most striking decorative detail being the red brick dressings and delicate cut-brick arches that frame each window opening. Red brick arch and dressing to window jambs form a simple and bold structural ornament that was to enter the vocabulary of London builders

and remain popular into the 1730s.
The function of the two residential ranges forming the central court is expressed – in a direct but subtle way – through the design and scale of their windows. In domestic architecture of the period the hierarchy of the occupation of a house could be read in the composition of its elevation. The more important rooms – dining room or best parlour – would have higher ceilings than the less important rooms, and so would have larger windows. The main rooms were almost always grouped on the ground or first floor – the *piano nobile* of the Renaissance *palazzi* (see page 92) – so the windows on these levels would be higher, although the same width, as windows on the floors above.

At the Royal Hospital Wren did not follow this convention – and for very good reason. The three main levels of the residential ranges are all of equal importance – they all contains wards for the pensioners – so to have made the ground- or first-floor windows higher would have been inappropriate. The practical and happy consequence of this rational decision is that all windows are as high as possible, allowing the maximum amount of the southerly light to flood into the wards. Above the cornice of the residential ranges rises a tall, pitched roof furnished with large dormer windows. This roof space contains a top, fourth tier of wards, creating the habitable space that was required to house the intended number of pensioners.

The range containing the Great Hall and the Chapel is in every way the centrepiece of the composition, as all its details proclaim. First, it is essentially a single-storey building – as its massive semi-circular arched windows reveal – and so there is no doubt that it contains the major, public rooms of the hospital. These huge, close-spaced windows give the building a dramatic transparency and allow light to flood inside.

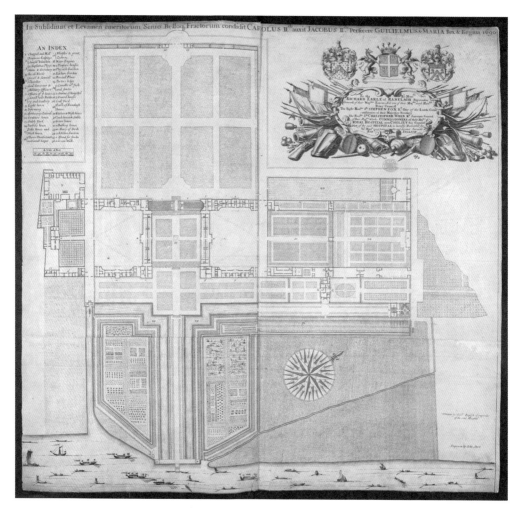

58. *Above*
The 'ground plot' of the Royal Hospital
buildings and grounds in c. 1690, as depicted
by Robert Inglish. To the north, beyond the
hospital's north range, is Burton Court. To the
south is the garden with its pair of mirror-plan
geometric canals, which brought the river to
the very walls of the hospital buildings. The
canals were filled in during the 1850s when
works were undertaken to the river wall.

The Doric frontispiece and portico – and their related internal and external details – form the great decorative, architectural and symbolic feature of the hospital. Built of stone and timber painted to look like stone, these monumental portals are in considerable contrast to the generally domestic character of the brick building they adorn. In fact, they can be seen as a triumphal arch sitting astride an axis that was, it seems, intended to run from the river to the north of the hospital. The orientation of these porticoes suggest that, from the start, Wren had the notion to extend the axis to Kensington, even before Nottingham House was acquired by the Crown in 1689 and transformed by Wren into Kensington Palace.

The large scale of the portals was utilised in a most practical manner by the pragmatic Wren, for he fitted cisterns within the pediments to supply water at pressure to the lower rooms of the Royal Hospital. In 1805 it was explained by Faulkner that the water 'is worked up from the river, by a patent engine placed in a small building erected for that purpose in the gardens, near the river side' (*Historical and Descriptive Account of the Royal Hospital and the Royal Military Asylum in Chelsea*). The 'patent' engine was, presumably, a steam-powered pump.

The symbolic importance of these great Doric porches is confirmed by the interior into which they lead. Here Wren created a stunning composition that possess the bold simplicity and clarity associated with late eighteenth-century neo-classicism. Octagonal in form and topped by a faceted dome that is top-lit – like the Pantheon in Rome – by a central oculus, it is effectively a temple to the military virtues – austere, simple, masculine. The walls are dressed in giant Doric pilasters that relate to the exterior columns and pilasters of the Doric porches. As well as being a military temple – and repository of trophies – this domed space also fulfils the more mundane

function of an entrance vestibule to both Chapel and the Great Hall. These are a pair of spectacular rooms. The Great Hall was organised in the manner of a college hall, with the pensioners dining at sixteen long tables – one for each ward – with the Governor, his staff and his guests seated at the high table, raised on a dais. A large mural painting in the hall is a most theatrical affair. It shows Charles II mounted on horseback and standing in the hospital's court, surrounded by cavorting and gliding allegorical figures, including a winged Victory. The artists were Antonio Verrio and Henry Cooke, and the work was completed by time of the official opening of the hospital in 1692.

The Chapel has a barrel vault with plaster embellishments. These are discreet but of high quality, with the oblong plaster panels set along the wall below the springing of the vault being especially good. Each panel is of broadly similar design but in its details individual and inventive, many with strange faces lurking in the foliage. The plasterwork in the Chapel, completed by 1687, was executed by Henry Margetts. The woodwork is also good, with oak panelling on which perch the heads of four-winged angelic beings, no doubt Seraphim. These heads and the 3:1 proportion of the Chapel's plan is a reminder that Wren, when designing and detailing it, had in mind the biblical description of the sanctuary of the Holy of Holies in Solomon's Temple in Jerusalem. Similarly proportioned, the sanctuary contained the Ark of the Covenant – God's throne on Earth – guarded by Seraphim. The Holy of Holies and sanctuary became the prototype for sacred buildings for Jews, Muslims and Christians alike.

The three ranges of the hospital were all conceived within the convention of a palace composition – that is to say each range was given a dominant pedimented feature in its centre with, in accord with Wren's theory published in *Parentalia*, the ends not being visually 'elevated' in design but treated as subsidiary pavilions. These end pavilions are essentially cubes, four windows wide, but each fulfilling very different roles. The pavilion to the northeast absorbs the apse of the Chapel and contains a most oddly shaped vestry room. The pavilion to the northwest was to contain the kitchen for the Great Hall. Those to the south were designed to contain apartments for hospital officers – with the pavilion to the southeast being the grandest of all, for it provided residential and reception rooms for the Governor. His parlour – at ground-floor level – is one of the best of Wren's surviving domestic interiors, executed by leading craftsmen. The oak panelling was provided by William Cleere, Master Joiner to the Office of Works, the overmantel was embellished with delicate carving by William Emmett and William Morgan, and the fine plaster ceiling is by John Grove, Master Plasterer to the Office of Works. The motifs in both the plaster and timber work date the creation of the room, for the ceiling contains elaborate mouldings displaying the cypher of James II, as does the carved overmantel revealing that the room was completed between 1685 and 1688 when James II was the monarch. Perhaps the most remarkable thing about the room is its volume. It measures 40 feet long by 30 feet wide and is almost as high as it is wide, creating a space that corresponds to Palladio's ideal proportion of a cube and a third. At the beginning of February 1685, just days before his death, Charles II visited the Royal Hospital, that was just being completed. He was pleased with what he saw, and declared that 'Fox and Hee had done that great worke ...'

The setting
The setting that Wren created for the Royal Hospital was of the greatest importance. The buildings were to sit within a bold and simple landscape that – it its orthogonal geometry – complemented the regularity of the buildings and reinforced the impression that the hospital was a key component in a great axial plan for west London. The organisation of the landscape is made clear in a plan of c.1690. Not only was the main axis of the hospital continued north to the King's Road across what is now Burton Court (laid out with oblong parterres divided by an orthogonal grid of gravel walks), but it was also extended south and used to organise the gardens lying between the Royal Hospital and the Thames.

The gardens were a restrained exercise in the French formal style with George London and Henry Wise being responsible for their design, cultivation and maintenance. The courtyard defined by the hospital ranges

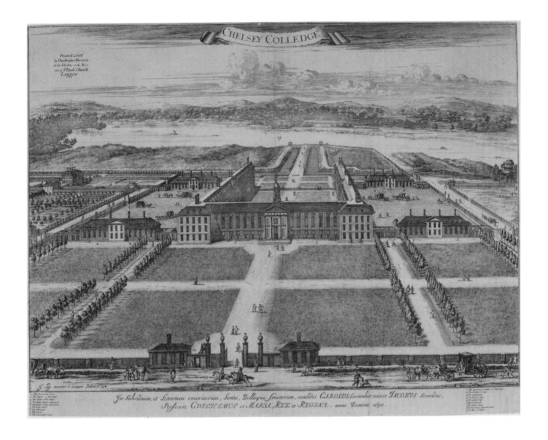

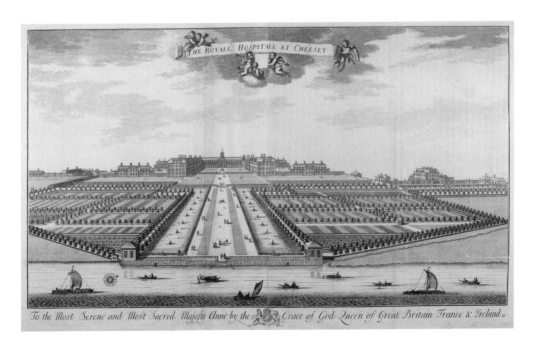

was echoed to its south by a square of identical area and design, but now unrestrained by buildings. This subtle bit of wit – making a play of negative and positive spaces (the buildings are the most important element in one square and the space in the other) – was continued south by a broad walk that continued the main axis of the hospital. This central walk was flanked by narrower straight walks shaded by avenues of trees. To the west and east of these walks were more utilitarian gardens used to grow vegetables, herbs and containing rows of fruit trees. The most spectacular feature of these southern gardens was a pair of right-angled canals that, in effect, brought the Thames right up to the southern terrace of the hospital. The river edge of the garden was terraced and walled to form a raised walk and furnished with a water gate and a pair of cubical end pavilions. It was all very handsome and useful.

Within three years of work starting on the construction of the Royal Hospital, the key man behind its foundation and financing was dead. Charles II died on 6 February 1685 and with his death – and the ascent to the throne of his brother James II – turbulent times rapidly returned to Britain. Foolishly, James attempted to re-establish Roman Catholicism and a type of absolute monarchy. He failed to realise the extent to which the times and the mood of the nation had changed. Nor did he seem to understand the essential weakness of his own position. Within three years the experiment was over and James had been forced to flee in 1688 – in most ignominious circumstances – to be replaced by the Dutch Protestant Prince of Orange, who from February 1689 reigned as joint monarch with his wife Mary Stuart, one of the daughters of James II.

James's three short years on the throne were eventful. Charles II's illegitimate son, the Duke of Monmouth, led a bloody and unsuccessful Protestant rebellion in the West Country. Monmouth's uncle, James, made the young man pay with his life for this adventure. This revolt no doubt confirmed James in his determination to enlarge the size of the standing army. This decision had a direct and dramatic influence on the Royal Hospital. First it meant that its revenue automatically increased since, with the growth of military manpower, there was an increase in the number of soldiers' salaries that, with mandatory contributions, provided the hospital with its income. Second, with an enlarged army, there was urgent need for additional accommodation at Chelsea because there would be more invalids qualified for entry than had been anticipated a few years earlier. So even before the building of the hospital was completed, it had to be enlarged to accommodate 500 men rather than the 422 originally anticipated. In November 1685 Sir Thomas Ogle was appointed Governor of the hospital by the already insecure James II, which was, essentially, a military appointment. Garrison towns and fortresses had governors, and the crown-appointed Governor of the Royal Hospital was to act like the colonel of a regiment and with his veteran troops was clearly expected to fulfil an active military role if necessary. With the need to expand the courtyard design of the hospital, Wren quickly saw that the solution lay in the fact that, from the start, he had conceived it as a family of buildings, with the three ranges of the central courtyard surrounded by minor buildings fulfilling subordinate functions. The extra accommodation could be provided by the addition of smaller-scale ranges to the main ranges. The need for the creation of a hierarchy of structures was also implied by the new requirement.

Wren did not only have to provide accommodation for more men but also for different types of men. So in his additional building at Chelsea, he provided rooms for gentlemen of the Life Guards. Now the men and NCOs of the hospital were to be

Soane was seeking to reinvigorate, almost to reinvent, the traditions of classical design.

61. Above
Peter Tillemans' early eighteenth-century view of the Royal Hospital from the south bank – looking along the hospital's main axis and with the canals, flanking the river entrance path, clearly shown. To the left (west) is an evocative perspective of the riverside frontage of Chelsea village, with its array of water gates, stairs and water-edge buildings.

62. Overleaf
Ranelagh House was built c. 1688, immediately to the east of the Royal Hospital, by Lord Ranelagh for his own occupation. The house was absorbed in 1742 into Ranelagh pleasure gardens and was eventually demolished in 1805. This view by Marianne Rush must have been made just before the house's destruction.

stiffened by a number of resident veteran cavalry officers and gentlemen. The four additional ranges Wren designed are of identical appearance that – although small in scale (only one storey above ground) – are noble in design, and with their two-storey, pedimented centres and high-pitched and dormered roofs and tall chimney stacks are, essentially, smaller versions of the main ranges. Wren placed these four new ranges or wings with a pair facing each other to the west of the main ranges and another pair facing each other on the east.

The pairs of wings, forming two additional courts of equal area to the main court, contained not only accommodation for veterans but one was also to serve as an infirmary, an innovation that seems to reflect a rapidly increasing concern for the welfare of the pensioners.

Although work on the building of the hospital was finished by 1689, the veterans were prevented from moving in by the deviousness and scheming of the Earl of Ranelagh, who in December 1685 replaced Sir Stephen Fox's son Charles as Paymaster-General.

137

If Sir Stephen Fox and his son had been discreet and restrained in their use of their position, Ranelagh was not. Ranelagh was among the first to realise the potential of the new hospital, which functioned as a noble public ornament while also, through its community of armed and disciplined veterans, ensured tranquillity from house-breakers and the mob. From the earliest days it was the duty of bodies of armed pensioners to safeguard the highway between Chelsea and Whitehall. In 1805, in his *Historical and Descriptive Account of the Royal Hospital and the Royal Military Asylum in Chelsea*, Faulkner claimed 'this patrole was established by royal mandate, on petition of the inhabitants of Chelsea, in the year 1715, the highways at that time being much infested with footpads, and very dangerous to passengers in the evening'.

One of Ranelagh's first actions was to acquire an official residence for himself in the grounds, and in about 1688 a fine, freestanding mansion was commenced (probably to Ranelagh's own designs), to the east of the main court. In April 1691, when William III dined at the hospital, the Paymaster-General managed to gain only one favour – the grant to himself as its Treasurer of a salary of £1 per day. Not only was the long overdue opening of the hospital not discussed at this meeting but it seems Ranelagh was doing his best to delay the opening. He realised that he would be unable to continue to embellish his own house and gardens (which he held on a long lease) at public expense once the hospital had been taken into use and its future revenue settled. This unpleasant situation was finally resolved, probably by Sir Christopher Wren working closely with Queen Mary and the Secretary of State, Lord Nottingham. First a Royal Warrant was issued that provided money to complete the hospital. Then, to ensure that Ranelagh had only a very limited opportunity to misbehave in future, another Royal Warrant was issued in August 1691 that transferred the management of the Royal Hospital from Lord Ranelagh to an executive committee that included Wren. Ranelagh proved himself to be the archetypal plausible rogue. He was constantly instructed to submit accounts but just as constantly failed to do so. In December 1702 he resigned as Paymaster-General and two months later was expelled from the House of Commons. Ranelagh moved gradually into a world of increasing debt although, despite his record, he managed to secure official appointments of an inferior sort. As for Wren, for his ten years of magnificent work, and upon the submission of his correctly audited bills, he had in June 1693 been awarded a modest £1,000.

Well over one hundred years after Wren's death, a Chelsea local made a most perceptive observation about this particular masterpiece. Having passed the hospital for many years, on a daily basis, 'without thinking much about it', the neighbour 'began to reflect that it had always been a pleasure to me to see it'. He looked at it 'more attentively and saw that it was quiet and dignified and the work of a gentleman'. The local was the philosopher Thomas Carlyle, who lived in Cheyne Row from the 1834 to 1881, and his measured compliment – itself clearly the 'work of a gentleman' – is much to the point. The Royal Hospital is such a pleasure to behold and it never becomes tiresome, because its power lies not in strident rhetoric or egocentric display but in simple, authoritative perfection.

Enter Sir John Soane
For over a hundred years the Royal Hospital functioned as intended. However, by the first decade of the nineteenth century Britain had changed. Her empire had expanded, as had her army, and she was locked in a prolonged war with Revolutionary and then Napoleonic France. So the hospital also had to change, and the man who gave the change

architectural expression was John Soane. In March 1807 he secured the position of Clerk of Works to the Royal Hospital and ushered in a twenty-year period of expansion that saw the design and construction of some of the most original and provoking architecture built in London during the Georgian epoch.

Soane's first hospital commission, in 1809, was to convert the eighteenth-century Walpole House, on the northwest corner of the hospital site, into an infirmary, to replace Wren's much smaller infirmary. This turned into a complete rebuilding, and on this small and utilitarian project Soane unleashed the full force of his unorthodox architectural thinking. The hospital was, it seems, to be an unsuspecting guinea pig for his radical ideas. Soane was seeking to reinvigorate, almost to reinvent, the traditions of classical design. To do this he stripped away much conventional ornament and relied on simple primary forms, on proportion and on almost abstract details to create structures that were novel and original, yet which still possessed a sense of classical nobility. He particularly avoided – where possible – the use of the familiar array of columns or pilasters, detailed in conventional manner, because he felt these spoke too much of the architecture of the past. He wanted his architecture to be modern, and startlingly so. With its simple brick elevations and arched ground-floor windows, the infirmary – built in 1810 – was a good example of Soane's spare and inventive manner.

Part of his strange style was to focus on seemingly unlikely details for special treatment. At this period he seems to have become obsessed with chimney stacks and chimney pots, and these became the infirmary's greatest single ornament. In a sense this was in the tradition of the Royal Hospital because Wren had given his buildings an impressive array of tall stacks, seemingly to offer a vertical counter-balance to the building's strong horizontal

lines. However, Soane went beyond the mere play of lines and with the infirmary initiated what turned out to be an increasingly bizarre collection of chimney stack designs. We cannot now judge for ourselves the architecture of the infirmary because it was bomb-damaged in 1941 and subsequently cleared away. The National Army Museum now stands on its site. However, the next major building Soane designed for Chelsea does survive.

The block of stables, designed in 1814 at the northwest end of the hospital, next to the infirmary, is one of Soane's most famous designs, spare and abstract with its main elevation defined by a ripple of concentric arches set around openings in the solemn brick elevation. This building is now perceived to mark a key moment in the progression of Soane's architecture, combing elements of Roman gravity – rendered in Roman-style pale yellow brick – with his very personal exploration, abstraction and reinvention of the language of classical architecture. Part of this exploration included experimentation in the ancient language of death, inspired largely by Soane's study of the often abstract ornament on Roman sarcophagi. When applied, his peculiar and most idiosyncratic language of design could give his architecture a strange, solemn, even uncomfortable feel and, as in the case of the stables, imbue even humdrum buildings with the quality of antique tombs.

The minimal architecture of the stables, its somewhat deathly appearance, and Soane's refusal to utilise the conventions of classical design – such as pediments and pilasters – to give a sense of dignity or bestow order, disturbed many contemporaries. Soane had been made aware of the effect his odd architecture could have when the recently completed, and very abstract, front elevation of his own house in Lincoln's Inn Fields was attacked in the press.

A·VIEW·OF·THE·NEW·BUILDINGS·FORMING·THE·PRINCIPAL·ALTERATIONS·AND·ADDITIONS·IN·THE·
ESTABLISHMENT·OF·THE·ROYAL·HOSPITAL·AT·CHELSEA·PARTICULARLY·THOSE·
·NOTICED·IN·THE·CHAMPION·OF·THE·TENTH·AND·TWENTY·FOURTH·OF·SEPTEMBER·

View of the Back of the Clerk of the Works' House

The Morning Post of 13 October 1812 dismissed it as 'a new-fangled ... ridiculous piece of architecture' and 'a palpable eyesore'. More seriously, Soane was prosecuted by the Holborn District Surveyor on the charge of having, by the construction of the façade, committed a 'common nuisance'. The hearing before the local magistrate was set to be a test case, with Soane calling numerous artists and architects to his defence. However, the case was dismissed on a technicality because the façade rose from Soane's own private forecourt, making it legally a private building beyond the jurisdiction of the District Surveyor.

One of the perquisites of the Clerk of Works' post was a house within the hospital grounds. In 1814 Soane started work on designs to enlarge the existing house – essentially rebuild it – to form a small villa. The design was most eccentric. It stood near the infirmary and stables and was distinguished by its cubical two-storey centre block flanked by single-storey wings from which rose exorbitantly tall, square-plan shafts of chimney stacks topped by large terracotta chimney pots in the form of antique funery urns. Soane's estimate of costs was approved by the hospital in September 1814, the final design in March 1815, with work starting the following month. In September 1815, just as the house was being completed, Soane and his work at the Royal Hospital became the focus of a vicious attack on 'The present low state of the arts in England ... particularly architecture.' The article was published in two parts in the September 1815 editions of a magazine called *The Champion*. The author, who was not named in the magazine, dismissed the new Clerk of Works' house as 'a monster in the art of building', while the infirmary was 'not a jot behind it in absurdity'. Soane was soundly brought to task for the perverse manner in which he plundered 'from the records of antiquity things in themselves absolutely good but which were never intended [to be] on the same place'. Soane's array of odd chimney pots at Chelsea were a particular target, particularly those on the Clerk of Works' house. The article concluded that, despite the 'depraved' state of contemporary architectural taste, 'such follies will not pass for wisdom; the public laugh at the extravagances which are too dull for madness too mad for the soberness of reason'.

Soane was shocked, not so much by the content of the article but by the probable identity of its author. He rushed to Cheltenham to show it to his wife. 'These are George's doings,' she declared of their younger son. 'He has given me

Chelsea Hospital.

Elevation of the East sia

Scale of

65. *Above*
Elevation of the east side of the Soane-designed stable block. The drawing is dated March 1818. The dominant features are ripples of concentric circles set around openings. The design – spare, abstract and solemn – is one of Soane's most striking and characteristic.

my death blow.' True to her word, Mrs Soane was dead within two months. Soane's relationship with his sons had long been difficult. No doubt his manic overwork, sombre and eccentric obsessions with antiquity, and his combative and intolerant character made him a remote and difficult father and caused his children deep resentment.

The aftermath of the *The Champion* article at the Royal Hospital appears to have been significant. Perhaps Soane took some of his son's criticism to heart; certainly he modified his architectural manner. Or perhaps the Royal Hospital Board had been rattled by the public criticism or already alarmed by Soane's odd-looking architecture because after 1815 Soane was instructed to design his Chelsea buildings

New Stables.

20   30 Feet

to look 'similar' to Wren's work. So the desire was that visual harmony should prevail and that the dominant character established by Wren should be protected and enhanced rather than diluted by new buildings. This policy is probably one of the reasons why the Clerk of Works' house was demolished as early as 1858. It did not seem part of the hospital's artistic identity. It was, presumably, only by good fortune that Soane's stables were suffered to survive. So after 1815 Soane worked, in most self-effacing manner, in the idiom of Wren's architecture. In 1818 he was commissioned to design the Secretary's office for a site, flanked by two Wren pavilions, on the east side of the hospital. He took his cue from these pavilions, producing a Wren style single-storey structure, built of brick with

stone corner quoins and red dressings around the windows. Only the interiors, with minimal details and semi-circular arched openings, are quintessential Soane, as are the tall and sculptural chimney stacks with their abstracted classical stone details.

Soane remained the Clerk of Works until his death in 1837 and produced modest design in comparison with his initial projects. Not all are slavishly in the Wren manner. The surgeon's house, on the west side of the hospital near the stables suggests a middle way, being an essay in the Wren manner but evidently no mere copy of Wren. Inside is a splendid staircase, displaying Soane's distinct architectural character and lightness of touch.

66. Above
The main elevation of the Royal Military Asylum
soon after completion in 1807 to the designs
of John Sanders. The asylum's inmates – the
children of the widows of regular soldiers – were
attired in patriotic military-style garb coloured
red, white and blue.

The Royal Military Asylum

In 1807, as John Soane took up the position
of Clerk of Works at the Royal Hospital, its
companion building – The Royal Military
Asylum – was being completed. The
Military Asylum's architecture and the
radical minimalist architecture pursed
by Soane could hardly be more different.
Soane eschewed the conventional use of
the Orders, columns and pilasters, and
rethought the manner in which elevations,
plans and interiors might be composed.
The Military Asylum does none of these
things. It is monumental in the old and
established manner, incorporating a
centrally placed pedimented portico
supported on giant Doric columns that
give the building a palatial appearance
and proclaims it to be a place of some
importance. In addition, the portico

It seems that what Sanders saw and learned in Soane's office wore off, certainly by 1801. Either it did not embed itself into his architectural persona or he did not like the abstracted Soane's style. This failure to follow Soane's lead is perhaps to be expected.

The purpose of the Royal Asylum was very specific. While the Royal Hospital was to house aged, infirm or injured 'Land soldiers', the asylum was to house, educate and train to a trade the orphaned or fatherless children of soldiers who had served in the regular army. Or, to be more precise, it was to take in children of the widows of regular soldiers. This might seem an odd way of stating things but there was a reason. If the mother of the child applying for admission to the asylum had to prove she was a soldier's widow, then she would have to prove that they had been married. Evidently, the asylum wished to avoid being inundated with applications from single women who were perhaps common-law wives or companions of dead soldiers or, indeed, common prostitutes seeking aid with the rearing of their illegitimate children.

also tells you where the main door is and offers you shelter from the rain as you prepare to make an entrance. This is all most charming and manages to combine symbolism and rhetoric with more practical considerations. The Military Asylum is not as architecturally clever or as original as Soane's best designs, but it is, nevertheless, strangely pleasing. These observations seem hardly contentious, in fact rather self-evident. However, there is one oddity about this story. The architect of the Military Asylum, which started on site in 1801, was John Sanders, who had been Soane's first pupil. He joined Soane's office in 1784 – by which time Soane had already started to plough his most individualistic architectural furrow – attended the Royal Academy Schools, won its Gold Medal and left Soane's office in 1790 to set up on his own.

Faulkner's 1805 *Historical and Descriptive Account of the Royal Hospital and the Royal Military Asylum in Chelsea* makes it clear that the asylum was yet to be completed. He describes it as an 'elegant structure', which does not seem particularly thoughtful. It is a solid Doric affair, with an arcaded ground-floor podium, wrought of beautifully crafted yellow brick against which are set the cylindrical and somewhat gouty stone shafts of giant columns. Elegant? Hardly. Impressive, solemn, authoritative, military in feel, even slightly daunting? Certainly. And one shudders to think what terrifying impression this building made on little children trembling before its commanding presence.

The central, porticoed block – thirteen windows wide and rising three storeys

67. Above
The Royal Military Asylum is now known as the
Duke of York's Headquarters Building and it
currently houses a museum of contemporary art.

above ground – is flanked by blocks of matching height and similar design, but astylar, all linked by exceedingly handsome brick arcades. The plans of these related buildings were organised to accommodate the boys and girls – strictly segregated in separate wards – and the staff. Faulkner records that the boys were taught reading and writing and four principal trades of shoemakers, 'taylors', saddlers and armourers. The girls were taught to 'cast accounts', as well as knitting, needlework and housework. The children's uniforms were quaint and carried a message. The boys wore red jackets, blue breeches, white linen and black stockings. The girls wore red gowns, blue petticoats, white aprons and straw hats. So, military looking and most patriotic in the choice and combinations of colours. For Faulkner this disciplined look and the sense of loyalty it could engender in young children, when combined with the trades and skills taught, meant the Royal Asylum was a 'nursery for honest and useful members of society'.

Unlike the Royal Hospital, which marvellously and almost miraculously continues to pretty much fulfil the function for which it was founded nearly 340 years ago, the Royal Military Asylum has undergone numerous changes of purpose. It now, in part, houses, for public enjoyment, a private collection of highly commercial contemporary art. It is a testament to Sanders' solid architecture that the building fulfils this seemingly unlikely function with aplomb, even with style, bestowing dignity on what can be seen as an ephemeral cultural activity. Contemporary art, despite being presented in museum conditions, can be a changeful business as fashions and fads come and go. This building does much to give the works it contains cultural pedigree and a sense of permanence.

CHELSEA'S SACRED LANDSCAPE

In the nineteenth century, as the population of Chelsea expanded, so did its sacred landscape.

68. Left
Chelsea Old Church from the northeast, painted
in the early years of the nineteenth century –
certainly before 1814 – by Marianne Rush.

Chelsea Old Church

A church has stood on the site now occupied by Chelsea Old Church since at least the twelfth century. It is possible that a church stood here before that date, or that this is an ancient pre-Christian sacred site, as pondered on page 41. This, however, remains in the realm of informed speculation. What is certain is that the site currently occupied by the church forms the focus of Chelsea's sacred landscape. The other components of this long-established sacred landscape were the fields in church ownership – the glebe lands – from which income for the parish could be derived, the rectory, burial grounds and perhaps other small and long forgotten fragments of Christian life such as wayside crosses and small shrines. There was, for example, the ancient Thame Shot cross that stood on what is now the burial ground of the Royal Hospital. In 1810 Thomas Faulkner, when speculating about the origin and purpose of the lost cross, observed that crosses such as this 'were frequently placed on the spot where any singular instance of God's mercy has been shown, or when a person has been murdered by robbers, or had met with any violent death [or] where the corpse of any great person rested as it was being carried to be buried' (*Chelsea, and its Environs*, pp. 236-7). The cross was dismantled in 1642 by Puritans who disapproved of such tokens of what they regarded as Roman Catholic superstition. In the nineteenth century, as the population of Chelsea expanded, so did its sacred landscape, as we shall see.

We have no idea why most medieval parish churches in Britain were sited in their specific locations but theories are many: they stand on the sites of pre-Christian sacred groves or henges, perhaps as is the case at Chelsea; they were placed to create an image of paradise on earth or to connect with God's creation with churches aligned with points on the horizon that mark the rising or setting of celestial bodies. Or their placing was more worldly and intended to enhance the claim to power of a feudal lord – temporal or spiritual – and reinforce his status. In the twelfth century the Abbey at Westminster claimed authority over the Manor of Chelsea from the time of Edward the Confessor, so it might have had a hand in resolving a site for Chelsea's parish church (*Chelsea Old Church*).

With somewhat more certainty we know that the precise placing of a church often had to do with its dedication. For example, the exact east–west orientation of a church might follow the line of a shadow cast by a staff erected at sunrise on the feast day of the saint after which the church was named. The Old Church

69. Above
Interior of Chelsea Old Church before the
Second World War, looking southwest from
the chancel through the More Chapel, with its
ornate Renaissance capitals of 1528.

70. Above right
The Old Church in 1941 after bomb damage.
Little survived beyond the walls of the
More Chapel, portions of the chancel and
the Lawrence Chapel. The 1680s houses of
Prospect Place in Cheyne Walk were also
grievously damaged.

at Chelsea had two dedications: to All the
Saints and to St Luke. Twin dedications
are unusual and if the association with
St Luke dates to the origin of the church
(it is documented only as far back as the
seventeenth century) then his feast day –
18 October – would no doubt have been,
in one way or another, enshrined within
the fabric of the church.

The church as it stands today is a
very compromised document and is
consequently hard to read. This is primarily
because the nave and west tower were
rebuilt between 1669 and 1674 and were
both – along with most of the chantry
chapel to the north of the nave, part
of the south chapel and much of the
chancel – destroyed by a bomb in 1941.
The chapels are said to date from the
fourteenth century and the chancel from
the thirteenth century. After the war all
that survived above ground were parts of
the chancel and the badly damaged south
chapel, which had been altered in the early

sixteenth century for Sir Thomas More (see page 42).

The 1669 rebuilding was fascinating, particularly when placed within the context of Sir Christopher Wren's sophisticated and near-contemporary rebuilding of the City churches after the Great Fire. Wren was inspired by the French Baroque and by specimens of Renaissance and antique Roman design. The details of his churches are refined in conception and execution, and many are faced with beautifully worked Portland stone. Furthermore, Wren explored numerous permutations of fundamental classical plan-forms, notably an oblong basilica plan (that is, a central nave flanked by lower-ceilinged aisles) and cubical 'centralised' plans of more symmetrical Greek cross form, sometimes with the central space topped by a dome. By comparison, the rebuilding of Chelsea Old Church was vernacular and rather old fashioned in its details. It is important to remember that when work commenced

in 1669 none of Wren's City churches had been completed, so there was not an existing, relevant and nearby body of exemplary work to which the Chelsea builders could refer.

After the war it was decided that the church should be rebuilt, largely because the More Chapel survived in reasonable condition, as did most of the church's rich collection of early and artistically important monuments, most damaged or dismantled but generally repairable. The rebuilding, undertaken in a most authentic and scholarly manner by architect Walter H. Godfrey, was completed in 1958. So, despite the church's war-time destruction, it is still possible – within limits – to assess its late seventeenth-century architecture. The most anachronistic element is the west tower, which was completed in 1674. With its corner newel staircase expressed externally and its corner buttresses, the broad outline of the tower looks

Walter W. Burgle.

Old Church Street.
Pattern proof. Coll. S. Cowden

71. Left
The tower of the Old Church from Old Church
Street in the 1890s, by W.W. Burgess. Most of
the buildings on both sides of the street have
long been rebuilt.

late medieval. Was an existing tower incorporated in the 1670s? There is no evidence to suggest so. The details are classical – round-arched openings with keystones and imposts, although there are pointed Gothic-style lancet windows in the upper window lighting the bell chamber. The bricks are laid in English bond, which – if Godfrey got this right – is odd because this bond was generally supplanted in London after 1630 or so by Flemish bond. Again, the bond helps to give the tower a look far older than the 1670s.

The nave is a slightly different matter. It is cubic in form, which suggests its designer might have been aware of the designs Wren was making for some of his centralised churches, for example St Mary-at-Hill that got underway in 1670 and which has a cubic central volume. So the nave's proportion – essentially 3:4 in plan and thus one of Andrea Palladio's 'ideal' shapes for a room – bears comparison with some of Wren's more advanced church designs, although Wren's plans are generally more complex because by the use of columns in various dispositions he created Greek cross plans within the cubical central volume. This was not attempted at Chelsea.

Also reminiscent of Wren's work are the nave's large arched windows, and in

particular its round windows, which is a detail found in several Wren churches. However, other details look earlier – for example the 1630s-style south door with its brick-made classical ornament – or appear somewhat unsophisticated, such as the large-scale concave external cornice. Together these plunge the church of c.1669–74 back to the status of being a charming but provincial design, hardly worthy of the architectural ambition of some of the great houses nearby. However, it must be said that the most fashionable late seventeenth-century specimens – notably Lindsey House – were being designed just as the church was completed.

On balance, the church is a most fascinating design, particularly the nave's cubical interior undivided by colonnades and with three wide and aligned arches opening from nave to chancel and chapels creating the imagery of a triumphal arch. The ceiling and roof must originally have been carried on well-engineered wide-span trusses. This is a rather Wren touch, for he was famed for such open and engineered interiors from the late 1660s Sheldonian Theatre in Oxford onwards. As the *Victoria County History* observed in 2004, the church, despite all it has suffered, preserves 'the atmosphere of the pre-Victorian village church crammed full of worthwhile monuments – the most evocative of such interiors in inner London' (*Victoria County History*, pp. 238–50).

St Luke's, Sydney Street

In 1818 the Chelsea vestry resolved that the parish needed a new church that was not only larger and capable of serving the ever-expanding population of Chelsea, but also set further inland where the expansion was taking place, mostly in the form of new terraces on, and just off, the King's Road. The new church was to be built on a 4-acre site east of Robert (now Sydney) Street that had been acquired in 1810 by the parish as an overflow burial ground. The Old Church was to be left standing, but reduced in status to being a chapel-of-ease, serving the residents of the old riverside village.

Money for the new church was to be raised by the parish but with one third of the cost of construction being borne by the Commissioners of the Church Building Act of 1818.

This Act had been passed as part of a national celebration to commemorate the successful conclusion of the Napoleonic war. The Tory government of Lord Liverpool deemed it not only patriotic and Christian to furnish the country with a new generation of churches in which the population could thank God for its victory but also politically expedient. Social and political unrest increased rapidly after 1815, initially in response to the imposition of the Corn Laws and there was mounting tension due to the prospect of full Roman Catholic emancipation and the increase in nonconformity. Building new churches was part of the government's response.

£1 million was set aside, and projects and sites were chosen with an eye to changing demographics so as to provide places of Anglican worship in rapidly growing cities or expanding urban areas such as Chelsea.

These 'Waterloo' churches – as they were soon called – were not just triumphalist manifestations of the state religion, but also a proclamation of the state's presence and control. It must be remembered that, at the time, the parish church was not only a place of worship but was also – since the parish was governed through the vestry – in certain senses the town hall. Within the vestry room of a parish church vestrymen would meet to fix local taxes and to organise the physical aspects of parish life, such as lighting, cleansing and watching the streets, and the maintenance of the poor. So these 'Waterloo' churches were not just religious architecture but also potentially potent political architecture.

However, a problem soon emerged after 1818. The ambitions for this building campaign were significant, but the money to realise it was not. Although this was not apparent immediately, it soon would be. The Commissioners turned to the government's Board of Works (BoW) to get the ball rolling and to devise architectural guidelines and models. What this meant was that the Board's three 'attached' or advisory architects were charged with the job of giving this vision a physical form. Unfortunately, these men did not get on particularly well, nor did they share architectural or professional convictions.

The three architects were John Nash, aged sixty-six in 1818, who had perfected a line in theatrical, often poorly constructed, speculative houses of conventional, classical design – much of it for the Crown and the Prince Regent personally; John Soane, aged sixty-five in 1818, noted for his obsession for solid traditional construction and highly idiosyncratic classical design; and Robert Smirke, aged thirty-eight in 1818, who had been apprenticed to Soane in 1796, but left the office after only a few months because of their mutual antipathy. Smirke was a solid classicist with a penchant for the Greek Revival. None of the men were Goths, although Nash and Soane were of the eclectic generation and dabbled in Gothic design, in a frivolous and ornamental manner, when required.

Consequently all three of the Board's architects were outside the mounting movement for a return to authentic Gothic design and construction. This movement, not hitting its stride until the 1830s, was championed most forcefully by Augustus W.N. Pugin. He argued that Gothic architecture – because of its structural excellence and because it had, in his view, been devised as a Christian architecture rooted in England – most convincingly expressed the Christian faith and national identity.

Classical or Gothic, all the early designs for the Commission have a penny-pinching feel. Quite simply, money was lacking for grand or generous gestures, and also, with all driven by grim economics, experimentation was brutally curbed. Even the churches by Soane, whose work is characterised by bold invention, abstraction and reinvention of the classical tradition (see page 141), are relatively tame. And this became the rule with the 'Waterloo' churches. Whatever the style in which they were designed, they tend to have a gimcrack and etiolated quality, even after 1824 when the Commission's initial budget was increased.

However, the church at Chelsea is different, for several reasons. First, its vestry had been quick off the mark and while the Board's architects – all busy men – took some years to produce their model designs, Chelsea rushed ahead and having announced its plans for a new church in 1818, had by 1819 appointed an architect and produced a design. Furthermore, money was not to be the defining factor because the vestry believed it could raise the additional money required, as indeed it did from Earl Cadogan. Consequently, the church the vestry proposed was ambitious in its design and in its scale. Perhaps one reason for this confidence was that the Rector at the time was the Rev. Hon. Gerald Valerian Wellesley. He had been the Rector since 1805, the husband of Lady Emily Cadogan since 1802 and was the brother of the Duke of Wellington, who was celebrated among the British as being the victor of Waterloo and thus, ultimately, the man behind the Commission's mission. Wellington was also in 1819, as Governor of Plymouth, part of Lord Liverpool's government.

Architecturally, the most significant thing about the vestry's chosen design is that it was not classical, like the vast majority of designs being developed by the Board's architects, but Gothic – and Gothic in a most forceful manner. The vestry's architect was James Savage. This was a fascinating choice, which suggests that the vestry understood – as did Pugin – that the true nature of Gothic lies in its structural character realised through a system of ribs, vaults, piers and buttresses, rather than in its picturesque or ornamental potential. Savage had designed a series of bridges after training with Daniel A. Alexander, an engineer and designer of utilitarian structures of heroic scale, notably Thames-side warehouses. In 1819 Savage had not designed a church nor, as far as it is known, worked in any significant way in the Gothic style. However, in competition with forty other designs, his was chosen despite a warning from the Board's architects that the design would be costly and difficult to construct. Presumably the deciding force behind Savage's selection was the Rev. Hon. Gerald Valerian Wellesley.

The design Savage produced is, in many ways, astonishing for its date. It not only possesses a high level of Gothic authenticity in its structure but it also anticipates some of the key Gothic Revival debates – promoted by Pugin and others – by a decade or so.

72. Left
St Luke's, Sydney Street designed in 1819 by
James Savage, in a photograph taken in the
1860s. The church was, despite its rather
machine-made look, a pioneering example
of Gothic Revival architecture that embraced
authentic Gothic techniques of construction.

73. Overleaf
The naves, aisles and timber galleries of
St Luke's looking east. The stone ribbed vault
of the nave is a splendid affair constructed
in true Gothic spirit but much of the detailing
of the interior is mean and repetitive.

St Luke's claim to Gothic structural authenticity is straightforward and dramatic. Gothic Revival buildings of the eighteenth and early nineteenth centuries are generally ornamental with characterful Gothic details used for visual effect. However, all the Gothic details at St Luke's are performing a structural job in true Gothic manner. The flying buttresses above the aisles are not simply there to achieve a pleasing Gothic appearance; they are there to resist the outward lateral thrust of the nave vault that is wrought of stone in proper medieval manner. Incredibly, this was the first Gothic style building built in Britain since the Middle Ages to be furnished with a large-scale stone vault of Gothic type.

The church is faced with Bath stone, but it is cut and laid in a somewhat mechanical way that – with the paucity of telling ornament – undermines the building's Gothic credentials and ambitions. For Pugin and later Gothic revivalists such as John Ruskin and William Morris, a return to the hand-crafted building practice of the medieval building was essential for an artistically inspiring and truly creative Gothic Revival. However, one look at St Luke's and it is clear that this church is modern Gothic that says more about the post-Industrial Revolution late Georgian age than it does about the medieval age.

What most impresses is the audacious height of the tower and nave, and what is most striking – in an unsettling way – is the architect's ruthless application of the principles of symmetry and repetition, the hallmarks of classical rather than Gothic architecture. The result is that the church feels little more than a standard late Georgian preaching box dressed in Gothic garb. Go inside and the experience is much the same. The nave, rising over 18 metres in height, is the loftiest of any parish church in London, and the ribbed nave vault of stone looks tremendous. However, the piers dividing the nave from the aisles again have a machine-made, mass produced appearance, while the timber galleries in the aisles are – despite their Gothic trim – a standard detail of Georgian church interiors. These features combine to give the interior an arid formality in stark contrast with genuine medieval churches. St Luke's was consecrated in 1824, by which time Savage's original estimate of £25,000, in addition to a parliamentary grant of £8,333, had been exceeded by around £7,000, making the total cost of the church about £40,000. Wellesley and his parishioners had to find the additional sum, which they eventually did with the Cadogan family largely footing the Trustee's bill. (*Victoria County History*, pp. 238–50).

161

St Luke's has a presence ... makes a most positive contribution to its setting and continues to fulfil ... the function for which it was created.

74. *Above*
The west front of Holy Trinity, Sloane Street. The church was designed in 1888 by John Dando Sedding in a permutation of the fifteenth-century English Perpendicular Gothic style. Commissioned by the 5th Earl Cadogan, Holy Trinity is now regarded as one of the finest English ecclesiastical buildings of its age and was dubbed by Sir John Betjeman 'the Cathedral of the Arts and Crafts Movement'.

Despite the ingenuity of its construction, St Luke's was not greatly admired, although some contemporary observers appreciated the sense of grandeur evoked by the church's generous scale and the evident expense. *The Gentleman's Magazine* noted that St Luke's 'would do honour to a cathedral' (*The Gentleman's Magazine*, XCVI (1), p. 201). Sadly, we do not know what Charles Dickens thought about the architecture of St Luke's but he apparently regarded the church enough to choose it as the location for his marriage in April 1836 to Catherine Hogarth. True, her family lived in Chelsea and Dickens had taken lodgings in Selwood Terrace, in nearby Brompton, so St Luke's was the logical choice. However, at the time Dickens also had lodgings in Furnival's Inn in Holborn, so other churches – dustier, darker and ancient – were options, but perhaps Dickens wanted a church that was bright and modern.

Later Gothic Revivalists saw little virtue in St Luke's, despite its pioneering stone vaults, because it lacked, in their view, the enduring, poetic and committed character of true Gothic architecture. Charles Eastlake, in his magisterial *History of the Gothic Revival*, published in 1872, offered a most astute appreciation of St Luke's. Despite the church's 'sound' workmanship and the expense of its construction, Eastlake observed that it is 'nevertheless mean and uninteresting in its general effect' and 'a failure from the artistic point of view'. This, argued Eastlake, was due to an 'unfortunate lack of proportion ... eminently noticeable in the lanky arches of the west porch ... a culpable clumsiness of detail, and a foolish, overstrained balance of parts'. He was in particular distressed by the building's overall 'cold and machine made look', the 'crude vulgarity of detail', and 'the cold formality of its arrangement'. It was, he wrote, 'astonishing' that 'the essential graces of mediaeval architecture' – its asymmetry and informality – 'at once necessary to convenience and the cause of picturesque composition' should have been 'so studiously avoided' (Charles Eastlake, *A History of the Gothic Revival*, London: Longmans, Green and Co., 1872, pp. 141–3).

These are good points, some of which even Savage might have conceded. However, they must be put in context. Savage was not trying to create an authentic, Gothic-style building as became the obsession with crusading later nineteenth-century Gothic Revival architects. He was creating a modern building, fit for the purpose of accommodating around 2,500 people of mixed social standing, in a way that was convenient, functional and safe. The style of the building was probably of secondary importance.

Eastlake's criticism of St Luke's set the pattern that reached its extreme in 1966 with Ian Nairn's brutal dismissal of the church. The building, with its 'mechanical' details, was, spouted Nairn (who was a most opinionated chap given to flashy and pithy put-downs), 'one of the most loveless in London', and had long got away with 'fraud' because whatever reputation it had was based on the fact that, when built, it had been a novelty (*Nairn's London*, p. 137). Nairn was, in my view, absurdly wrong. Of course the church is flawed, as Eastlake explains in measured manner, but like all good public architecture, St Luke's has a presence, remains solid, makes a most positive contribution to its setting and continues to fulfil – effectively and with character – the function for which it was created. One cannot ask, nor expect, any more of architecture. The Roman architect Vitruvius in the first century BC defined good architecture as possessing 'firmness, commodity and delight'. St Luke's possesses all these virtues.

St Simon Zelotes, Milner Street and St Mary's, Cadogan Street

Chelsea's later sacred buildings are a mixed bag, but with highlights, depending on one's artistic points of view. St Simon Zelotes, on the corner of Moore Street and Milner Street, built in 1858–9, continues to offer an extraordinary and most revealing vision of the mid-nineteenth-century city. The church, the focus of a collection of small and related structures of Gothic form for Anglican worship, was designed in a most individual manner by a railway architect named Joseph Peacock. It is built of Kentish ragstone, with a tall nave and a very large west window arch within which are placed two narrow traceried windows separated by a niche and topped by a small round window, also traceried. There is no tower but a tall and paper-thin bellcote which, when seen from the side, gives the little church a most fragile, paste-board appearance, making it look not unlike the gimcrack Georgian Gothic churches that A.W.N. Pugin loved to mock. This is unfair because St Simon's is, in its way, a good and learned Gothic essay but its setting undermines the seriousness of its

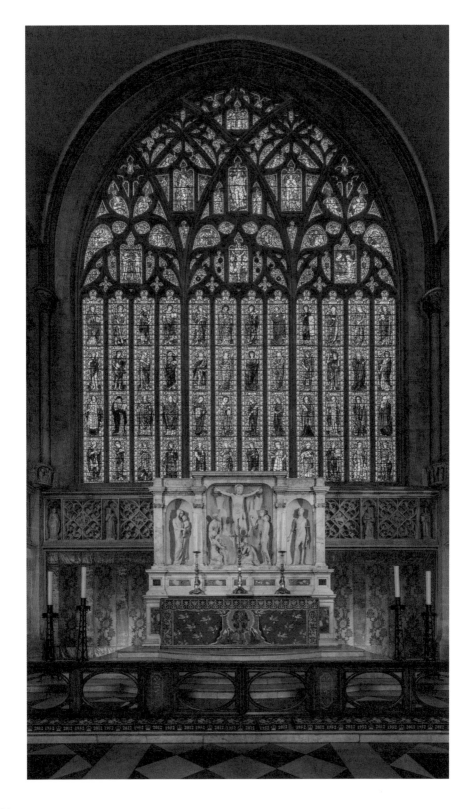

intentions. Cheek by jowl in Moore Street, in glorious and almost absurd juxtaposition, is a standard uniform classical terrace that cannot be much earlier than the church, with another – larger – classical terrace facing in on Milner Street. The little church, for all its bluster, is not quite able to defend itself or assert its ideals. And so its stands sadly muted, just part of a strangely conflictive mid-nineteenth-century building world, marooned amongst Palladian classicism, Queen Anne and Flemish Renaissance Revival and even – on the opposite side of Milner Street, at number 67 – a mid-nineteenth-century brick-built, polychromatic evocation of Venetian Gothic.

At the opposite end of Moore Street is another piece of nineteenth-century Gothic that has a very different character and presence. St Mary's, Cadogan Street is long and low, wrought of not very attractive pale yellow and mechanical-looking brickwork, and is simple and sculptural in design, all of which conspires to make it look broody and not quite complete. The Gothic is erudite, simple and a trifle mixed, combining lancets of Early English type and some 'Middle Pointed' details. The church was mostly constructed between 1877–82 for the Catholic diocese and was conceived to be part of a community of buildings – many of which survive although altered – that

were to sustain the Catholic congregation and, in their way, echo medieval Catholic life. This group of buildings was, in a very direct way, intended to be a key part of the nurture and rekindling of the old faith, after the 1829 Roman Catholic Relief Act, through the creation of a modern sacred site in the heart of Chelsea. The uses envisioned catered for most of the ages of man. As well as the church, there was to be a convent, a school, an almshouse and a cemetery. The architect was John Francis Bentley, following initial work of the mid-1840s by A.W.N. Pugin, including the south chancel chapel and its altar. Bentley was soon to abandon Gothic in favour of the application of Byzantine Romanesque architecture to the challenges of modern ecclesiastic design.

Holy Trinity, Sloane Street

The most universally admired of Chelsea's Victorian churches is Holy Trinity, Sloane Street that was designed in 1888, having been commissioned by the 5th Earl Cadogan to replace James Savage's Gothic-style church that stood on the site. This was a generous gesture on the earl's part. At the time he was involved in the expansion and large-scale rebuilding of Hans Town as an exemplary high-class residential area in the then-avant-garde Queen Anne and Flemish Renaissance styles (see page 205). These were the domestic equivalents of the ecclesiastic Gothic Revival and to attract investors and residents to the area he needed a new church, of obvious quality, designed in an appropriate and contemporary style. The new Holy Trinity possesses many of the Gothic qualities that Eastlake felt Savage's St Luke's lacked, notably finely crafted Gothic details. Holy Trinity also possesses some of the characteristics – such as symmetry and a certain formality – that Eastlake found offensive at St Luke's. However, this is due to the fact that the Gothic Revival had moved on significantly between 1872, when Eastlake's book was published, and 1888. Holy Trinity was designed by John Dando Sedding, who was a pivotal figure in the late phase of the nineteenth-century Gothic Revival. Sedding drank deep at the Gothic fountainhead of Pugin and Ruskin, and worked with the great mid-Victorian Goth George Edmund Street, whose practice became a hothouse for the Arts and Crafts Movement, which was the final expression of the nineteenth-century Gothic Revival. Inspired by craft and handicraft, and by the practice of William Morris, Arts and Crafts designers looked to all manner of vernacular architecture for inspiration.

Part of this reassessment of the relative worth of historic precedents in the design of new buildings led, from the early 1880s, to a renewed interest in the potential of Perpendicular and early Tudor Gothic that had been eclipsed in the mid-nineteenth century by a preference for 'Middle Pointed' or Decorated Gothic. The sense of organisation and of symmetry – which had alarmed Eastlake – found in authentic Perpendicular Gothic architecture, along with its use of large windows and minimal structure, seemed most appropriate to the modern age. So Holy Trinity is, externally at least, in the late fifteenth-century symmetrical Perpendicular manner of King's College Chapel at Cambridge and St George's Chapel, Windsor Castle, having, like them, a tall nave with a large traceried window flanked by slender octagonal towers. However, as Sedding demonstrated so convincingly at Holy Trinity, any tendency towards mechanistic design that strict symmetry might imply can be mitigated by the use of an array of well-crafted details and – as with the west front of Holy Trinity with its banded decoration – by the use of a rich mix of materials. Sedding died in early 1891, just after Holy Trinity had been roofed, so what you see today when you enter he never saw. However, it is the child of his imagination and a vivid expression of the Arts and Crafts aesthetics he helped to hone and that he held sacred. It is a testimony to the basic idea underlying the Gothic Revival and the Arts and Crafts Movement: that God's spirit can lie in man-made beauty if that beauty is achieved and expressed in truth and honesty and in accord with the principles of Divine creation. Such wonders cannot only delight the eye but can raise man's soul to a higher, spiritual plane.

So enter the church and meditate upon its treasures, each beautiful and each carrying a divine message, some overtly so because of the subjects they depict but others by virtue of their craftsman-like creation. The east window is both. It was designed by Edward Burne-Jones and made by Morris & Co. The stone tracery is slender and ornate and the glass – of deep hues placed carefully to create a harlequin display of contrasting colours – shows four tiers of exemplary figures, with forty-eight in total. These include, top centre (left to right) St Thomas, St James the Less, St Philip and St Bartholomew. Above these are other images, including the Nativity, a guardian angel and the Annunciation. On the chancel gates are bronze angels by Frederick Pomeroy. Henry Wilson – who took on the completion of the church after Sedding's death – designed the screen in the north aisle in Byzantine style, which in the 1890s was seen as preferable alternative to more conventional classicism. In the north aisle is more outstanding stained glass of deep and strong colours, showing Patriarchs and saints, with their attributes and scenes from their lives. One window shows Abraham, who represents wisdom, St Paul representing fortitude, and St Francis of Assisi representing patience.

The life of Holy Trinity after completion in the early 1890s was not without incident. In the 1920s much of the interior was covered with whitewash because the ornate scheme was too oppressive for contemporary taste, during the war the roof was damaged by bombs and in the 1970s the diocese proposed to rid itself of the upkeep and further expense of restoring the church by demolishing it and replacing it with a block of flats and offices. This led to a most unholy battle, with opponents of demolition led by Chelsea resident Sir John Betjeman, who in most memorable manner characterised Holy Trinity as 'the Cathedral of the Arts and Crafts Movement'. The church was saved and it now recognised as one of Chelsea's great architectural jewels.

The First Church of Christ Scientist, Sloane Terrace and St Columba's, Pont Street

Chelsea's sacred landscape was extended in 1907 when, in Sloane Terrace, around the corner from Holy Trinity, a very large building was completed for the Church of Christ Scientist. The church, with a soaring slender tower topped with a small stone dome of somewhat Moghul character, is a most peculiar affair, as is the permutation of Christian faith it was designed to accommodate. The Church of Christ Scientist was founded in Boston, Massachusetts in 1879 by Mary Baker Eddy who, as a fervid and evangelical champion of 'primitive' Christianity, believed the Bible possesses mystic powers to heal the body and the mind. She inaugurated 'testimony' meetings at which congregations, after listening to readings from the Bible and the Christian Science textbook, were invited

to offer personal evidence of healing resulting from Christian Science prayer. The movement's motto and registered trade mark – 'Heal the sick, raise the dead, cleanse the lepers, cast out demons' – reveals the literal and magical manner in which the New Testament is taken.

In the early twentieth century the movement grew rapidly in popularity and so this huge Portland stone and granite-clad church was built in Chelsea. The style of its architecture has little or nothing to do with local or British building traditions, being, in rather ruthlessly abstracted way, a derivation of early medieval Byzantine design. The architect was Robert F. Chisholm. He was around sixty-five years of age when the church was designed and had just retired to England after a forty-year career in India, based in Madras (now Chennai) where he was head of the school of industrial art. Subsequently he practised as an architect and was responsible for much government and institutional architecture, as well as palatial architecture for the princely states, notably a large portion the Chepauk Palace, built in 1868–71 and once the home of the Nawab of Arcot. Chisholm is now regarded as being instrumental in the development of 'Indo-Saracenic' architecture, a hybrid style that fused elements of Mughal and Hindu architecture with western classical and Gothic in an attempt to create a distinct national architectural style for Imperial India. At best the result can be a whimsical and charmingly eccentric oriental equivalent of the Gothic Revival, but often Indo-Saracenic buildings are far from convincing in their mix of styles and motifs.

Presumably Chisholm had in mind the ethos of Indo-Saracenic when he designed this church which – one has to assume – was his shot at forging a modern, history-based ecclesiastical style for London. His choice of the Byzantine was not entirely novel

76. Right
The First Church of Christ Scientist
(now Cadogan Hall) in Sloane Terrace.
This strange fusion of a building, in which
Byzantine-style architecture is enlivened
with a sprinkling of Indo-Saracenic detail,
was completed in 1907 to the designs
of Robert F. Chisholm.

because, as already explained, many at the time saw it as the happy compromise between Gothic and Renaissance classicism. To put it simply, Byzantine architecture was seen to be Gothic in its free and creative spirit of invention and in its opportunity for honestly expressed construction (with which Victorian Goths were besotted), and yet with the practical underlying discipline appropriate for the industrialised construction of modern building. In most spectacular manner the architect John Francis Bentley had demonstrated – on a sublime scale – the potential of Byzantine architectural sources in 1895 when construction started on Westminster Cathedral in Victoria. The cathedral was nearing completion (it was consecrated in 1910) just as Chisholm was getting to work in Chelsea in 1904. So he had a nearby prototype, but Chisholm's Byzantine style could hardly be more different. Bentley's cathedral is, externally, banded with red brick and white stone in most ornamental manner, with an array of small domed towers and large lunettes flanking a huge brick-built shallow dome, in the manner of the sixth-century Hagia Sophia in Istanbul. By contrast, Chisholm's church is, externally, white and simple, with round arched windows and arcade, as found in eleventh-century Byzantine-style architecture in Venice. Chisholm's building is certainly interesting and

visually striking, but it is hard to see it as a great success and, in its forms, seems to stand aloof from London's architecture. Chisholm's determination to plough his own furrow and his refusal to integrate his architecture with its surroundings does not seem to have done the Church of Christ Scientist any favours. Perhaps, like its church building, it also failed to integrate or become a much-loved part of Chelsea. By the mid-1990s the congregation had dwindled to the point where it could no longer support this grandiose building. It was sold and eventually acquired by the Cadogan Estate that – in a most unusual turn of events – came up with a new use for the building that is arguably more suitable than the use for which it was created. The estate has re-launched the church as the Cadogan Hall, now home of the Royal Philharmonic Orchestra, a rehearsal and performance space with an outstanding programme of classical music. The hall's acoustic qualities have been refined, it has been insulated to exclude external noise, and now it is one of the best examples of its kind in the capital. This makes the point that sacred spaces are not only about religion. They can also, quite simply, be about beauty – as Holy Trinity makes clear – which, if you are so minded, can be seen as a divine gift, an inspiration and a guiding light.

77. Left
St Columba's Presbyterian church in Pont Street, completed in 1955 to the designs of Sir Edward Maufe. The church is a strikingly odd mix of historical styles, including Romanesque, from which the architect evidently hoped to mould a modern ecclesiastical style.

A footnote to the First Church of Christ Scientist is St Columba's Presbyterian Church in Pont Street. The late nineteenth-century church on the site was destroyed during the war and a new church was built in 1950–55 in a style as strange – if not stranger – than Chisholm's church. Although significantly different in many ways, the two churches have aspects in common that, superficially at least, suggest far stronger architectural connections than in fact exist.

Both are clad in Portland stone, have tall, square-plan, asymmetrically placed campanile and both possess an almost abstract external simplicity and flirt with Byzantine and Romanesque tradition. St Columba's was designed by Sir Edward Maufe, a somewhat late proponent of the Arts and Crafts Movement who spent much of his career – as did architects a generation or two before him – attempting to extract a modern British architecture from a myriad of historic building styles and traditions.

Guildford Cathedral – a sort of machine age Gothic that gives a spiritual powerhouse a more than passing resemblance to a brick-built power station – is Maufe's best-known effort. St Columba's is not so well known, but arguably a better, or at least more intriguing, piece of architecture.

The outside, with its elemental Romanesque entrance façade, does tend to stop one in one's tracks – not necessarily a good thing – while the interior is marginally more subtle and perhaps more satisfying, with an arcade formed by round arches supported on square piers and a scattering of Romanesque style capitals. What cannot be in doubt is that this building, idiosyncratic as it may be, holds its own in the landscape, and few who pass by would not appreciate that it is marking a sacred site.

ARTS IN CHELSEA

78. Above
John Singer Sargent's studio in a purpose-
designed block of artists' studios in Tite
Street. Named 'The Studios', the block was
built between 1878 to 1880 to the designs
of R.W. Edis. This photograph of Sargent's
studio was taken shortly before his death
in Chelsea in 1925.

During the late nineteenth and early twentieth centuries Chelsea became a favoured location in London for the construction of purpose-designed and built artists' homes and studios. Some were commissioned by individual artists from specific architects but many were mass-produced as speculations, either as single studios or, more commonly, as blocks of studios. Clearly, since such speculations were seen as sound and potentially profitable, they confirm the intensity of the demand in London's late Victorian and Edwardian artistic community for a base in Chelsea. The *Victoria County History* estimates that during the sixty years prior to the First World War over 1,300 domestic artists' studios were erected in London as a whole, with Chelsea the 'favoured' location, with nearly 300 individual studio units by 1914 because 'it had sites available for building at reasonable cost, while still being close to the West End and the picture-buying public' (*Victoria County History*, pp. 102-96; and Kate Orme, 'Artists' Studios, Supplementary Planning Guidance', 2004, p. 11, who identifies fifty-four purpose-built groups of multiple studios in the borough containing 293 individual units).

The rise of this building type with its distinct features – characteristically, a big double-height studio with a large window, sometimes virtually a wall of glass, and often a mezzanine gallery – is a fascinating testament to the rise of professionalism in the artistic community and to the level of money that could be generated by artists attuned to the tastes of a public evidently ready to spend large amounts of money on a contemporary art that, today, would hardly be considered art at all. Much of the more popular offerings depicted saccharine landscapes or took the form of sentimental and patriotic history painting, often technically able but little more than illustration and lacking the intellectual challenge or rigour or psychological insight that is now expected from fine art.

Late Victorian military paintings became something of a national addiction, with its high priestess being Lady Butler, whose latest military epic painting – showing the self-sacrifice and stoic suffering of sometimes traumatised heroes of the Napoleonic, Crimean or Zulu wars – could get crowds queuing in the street outside West End galleries. When *The Roll Call*, depicting wounded, exhausted and shell-shocked Grenadier Guardsmen after a Crimean engagement, was shown at the 1874 Royal Academy Summer Exhibition, police had to be posted next to the painting to control the crowds that flocked to see it. After touring the country, the painting was purchased by Queen Victoria, with coloured prints of it and its kind adorning many a Victorian parlour. The readiness of the Victorians – from lower middle class to royalty – to spend money on newly minted art meant that more artists than ever before could earn a reasonable living from their work and enjoy the status of a skilled professional rather than a tradesman. It also meant that a larger number of artists than ever before could afford to build or rent well-appointed studios in which to live and work (see Donald Insall Associates, 'Historic Building Report on Rossetti Studios, 72 Flood Street, Chelsea' for the Cadogan Estate, 2016, p. 11; Anne Helmreich and Pamela Fletcher, *The Rise of the Modern Art Market in London 1850–1939*, Manchester University Press, 2011, p. 24). The *Victoria County History* suggests one reason why Chelsea was popular: there was building land available at a reasonable cost yet it was near central London where potential clients and galleries were located. However, there is an additional reason that made Chelsea popular: the quantity of building sites and the quality of the light. A large proportion of the available sites had only recently been created and their location was perfect. When the Chelsea Embankment was constructed in the early 1870s – moving west from Grosvenor Road and Chelsea Bridge to Cheyne Walk – building land that had been acquired or created by land reclamation by the Metropolitan Board of Works (MBW) and what proved 'surplus' to requirements for road construction was leased to speculating builders or individuals wanting riverside homes with good prospects and clear light. One of these was the artist James Abbott McNeill Whistler, who acquired a site at the Embankment end of Tite Street from the MBW and in 1877 commissioned a studio home from the progressive architect E.W. Godwin.

The quest for light
Light was the issue. It had drawn J.M.W. Turner to Chelsea in the 1840s when he lived and worked in what in now

119 Cheyne Walk, one of a group of modest late eighteenth-century houses, much altered and rebuilt, and with a roof-top studio and balcony with a cast iron balcony railing, presumably added by Turner so he could gain and enjoy the prospect and the pure light reflected off the supple surface of the Thames. One of the odder ironies of the construction of the Chelsea Embankment in the early 1870s is that it inadvertently created opportunities for the construction of artists' domestic studios but also destroyed the peace, solitude and the picturesque working riverside community that had attracted Turner and the Greaves brothers (see page 77).

There are few examples of notable pre-Victorian painters choosing Chelsea as a base from which to live and work, although some chose it or its buildings as subjects worth painting, for example Giovanni Antonio Canaletto's 1754 painting of the rotunda in Ranelagh Gardens (see page 240). Artists who did venture to use Chelsea as a base were the sporting painter John F. Sartorius, who in 1806 had a studio in the King's Road and was soon joined by his brother, C.J. Sartorius, a painter of marine subjects, who settled near the Queen's Elm pub. Sir David Wilkie, the genre painter, lived in both Hampstead and Chelsea before settling in Kensington High Street in 1811, while Sir Francis Chantrey at about the same time bought a house and land near the Thames in 'lower' Belgravia, a good location for the delivery of the large blocks of marble that his work demanded, especially after the Grosvenor Canal opened in 1824 (Giles Walkley, *Artists' Houses in London, 1764–1914*, Scolar Press, 1994, p. 25). By the mid-nineteenth century artists and craftsmen started to appear in ever-increasing numbers in Chelsea. Edward Burne-Jones found his first London studio in Sloane Terrace in 1856, near the artisan quarter in and around what is now Pavilion Road, and in 1862 Dante Gabriel Rossetti established himself in the vast and sprawling early eighteenth-century

Light ... had drawn J.M.W. Turner to Chelsea in the 1840s ... and ... Whistler delighted in the shifting moods of the light playing upon the river's surface.

79. Above
A group of small late eighteenth-century houses on Cheyne Walk with, in the centre, number 119, which was rented to J.M.W. Turner in the 1840s and where he died in 1851. The balcony on the roof seems to have been added by Turner to allow him to enjoy a wide prospect of the Thames.

16 Cheyne Walk, but which he found 'too dim to paint in even in mid-summer' and tried to commission Philip Webb to design him a garden studio (Walkley, p. 80). And then, of course, from 1866, Whistler lived and worked in a portion of Lindsey House, overlooking the Thames and a stone's throw from the house in which Turner had died just over a decade earlier. Like Turner, Whistler delighted in the shifting moods of the light playing upon the river's surface.

Chelsea Porcelain Factory
However, not only artists need light to see what they are doing. Many crafts have the same requirement, as made clear by the wide windows on the houses in which silk weavers lived and worked in the weaving districts of Spitalfields, Bethnal Green and Shoreditch. The desire for good daylight was, perhaps, one of the key reasons that the Chelsea Porcelain Factory was established in 1743 or 1745 at the north end of Lawrence Street. The porcelain was

80. Above
'The Music Lesson', being given by a shepherd
to a shepherdess, is faintly erotic, Rococo in
style and typical of the wares made by the
Chelsea Porcelain Factory. It dates from about
1765 and was modelled by Joseph Willems
after an engraving by François Boucher.

known for its fine and delicate modelling and detailed colouring achieved through the meticulous and skilled application of pigments and glazes. All this, of course, demanded bright and clear light. The factory specialised in the production of small polychromatic porcelain ornamental figures, some of which were also *bonbonnières* suitable for scents or needle-cases, and generally inspired by Meissen porcelain. All was playful, fashionably Rococo in manner and often softly erotic, with many pieces furnished with amorous mottos, invariably in French and often misspelt. It is generally assumed, and with good reason, that the factory's fortunes were linked to those of Ranelagh Gardens, which opened in 1742 and whose clientele, drawn to Chelsea for the playful pleasures of the place, would feel tempted to purchase equally playful local porcelain. So, at one level, Chelsea porcelain can be seen as highly superior tourist tat.

The factory appears to have been started by Nicholas Sprimont, an entrepreneurial Huguenot silversmith from Soho, or at least by 1750 he was its director and the moving force. Another Huguenot silversmith, Charles Gouyn, was involved but his precise role remains unclear.

There was another reason – besides clear light and a potential market for its wares generated by Ranelagh – that attracted Sprimont to Chelsea, and that was the body, or 'paste', from which the factory's charming objects were made.

Since at least the sixteenth century imported Chinese porcelain had been highly regarded in Europe, not only for the excellence of its design and colouring but because of the delicate but immensely tough fired material out of which it was made. The material was obviously a form of clay, but there seemed to be ingredients added that allowed the fired object to be delicate in detail and thin to the point of translucency yet strong enough to survive day-to-day usage. There were many attempts to discover the formula and to make in Europe fired clay products as good as Chinese imports that would divert porcelain lovers' money from Chinese pockets into European pockets. Meissen was an attempt to simulate Chinese porcelain, as was English Royal Worcester, Derby, Bow and Chelsea porcelain manufactories, most of which flourished in the 1740s and 1750s (Meissen, near Dresden in Germany, was a pioneer, getting underway in 1708). They all made reasonable imitations of Chinese porcelain, even though none of them knew the Chinese formula.

In the 1730s, a Jesuit missionary in China named Père François d'Entrecolles had found out the nature of the paste using kaolin clay, and had informed his friend Jean-Baptiste Du Halde of his discovery. Du Halde wrote a pamphlet on this, entitled *A Description of the Empire of China and of Chinese Tartary*. However, it was not until the early 1760s that a series of odd circumstances led to d'Entrecolles' discovery being applied, initially by the Englishman William Cookworthy.

In 1750, having been told about kaolin by a Huguenot potter familiar with Du Halde's pamphlet, Cookworthy discovered by chance a supply of kaolin-type clay and petuntse in Cornwall – a material now known as China Clay. Cookworthy was busy and somewhat distracted at the time and it was not until 1768 that he took out a patent and started a commercial porcelain works producing Britain's first, authentic, homemade porcelain goods.

However, by this time the Chelsea Porcelain Factory was winding down. In 1770 it merged with the Derby porcelain works, which itself closed in 1785. The Chelsea manufactory seems to have finally closed in the same year, with now no significant physical trace of its existence surviving in Lawrence Street beyond a blue plaque marking the factory's location.

Chelsea's location must have played a key role in the complex business of obtaining the materials required to allow the factory to function, initially successfully. A chemist would have been employed to devise the formula for the paste, the glazes, the colours and the firing times required. This could have been Gouyn, or Thomas Briand, who in 1743 demonstrated a sample of porcelain at the Royal Society that was said to be an 'earthenware Little inferior to Porcelain or China ware' (W.B. Honey, *Old English Porcelain*, 3rd edition, Faber and Faber, 1977, pp. 18-20). The chemist would have required a wide range of specific ingredients, principally of course the primarily clay-based paste. Chelsea, with its long association with the supply or trade in chalk, lime or clay (see page 13) might perhaps have been chosen as a location for the factory because some of the key ingredients for the paste could have been found locally. However, more likely it was the proximity of the river, providing the highway along which clay and other ingredients could have been delivered with relative ease.

This all gives the product of the Chelsea porcelain factory a most elemental quality: water to transport the clay – that had been won from the earth – to Chelsea, where it was mixed, modelled and transformed by fire into durable and beautiful ware. And, of course, air – or more specifically uncorrupted light – to allow craftsmen to fashion and decorate the objects with precision.

Light, as well as the convenience of river and road communications, and perhaps the supply of local materials, was no doubt one of the key reasons the potter William de Morgan, friend of William Morris and Rossetti, established himself in 1872 at the north end of Cheyne Row. The production of his polychromic glazed 'lustreware' tiles, vases and plates demanded a high level of craftsmanship and, of course, skilled craftsmen doing meticulous work needed

good light. In 1881 de Morgan moved his factory, warehouse and showroom to Merton. Eventually these buildings were replaced by the Roman Catholic Church of the Most Holy Redeemer, which since 1895 has held court on the site in a rather grand and lofty Italianate manner.

Domestic artists' studios

Domestic artists' studios are a fascinating building type that emerged in London in the mid-nineteenth century. As pointed out, there were two basic types. First, there were the individual studio houses, generally commissioned by an artist or built as a speculation for occupation by an individual artist – either way the artist needed to be of considerable means and fairly confident in the ready sale of their work. Secondly, there were blocks of 'mass-produced' studios built to rent – almost invariably built as a speculation and less spacious, less ornamental and consequently less financially demanding to occupy. These studio complexes could take the form of individual studios with large windows and roof lights grouped together around a courtyard or narrow road to form a community of low-rise studios. Or they could take the form of multi-storey blocks furnished with a series of large windows lighting individual studios juxtaposed with windows of conventional size serving domestic interiors.

The most spectacular examples of the affluent artist's mansion, incorporating luxurious studios, rose along and near Melbury Road, Holland Park, during the 1860s and 1870s, notably the houses and studios designed by Norman Shaw in 1876 to 1877 for Marcus Clayton Stone and for Sir Luke Fildes and, in Holland Park Road, the exotic oriental wonder that Lord Leighton designed with George Aitchison from the mid-1860s into the late 1870s as an almost impossibly romantic setting for his work and life. As Ian Nairn observed most perceptively in 1966, Lord Leighton's house 'has the wholeness and excitement

... so conspicuously absent from his paintings' (*Nairn's London*, p. 155 of 1988 edition). An odd situation but evidently Leighton put the fire of his imagination into his architecture rather than his art.

Although Chelsea has nothing to quite match these excesses, it is rich in studios that were bespoke by artists or that were designed as speculations to be occupied by individual artists. Chelsea also has a fascinating stock of more modest mass-produced studio complexes.

Most of these studios date from the late 1860s into the 1890s when building studios became a major construction project in several parts of west London and when the universally preferred style was the relaxed asymmetrical and often whimsical vernacular classicism of the Queen Anne Revival. This is hardly surprising, since this style – with its moulded and rubbed red brick ornament, including such motifs as sunflowers – was the preferred style of the Aesthetic Movement, of which many Chelsea-based artists or writers were part. Notable, of course, was Oscar Wilde, who from 1884 lived in the newly completed and speculatively built 34 Tite Street (see page 188). The house has an extraordinarily dull and diluted 'Queen Anne' exterior, but Wilde compensated by commissioning a startling Japanese-inspired interior from Godwin that was intended to serve as a demonstration of the Aesthetic Movement's artistic principles and as a setting for Wilde's elegant receptions. The circumstances of Wilde's fall from grace and sudden exit from the house meant that his contribution was little valued or protected, and all trace of the remarkable interior has long gone.

The first purpose-designed, speculatively built 'mass-produced' studio complexes in the Chelsea area were started in 1869. Named 'The Avenue', the studios – set behind 76 Fulham Road – take the form of a mews or group of workshops. The developer

was Sir Charles Freake. The Avenue consists of two-storey houses along its south side that are of simple but unusual asymmetrical design – purely the result of function rather than affectation – with large ground-floor windows and a single large first-floor window set above and between the two. An early artist working in The Avenue in the mid-1880s was M.R. Corbet ARA, who specialised in the production of softly romantic Italian landscapes, a sure seller on the middle-class art market. Other artists in occupation included Lady Butler, who painted *The Roll Call* here in 1874 (see page 177), Sir Alfred Gilbert, who in his studio in The Avenue sculpted the Shaftesbury Memorial, now better known as 'Eros' that stands in Piccadilly Circus, and John Singer Sargent (Walkley, pp. 140–42).

The best way to explore Chelsea's domestic studios, to consider their varied design and see which artists were attracted to the area, is to walk along three streets – Tite Street, Glebe Place and Flood Street – all with a good collection of studio houses.

Tite Street
Tite Street was laid out by the Metropolitan Board of Works (MBW) at the time it constructed the Chelsea Embankment in the early 1870s. The idea was that the new street would help connect the Embankment to Chelsea's existing network of streets, notably the King's Road.

The 1799-1819 edition of Horwood's map gives a good idea of the situation in the late 1860s when the MBW moved into action. There were a number of property boundaries running from Paradise Row down to the river and on the narrow plots were a scattering of buildings. Tite Street – named after William Tite, one of the commissioners of the MBW – followed the line of one of these boundaries. The street's main feature when laid out was that, to its east, was the detached eighteenth-century Gough House and its garden, deep and

81. Above
Gough House from the Thames, built in 1704 for the Earl
of Carbery to the south of Paradise Row and not finally
demolished until 1968. This view was painted by Marianne
Rush in around 1800–10 and confirms that many of her
depictions of Chelsea locations are almost as much
imagined as they are real. This portrayal of the house is
reasonably accurate, but its detached setting and terraced
garden is poetic licence.

narrow reaching south to the Thames. Gough House is one of the great lost houses of Chelsea. It was built in 1704 for the 3rd Earl of Carbery who was the Governor of Jamaica. The main elevation, facing the river, was seven-windows wide with a pediment over the three centre windows. The north elevation was more interesting. With end bays breaking forward slightly, it looked like a compressed version of Clarendon House, Piccadilly, which was designed in 1664 and architecturally one of the most influential houses of its age. Carbery's house was acquired in 1713 by Richard Gough, a wealthy East India merchant, but it gradually slid down the social scale, becoming a girls' school in the 1790s, a boys' school in the 1830s and a children's hospital in 1866, at which point the house and its long garden were acquired by the MBW. The house was spared (in fact it survived, much altered, until 1968) but the southern end of its garden was used for the construction of the Embankment with the garden's west edge added to the MBW property portfolio and earmarked for development as land that was 'surplus' to the requirements of road construction. Prospective builders were most happy to snap up leases on this newly available and prime land. However, the MBW, as the freeholder, was able to impose certain covenants, conditions and aesthetic controls that were soon to prove onerous and the cause of great friction.

One of the first to lease a site from the MBW was Whistler. This was in 1877 when his work was selling and his prospects were good. His ambitions were high. He commissioned Godwin to design the White House, a studio and house combined. The building was large and radical in its pure simplicity. The MBW, exercising its right of aesthetic control, objected to the design, which it thought too crude and unbeautiful, and which it feared would lower the tone of the up-and-coming Tite Street and prove difficult to let in

82. Right
A drawing of 1877 by E.W. Godwin showing the Tite Street elevation of the White House that he had designed for J.M. Whistler. The unusual simplicity of the house and studio greatly alarmed the landlord, the Metropolitan Board of Works.

83. Below right
Following his costly libel battle with John Ruskin, Whistler was compelled to give up the White House in 1879, after less than a year in occupation. It was soon altered by its new occupant, as shown, to the outrage of Godwin and Whistler.

the future. Battle began, a compromise reached and the house completed, just in time for Whistler to face another battle. This – his 1878 prosecution of John Ruskin for libel – he was to win, yet to all intents and purposes lose (see page 74). These two cases make curious companions. In the first, Whistler and his architect – evidently artistically adventurous free spirits – were apparently dogged by MBW dullards who wished to impose aesthetic control to enforce a more conventional design. In the second case, Whistler wished to impose control over Ruskin's opinions about aesthetics after the latter was biting and patronisingly critical of the former's art. Presumably in both battles Whistler saw himself as taking on the philistines.

The consequence of Whistler's ill-advised action was that he was bankrupted by his very costly pyrrhic victory in court and in 1879 was obliged to move out of the White House almost before he had moved in. There is no record that the MBW found it difficult to let, although its next tenant did make some additions that outraged both Godwin and Whistler. Ultimately, the house's odd and simple design might have been its undoing and one of the reasons for its demolition in 1968. Even by that time, few, it seems, understood it. Despite Whistler's public discomfiture, other artists soon followed him to Tite Street,

and most of them hired Godwin as their architect, who was the architect of choice for progressive – or at least aspirational and experimental – artists, as opposed to the massive establishment artists domiciled in Holland Park. To a degree Godwin's lifestyle matched that of his Chelsea clients. He was not only an architect but also a designer of theatre costumes and sets, fabrics and furniture, and for six years until 1874 had lived with the actress Ellen Terry. It says much about this curious interwoven world that Godwin's second wife (he never married Terry) went on to marry Whistler after Godwin's death in 1886.

In 1878, while the White House was under construction, Godwin was commissioned to build a double studio on the Tite Street site opposite. The client was the Hon. Archibald Stuart-Wortley, who wanted a studio for himself and for his artist friend Carlo Pellegrini, who displayed his talents as 'Ape', a caricaturist for magazine *Vanity Fair*. Called Chelsea Lodge, the studio block is designed in an early seventeenth-century version of the Queen Anne Revival, with a bay and large chimney stack to turn the corner with Dilke Street, myriad mullioned and transomed windows including three at second-floor level, topped by pedimeted gables, that lit the studios. Stuart-Wortley and Pellegrini's relationship, professional or personal, did not – despite their shared

work-place – prove enduring. By August 1879 Chelsea Lodge was on the market, but perhaps it had been a speculation all the time.

In 1878 Godwin started work on a Tite Street studio home for Frank Miles, an independently wealthy and socially well connected artist with something of a reputation for the darker, more decadent aspects of late Victorian London life, a reputation that outlived his death, causing him to be proposed – in the face of compelling evidence – as a contender for the identity of Jack the Ripper. The design was to prove a struggle. Once again Godwin had to contend with the MBW, which was again the freeholder of the site and, again, suspicious of unconventional architecture. And once again Godwin's design was unusual – in the circumstances bravely so. Its Tite Street elevation , number 44, had horizontal emphasis, with bands of brick enlivened with areas of ornate decoration. It was asymmetrical, with two tall second-floor windows rising through the eaves to light the studio. The MBW refused to pass the design. As Giles Walkley points out, 'Godwin thought it the best design he had ever produced. He had good reason ... it could be mistaken for a sketch of around 1905 by Frank Lloyd Wright' (Walkley, pp. 88-9). Again there was dispute and delay, and again a compromise was finally reached, with Godwin eventually producing a simplified Flemish Renaissance style design, one of the popular strands of the Queen Anne Revival. The elevation is again asymmetrical, with on one side the front door topped with a segmental pediment supported by large brick-wrought scrolls. On the opposing side is a tall bay containing the large second-floor studio windows, set behind a small balustraded balcony, that breaks above the eaves in the form of a tall Baroque gable. All this is pretty predictable – and perhaps more to the point beyond objection. More exciting by far is the plan Godwin devised, very

modern in its interplay of volumes and sense of space and light. Miles specialised in pastel portraits of society ladies and botanical illustrations and formed a firm friendship with Oscar Wilde after meeting him in Oxford in 1874. When new in London, with little money and few friends, Wilde relied on Miles for financial support and for those introductions into society that were as life's blood for the socially aspirational young Irishman. Wilde lodged with Miles in his rooms off the Strand after leaving Oxford in 1878, moved with him to Tite Street in 1880 and later, of course, became Miles's near neighbour in the same street. However, despite his growing success, Wilde was obliged to occupy a more humble off-the-peg home, although he managed to persuade Godwin to redesign the interior.

The artistically and socially elevated world of Wilde's Tite Street did not last long. In 1887, Miles – just before his marriage – was committed to a lunatic asylum near Bristol, which surely puts him out of the frame for the 1888 Ripper murders. He died in 1891 of an ailment diagnosed as 'general paralysis of the insane'. Four years later Wilde found himself in Reading Gaol, a long way, in every sense, from exquisite Tite Street.

Numbers 31 to 33 Tite Street are an interesting example of upper-end speculatively built studios, intended for occupation by a small number of eminent artists rather than by a larger community of more modest artists. Godwin produced a design for the site, immediately to the north of the White House, in the late 1870s that envisaged the creation of a terrace of relatively small studio houses. However, the site was sold to speculators who resold part of the site to artist Frank Dicey and then employed the architect and amateur soldier Colonel R.W. Edis to produce an overall scheme. Built between 1878 and 1880, the block – christened 'The Studios' – is self-consciously divided to appear to be four separate structures, each crowned by a gable, all of which are of slightly different

In 1895 Wilde found himself in Reading Gaol, a long way, in every sense, from exquisite Tite Street.

84. *Above*
A curious perspective of 'Artists' Houses' at the southeast end of Tite Street, published in the 14 May 1880 edition of *The Architect*. The drawing is partly visionary, showing recently completed buildings as well as those proposed. For example, at the far right is a group of designs credited to Godwin, including the White House. In the centre is a gabled structure by R.W. Edis, which eventually expanded to the south to form 'The Studios' complex. To its north is a set of ornate residential studios, also designed by Godwin.

heights, widths and designs but all in the approved Queen Anne style. The block is big, with tall studio windows, mostly at first- and second-floor levels. John Singer Sargent moved into number 33 in 1885, bringing of course some of the grandness of Holland Park to Tite Street, and in 1901 expanded into Dicey's studio in number 31. Here the greats of Chelsea and of London made their way to be immortalised by one of the greatest portrait painters of the age. These included Henry James, who would have strolled from his flat on Cheyne Walk (see page 100) and Ellen Terry, who ensured the world of Sargent overlapped with that of Godwin – and of the afflicted Miles and the stricken Wilde. Even Whistler again become part of the scene, when in 1881 after some time recuperating in Venice, he took a studio in the block so he could 'live next door to himself'. Godwin's last significant architectural foray in Tite Street was number 46, The Tower House, which was conceived as a block of studios.

FOR F. MILES ESQ.

TREET, CHELSEA.

FRONT ELEVATION

¼ scale

85. *Above*
The initial design of 1878 by Godwin for Frank
Miles's studio house at 44 Tite Street. Ahead
of its time, the design proved too much of a
challenge for the landlords, the Metropolitan
Board of Works (MBW), who duly rejected it.

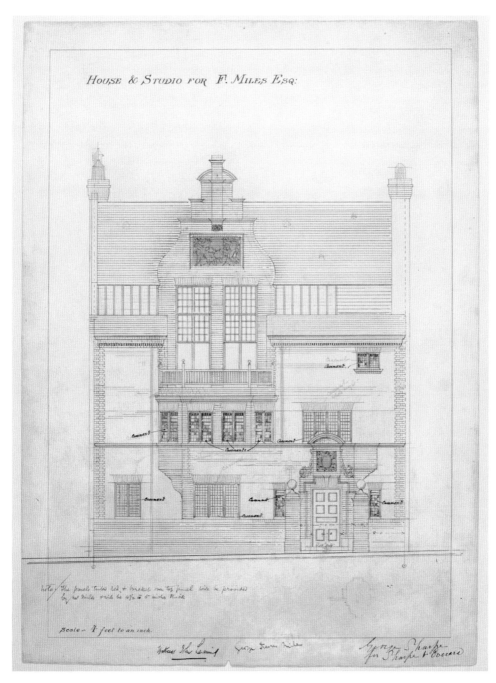

HOUSE & STUDIO FOR F. MILES ESQ:

86. Above
Godwin's revised design for the Miles house in
Tite Street, of 1878, in a far more conventional
gabled Flemish Renaissance revival manner
that the MBW found acceptable.

However, he seems to have been running out of steam. It was designed in 1884, incorporates four tiers of huge studio windows, alongside of which are stacked-up small windows and bays serving the building's eight floors. The design was executed by Denton, Son & North, to whom Godwin had sold construction rights.

Glebe Place

Glebe Place runs north from Upper Cheyne Row. The short south part of Glebe Place is a continuation of Cheyne Row, built in 1708 (see page 91) but it then makes a right-angled turn and heads east before making another right-angled turn to continue north to the King's Road. The line of Glebe Place is continued north of the King's Road by Manresa Road. As the road's name suggests, it runs across parish-owned glebe land, with part of it indeed once bordering the garden of the rectory fronting on to Old Church Street. Emblazoned over all – on Richardson's 1769 estate map – is the word 'Glebe', so there can be no misunderstanding about its ownership. Richardson's map also shows the characteristic zigzag form of Glebe Place already established, presumably as a path around discreet packages of land that served a scattering of freestanding buildings. One of the early buildings might survive – the diminutive number 51, which with its large chimney stack and gambrel roof looks like an early eighteenth-century cottage, and a building on its corner site is shown in Richardson's map.

The zigzag path seems to have been gradually lined with buildings, for example numbers 36, 37 and 38 form a short terrace dating from the early nineteenth century. However, building along the edges of the path in continuous manner seems to date from the 1850s, at which time a uniform and standard terrace was constructed on its west side and, a few years later, small individual studios or small block of studios, then becoming a favoured building enterprise in much of Chelsea,

were run up along its east side. The most architecturally interesting of these studio houses in Glebe Place is, as it happens, the earliest purpose-built and designed domestic studio in Chelsea. Number 35 Glebe Place – known as West House – was designed in 1868 by Philip Webb for an artist that one must regard on the very periphery of the art world, now of course more than then. George Boyce, who specialised in the production of watercolours of English landscapes and vernacular architecture, and was one of Rossetti's hangers-on, thought long and hard before acquiring a lease on the site and employing Webb. He was that sort of meticulous fellow. In 1864 Webb had just completed, most successfully, a studio house in Holland Park for Val Princep. This was designed in a much-reduced vernacular Gothic style, almost abstract and with little external detail, with large studio windows placed within simple gables. This quest for a modern English architecture within the rational tradition of the vernacular Gothic was a logical development of the architecture of the famed Red House at Bexleyheath that Webb had designed in 1859 with, and for, William Morris. So Webb was a most reasonable choice for Boyce, not least because Webb was on easy terms with Boyce's hero and now near-neighbour Dante Gabriel Rossetti. Webb was commissioned and by March 1869 the design was completed, agreed and an estimate submitted and approved. A year later Boyce moved into his new home and studio. So all proceeded in a quietly practical, efficient and speedy manner, unlike Godwin's work in Tite Street. However, perhaps surprisingly given the no-nonsense construction, Webb's design was also quietly revolutionary. His simplified Gothic had evolved into simplified Queen Anne Revival. With its rudimentary vernacular classical details, red brick and white painted joinery, this is one of the earliest examples of the style that was to become hugely popular, particularly in the

87. Above
The West House, at 35 Glebe Place, designed in 1868 by Philip Webb in a pioneering Queen Anne Revival style. It was one of the first purpose-built and designed studio houses to be built in Chelsea. The wing, topped with diminutive gables, was added by Webb in 1876, giving the building a more fashionably asymmetrical appearance.

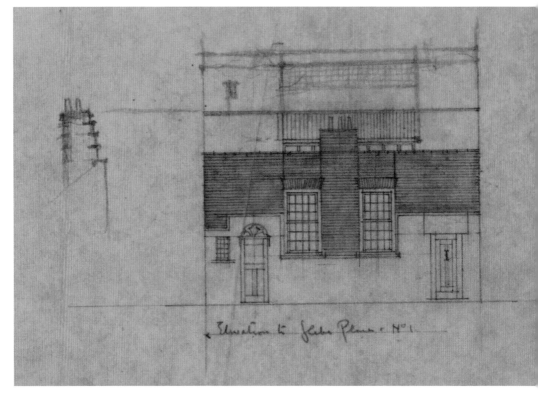

88. Above
Alternative elevations for 49 Glebe Place designed in 1920 by Charles Rennie Mackintosh as a studio house for artist Harold Squire. The design on the left was built but soon greatly altered by the addition of a brick-built and cornice-topped first floor. The house survives in its altered state.

Cadogan Estate's development of Pont Street and Cadogan Square. However, this was nearly a decade in the future (see page 205).

So while Oscar Wilde was still a fifteen-year-old schoolboy mooning around Dublin and Enniskillen, Webb was forging the architectural style that just over a decade later Wilde – the personification of the Aesthetic Movement and the House Beautiful obsession – would do much to make his own. It is strange when you realise that this complex tale of late nineteenth-century taste and morality begins, in many ways, with this building, secreted down a Chelsea back street. West House is solemn, with little of the whimsical or playful moulded detail of later Queen Anne Revival buildings. It is square in plan – almost cubical in volume – containing a sequence of square rooms, including (originally) an extremely lofty studio. The two-storey porch – advancing forward into Glebe Place

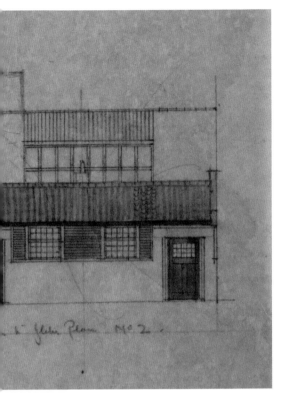

– is also cubical, or rather one cube set upon another with the composition made asymmetrical by the addition of a service door next to the front door. Above porch and main house perch pyramidal roofs, large and small.

After the West House was completed in 1870, it would be almost a decade before the next architecturally significant purpose-designed bespoke domestic studio would be built in Chelsea – and that would be Godwin's White House. However, before that Webb did much to reduce the severity of the original design and bring the West House more into line with Queen Anne Revival picturesque sensibilities by, in 1876, adding a wing topped by miniature tile-hung gables, incorporating a tall chimney stack and served by a door added alongside the main porch. The opportunity for this amendment was Boyce's marriage and his desire for an additional dressing room and a new dining room.

The remaining studio houses in Glebe Place are very much a mixed bag. Most curious is number 49, which is the only London building designed by the Glasgow-based Charles Rennie Mackintosh who lived and worked at number 43 Glebe Place from 1913 to 1923. Number 49 is a late work – designed in 1920 – externally very simple, and significantly altered in 1924 when a top floor was added. It has something of a modern feel, its ground-floor elevation rendered and, along with the brickwork above, painted white like some of the white-box architecture being designed in the early 1920s by Le Corbusier. And the design also, in an odd way, anticipates Art Deco, which emerged as a popular ornamental style after 1925 and generally incorporated abstracted classical details. The elevation of the studio include a cornice – not what Mackintosh intended – and a stringcourse. This is a traditional vernacular classical detail design, but here handled in a rather surrealist or abstract Art Deco manner because it passes in conventional manner above the doors which frame the façade and then – seemingly a later addition – continues between the central pair of ground-floor windows while also diving down to pass below them.

Inside the building is much more assured, with a large studio room forming the working and convivial heart of the building. The client was Harold Squire, a Chilean-born painter who had lived in London since 1891. He met Mackintosh through the idealistic Arts League of Service, of which both were members (along with Wyndham Lewis, T.S. Eliot and Duncan Grant), that had been founded after the First World War to place 'within the reach of everyone higher forms of entertainment, and opportunities for the enjoyment of any art or craft'. The League's motto was 'Bring the Arts into Everyday Life.'

So this little building, founded on a most sound and admirable set of principles, was – presumably – intended to be something of a demonstration project. Later residents include Augustus John in the mid-1930s and the painter Edward Le Bas in the 1940s. Numbers 66 to 70 (inclusive) is a uniform two-storey group named the Turner Studios. On it an unofficial blue plaque states that it was the studio of Joseph Turner – presumably J.M.W. Turner – from 1811 to 1829, which is a perplexing claim since the building, to judge by its pretty but modest Queen Anne Revival façade, was constructed fifty years or so after Turner is supposed to have ceased working on the site, and about thirty years after he died in Cheyne Row (see page 69).

Flood Street

Flood Street makes a fascinating contribution to the story of Chelsea's domestic studios. Located behind number 72 are the Rossetti Studios, which are an excellent example of a speculatively built, purpose-designed multi-studio complex. A date stone suggests that the studios were built in 1894 but, as Donald Insall Associates points out in their historic building report on the studios, the 1894–6 Ordnance Survey map does not depict the studios, and records the area as part of the 'Oakley Works' with the 'studios not listed in Kelly's Directory of Chelsea until 1896' ('Historic Building Report on Rossetti Studios, 72 Flood Street, Chelsea', 2016, p. 13). The studios were developed by Edward Holland – mentioned on the plaque – and it is assumed he designed them. The complex consists of three two-storey studios and four one-storey studios – separated by a corridor – all with large north-facing windows carefully oriented to allow soft, even light into the studios. The architectural style adopted is Queen Anne Revival, but embellishments are minimal and largely reserved for the external portion of the complex that most visitors would see. The formal entry to the complex is from Flood Street by way of an arch embellished with engaged Doric columns that is set within a handsome street block, also Queen Anne in character, named Rossetti House. The arch leads to a small court, where the main elevation of the studios – wrought of red brick with a rendered first floor – is embellished with moulded brick swags and a stunted corner tower supported on stone corbels. On the north side of the court is an impressive brick-made Baroque pedimented arched entrance that leads to the corridor serving the studios.

Upon contemplation it is clear that the complex is a subtle machine that offers a most revealing vignette of the workings of London's late nineteenth-century art world. The entrance is ornamented because it was assumed that artists using the studios would occasionally invite clients or patrons to visit them to see work in progress or to secure commissions. Consequently, it seemed only right and proper, for the sake of decorum at least, that the artists should appear in the guise of prosperous professionals, even gentlemen or gentlewomen working in a place of fashionable architecture rather than as mere tradespeople toiling in a utilitarian workshop. Needless to say, the portions of the complex not readily seen by visitors look very much like workshops. There is also a system of discreet routes within the building to segregate its users and visitors. Essentially, in opposition to the main entrance for polite visitors, there was a back entrance, with related passages, seemingly originally overseen by a caretaker or gate guardian, that would have been used by servants or – more particularly – by artists' models. Although vital to the creation of the great art of the time – indeed often artists' muses – models were not regarded a respectable, especially those who might pose naked, and so had to be kept away from clients of patrons to avoid causing offence.

The two types of studios are also revealing. The two-storey studios contain living accommodation on the ground floor with a high ceilinged, well-lit studio on first-floor level, furnished with a mezzanine gallery. This was a standard studio detail; evidently a desirable device providing a platform from which clients could view larger-scale works, presumably while being regaled with champagne. The studios also possess a very useful specialised detail, slit-like windows allowing large framed canvases to be transported into or out of the studio. The single-storey studios contain no living accommodation but they do have mezzanines, and each has a small room in which models could undress. Evidently Holland envisaged his complex of studios serving a fairly broad community of artists, which of course meant that he had a better chance of finding tenants. Some artists were evidently meant to make Rossetti Studios their homes while others, it was assumed, would use it only as a place of work. Donald Insall Associates' research through *Kelly's Directory* from 1899 to 1900 has revealed early artists in occupation, including, in studio number 2, Robert Brough, a most talented painter and political cartoonist who was himself painted by Sargent but was killed in a railway accident in 1905. Also in occupation in separate studios, in the early years of the twentieth century were Henry Jones Thaddeus, an Irish-born 'Realist' and portrait painter; George Washington Lambert (probably in 1902 or 1903), an Australian portrait painter, RA medallist and war artist known for his paintings of Gallipoli; and Arthur Stanley Young, a Chelsea-born sculptor, the son of Richard Henry Young, a bronze founder and iron moulder who lived north of the King's Road in Trafalgar (now Chelsea) Square. *The Morning Post* of 31 March 1900 (page 3), records that Thaddeus had his works on public display in his Flood Street studio, confirming the studios' role as an occasional gallery.

In 1904 the artists Augustus John and William Orpen established the Chelsea School of Art in studios 4 and 5. The school lasted only until 1908, with Orpen teaching life drawing (a model posed daily) and John acting as drawing master, teaching by demonstration. Although short-lived, students were notable. They included Gwen John (Augustus John's sister), Wyndham Lewis, Jacob Epstein and Henry Lamb, a founder of the Camden Town Group and the London Group (information thanks to Donald Insall Associates; and see Michael Holroyd, *Augustus John*, London: Pimlico, 2011, pp. 140–44).

The Chelsea Arts Club

Just before John and Orpen launched their admirable but short-lived Chelsea School of Art an event took place that – like the school – confirmed Chelsea's role as home to London's most numerous, closely knit and vociferous community of artists. The studios on and off Manresa Road were numerous and often interlinked around courts, stable yards and workshops. This intensified the sense of community and common cause, and seems to have made Manresa Road into something of a breeding ground for ideas. The sculptor Thomas Stirling Lee was one of the denizens of this hive of artists and in September 1890 proposed, along with painters Percy Jacomb-Hood and Jimmy Christie, that a Parisian-style independent 'exhibition society' should be organised to display and promote the works of local artists. The idea took off but rapidly evolved in a way that captures the unquenchably high spirits of the community that, beyond success, valued conviviality, shared endeavour and mutual support. A meeting was soon held, on 25 October 1890, at which Theodore Wores, a visitor from San Francisco and friend of Wilde and Whistler, suggested that what the artists of Chelsea needed more urgently than an exhibition society was a club. The suggestion gripped the imagination of those at the meeting. Whistler, who was present, supported it and he, along with Jacomb-Hood and Christie formed a committee, with Lee as chairman, to pursue the idea. Interestingly, there seems to have been little obviously Bohemian about the proposition that emerged, which was evidently inspired by West End professional and gentleman's clubs. Women were not to be permitted as members (indeed, they could not enjoy full membership of the club until 1976), and Jacomb-Hood, a wealthy friend of Frank Miles and who was to join the Prince and Princess of Wales on their 1905 tour of India, was rather a grand figure. However, it must be assumed that he played an important role in the foundation of the club because he was an artist rather than because of his connections – and because of his love of Chelsea. He went on to be a founding member of the Chelsea Society in 1927.

On 18 March 1891 the Chelsea club, 'for professional architects, engravers, painters and sculptors' was launched, with fifty-five members, at 181 King's Road – Christie's home – with the aim of advancing 'the cause of art by means of exhibitions, life classes and other kindred means and to promote social intercourse amongst its members'. It was agreed that the club should be named the Chelsea Arts Club to distinguish it from the existing Arts Club in Mayfair, of which Whistler was a most dissatisfied member. He, no doubt like many of the members of the new club, believed the Mayfair club did little for the artists of Chelsea. But no matter, now they had their own club that not only reflected but also did much to establish the Chelsea artists' sense of their own identity and worth. In 1902 the club, that had thrived from it launch, moved to a larger building, with a handsome garden at 143 Old Church Street where it remains, still thriving.

The club's members are still mainly from the arts, and now nearly 4,000 strong and ever rising. Although many of the members now live and work farther

afield than Chelsea, the club's continuing healthy existence does much to confirm that the late nineteenth-century dream of Chelsea as a vibrant and self-sustaining artists' community remains alive and well. Whistler and friends were not wrong in their ambition to give the artist community of Chelsea a living heart by founding a club in which members could enjoy all the convivial pleasures of unbridled 'social intercourse'.

Art in the Old Town Hall
On the King's Road between Flood Street and Glebe Place stands Chelsea Old Town Hall. Its frontage to the King's Road is a remarkable design, constructed between 1906 to 1908 in an English Baroque style that recalls Wren and Vanbrugh. It is vigorous, symmetrical and assertive – indeed rather imperialistic – and is a manifestation of the odd return to more orthodox classicism that became fashionable around 1900 and that put an end to the whimsical, gentle and inventive classicism of the Arts and Crafts-based Queen Anne and Flemish Renaissance revivals.

The architect for the King's Road portion of the Town Hall was Leonard Stokes, who specialised in the design of Roman Catholic churches, country houses and telephone exchanges, and who in 1919 was awarded the Royal Institute of British Architects' Gold Medal. The town hall is one of Stokes' more interesting works, not least because it has two pedimented centre features, neither of which are actually in the centre of composition but both pushed to its two outer ends. Rather odd, but this is in the Baroque spirit of the perverse and is in fact logical because each serves one of the town hall's major functions. One leads to what is now the library and registry office, and the other to the building's splendid, pilastered great hall, with its ceiling embellished with a series of saucer domes. The great hall is an imposing piece of civic architecture constructed in 1885–7 to the design of John Brydon and somewhat anticipating the coming Baroque Revival. It was built to the south of the 1860 Vestry Hall on the King's Road (see page 274) that was replaced by Stokes' building. The south elevation of Brydon's great hall – in fact the main elevation – is very fine, built of brick with stone dressings in the manner of Wren's Royal Hospital, with good Baroque detail and a pediment and Venetian window embellishing the hall's elevation. The rebuilding of the Town Hall was financed by the 5th Earl Cadogan.

As well as being a fine and early piece of Baroque revival architecture, Brydon's hall is also a monument to Chelsea's proud tradition as a place of art and craft. In May 1911 the Borough Council organised a competition for the execution of four large murals for the hall depicting 'Chelsea celebrities' through the centuries, grouped under the headings of Literature, History, Art and Science. The competition was managed by the Chelsea Arts Club, and open to all its members and to other 'artists domiciled in Chelsea'. A £200 prize was offered for each of the chosen designs, with Lord Cadogan undertaking to donate the prize money for one of the murals while the remainder were to be paid for by other local worthies. Much was made of the fact that local ratepayers would not be paying the bill. The result of the competition was announced in December 1911, with the successful artists getting to work, it must be assumed, in early 1912 (see 'scrap book' in Local Studies Library, Kensington and Chelsea Library, catalogued under 'Chelsea Miscellany', 1504-1567 12(1)). The murals are not now much noticed but they do – in their way – express the heart, soul and pride of Chelsea when it basked in its history and high place in the culture of the country just before the First World War cast its deadly shadow over the nation. The mural entitled 'Literature' was painted by George R. Woolway, a now rather obscure artist who specialised in landscapes and architectural views. The mural shows an interesting group with Thomas Carlyle in the centre

and Leigh Hunt, Mary Ann Evans and Oscar Wilde placed together to one side, all in their different ways 'radicals' – Evans if only because she published under the pen name 'George Eliot'. The history of Wilde's portrait is salutary.

Wilde's inclusion among the 'celebrities' to be depicted was quite a bold gesture in 1911 because it was little more than fifteen years since he had been imprisoned for 'gross indecency' following his arrest in the Cadogan Hotel. Clearly some local politicians had resented the decision and in May 1914 a Councillor G.J. Wright submitted a motion to the Borough Council requiring Woolway to substitute the portrait of another Chelsea 'celebrity' in place of Wilde or, if the artist was unwilling or unable to do so, Wright argued that the 'panel' should be removed. Quite a tough request since the panel was in fact a mural. A Councillor Strutt went one better in his display of philistine contempt for his own council's artistic patronage, for those who had donated the prize money and for the competition winner. He said that he did not care about Wilde's inclusion but tabled a motion that the mural should be removed on artistic grounds because it was 'a disgrace to the town hall'. Most depressingly, Strutt's motion was carried by a large majority (The Times, 14 May 1914 and Chelsea Miscellany, 1504-1567 12 (1)). However, the mural was saved by history. Soon after the vandalistic and shameful decision was taken, Chelsea's councillors – along with the rest of Europe – had other things to fret about. By the time the First World War ended the decision was forgotten and the mural – and Wilde – were left in peace (see Chelsea Society Report, 1966, p. 33). Such vitriol was not, in 1914, poured by craven councillors upon the other murals. Of course they were not – in their subject matter – so provocative for small-minded local politicians.

'History', painted by Charles Sims, is dominated by Tudor and Stuart characters

– always popular subjects. Queen Elizabeth smiles to herself in the centre of the painting in the guise of the Virgin Queen. To one side lurk Charles II and Nell Gwyn, appearing to want nothing to do with the preying queen. Sims is a most interesting artist. His strengths were sunlit landscapes and portraits, he was a Royal Academician and in his day most successful. However the First World War, and the death of his soldier son in 1914, changed everything. His work became darker and more idiosyncratic, which was a problem for his large mural in the 'Building of Britain' series commissioned for St Stephen's Hall in the Palace of Westminster. When it was unveiled in 1927, few could understand it. The following year Sims painted the disturbing *I am the Abyss and I am Light*, and then he took his own life by drowning.

'Art' focuses on a throned personification of the 'muse of art' sitting below a canopy, around which are clustered Wren, Rossetti, Whistler, Turner and many others. The faces are not very convincing. The artist was Frank O. Salisbury, who became a stalwart traditionalist and in the 1920s an outspoken critic of contemporary 'Modern' artists such as Picasso. He rose among the ranks of 'society' artists, becoming successful on both sides of the Atlantic. He painted Winston Churchill (more than once) and Franklin Roosevelt.

The final mural depicts 'Science', and in some ways it is the most interesting and original, certainly as a composition, and with faces rendered in a slightly rough but most characterful manner. In the centre sits Sir Hans Sloane, in the posture of a man squatting on a kerbstone, looking towards a winged 'Figure of Wisdom' prancing within a Renaissance loggia. Near Wisdom are Sir Thomas More, Erasmus (who probably never came to Chelsea to see More) and Sir Isaac Newton. Other figures include Elizabeth Fry, Dr Johnson, Sir Robert Walpole (who had a riverside house near the Royal Hospital) and the

potter Nicholas Sprimont. The artist was Mary Sargent Florence, a specialist in murals and frescoes, who had studied at the Slade and became an ardent suffragist and was active in the Women's Tax Resistance League.

These murals placed in the four corners of the hall are an impressive monument, realised through art, to the aspirations – and achievements – of generations of people who have lived and worked in Chelsea. The place had and continues to have a pride in itself. However, there is one other thing to see on the wall of the hall. In 1915 a panel was put in place 'To the Honoured Memory of George Henry Fifth Earl Cadogan.' When Chelsea was established as a borough in 1900, the Earl – by tradition the Lord of the Manor of Chelsea – had been elected the borough's first mayor. In his capacity as a major landowner in the new borough he 'gave the sites of its Town Hall, its Library, its Polytechnic' as well as 'many other generous benefactions'.

So this splendid building was the gift of the 5th Earl who, as the panel puts it, 'seeing in rank an obligation, in possessions a trust and in duties a privilege he sought steadfastly the good of Chelsea'. This is the creed of the Edwardian Gentleman. Possessions carried with them a duty to serve, and art and architecture were part of the way in which a better world – more beautiful, healthier, more ennobling – could be created.

89. Above
The mural depicting 'Chelsea celebrities'
involved with 'Literature', painted in the
hall of the old Chelsea Town Hall in 1912
by George R. Woolway. The figures include
Thomas Carlyle (centre) Leigh Hunt, George
Eliot and – seated on the left – Oscar Wilde,
who in 1914 a majority of councillors voted to
expunge. The intervention of the First World
War saved Wilde, who continues to stare upon
his fellow literary celebrities in a wonderfully
supercilious manner.

PONT STREET DUTCH

90. Above
18 and 19 Hans Place, left, 26 to 30 Pont
Street, centre, designed by Charles William
Stephens. To the far right are 18 to 24 Pont
Street. All were built in the mid- to late
1880s as speculations, with good if relatively
restrained Flemish Renaissance detail.

To walk down Pont Street and around Cadogan Square and Hans Place remains one of the oddest architectural experiences in London. The houses – built mostly from the late 1870s into the 1890s – are tall, many are topped by curvaceous Baroque gables, with exteriors ornamentally crafted in a seventeenth-century Renaissance style with a preference for asymmetry that – superficially at least – appears to owe little to London's building practice. Also, in a further break with the tradition of London's domestic architecture, most of the elevations are assertively individual in their detail, although unified generally by a broadly shared aesthetic and by a preference for red brick that only a few years earlier had been regarded as hopelessly rustic and woefully out of place on the urbane streets of London. This aesthetic represented – no more and no less – an architectural revolution, with the comfortable streets of the Cadogan Estate in the vanguard. This was an architectural revolution that was not only to do with taste but also with the way people lived in cities in the late nineteenth century – or at least in smart and affluent areas of city, such as this quarter north of Sloane Square – and with the evolving nature of the way buildings were made and in the role and responsibilities of the architect. Was he primarily a tradesman, a technocrat or an artist with poetic vision? Most important,

was an architect to be regarded as a disinterested professional, whose business above all was the welfare of his client and the promotion of the art and science of architecture rather than the pursuit of personal profit?

To appreciate the dramatic nature of this revolution, it is necessary to put it in context. Since the early seventeenth century in London the dominant urban and architectural ideal had been to create an orthogonal and integrated grid of streets lined with terrace houses of different scales, and incorporating squares as the focus for main architectural effort. Elevations were increasingly designed in a restrained classical manner, tending towards uniformity, with individual flourishes – of the sort seen on house in Cheyne Walk (see pages 94-5) – replaced by a subdued form of classical design that became known as Palladian. This was an architecture that venerated exterior simplicity, and that relied for visual power not on ornament but on the applications of a system of harmonically related proportions and on rigid symmetry. It was an architecture that recognised the sublime potential of repetition on a large scale and that, when possible, organised numerous separate buildings to form a unified palatial composition, usually with a central pediment and end pavilions.

The preference had also evolved for cool colours: in London Portland stone, and from the mid-eighteenth century grey, yellow and even white bricks. The ideal was launched in London by Inigo Jones in the early 1630s when he designed the Piazza in Covent Garden for the Earl of Bedford, and was pursued throughout London during the following 200 years or so, notably in Bloomsbury and on diverse estates in Canonbury and Barnsbury and, outside the metropolis, in Bath and Edinburgh New town. Indeed, one of the epitomes of this approach was Henry Holland's Hans Town of the 1770s and 1780s (see page 111), and it was the simple but sophisticated terraces erected under Holland's control, of refined Palladian designs and wrought of very pale yellow and white brick – now best seen in Cadogan Place – that were being replaced by what Mark Girouard has described as a domestic architecture of a north European seventeenth-century character that was reminiscent of 'a hyper-concentrated canal-side in Antwerp' (Mark Girouard, 'Cadogan Estate, Chelsea', *Country Life*, 23 November 1978, p. 1724, quoted in Alan Powers, *Cadogan & Chelsea: The Making of a Modern Estate*, ed. Anjali Bulley, London: Unicorn, 2017, p. 142. See also Girouard on the Cadogan Estate in *Country Life*, 11 November 1978, pp. 1602–1605).

The dramatic transformation of Hans Town commenced during the mid-1870s, just as the initial ninety-nine-year leases started to terminate on the houses built under Holland's control. For a bold landlord much was possible and the 5th Earl Cadogan was bold indeed. He had inherited the estate in 1873, was aged thirty-three and at the height of his powers. He was politically active in the House of Lords, deeply interested in the improvement of his land in Chelsea and was an advocate of aspects of housing reform. So the Earl wanted not only to build large, comfortable, fashionable and potentially profitable new homes for the middle and upper classes but he also wanted to pursue a policy of

'slum clearance' and to provide hygienic 'dwellings' for the 'industrial' classes in conjunction with trusts dedicated to the construction of artisan and working class housing (see page 281). He seems to have been happy to accept a financial loss in the creation of a mixed community on his Chelsea estate.

In 1875 the Earl was involved in the establishment of a limited liability company – Cadogan and Hans Place Estate Improvements Ltd – which was intended to offer some protection from builders going bankrupt, as had often dogged the eighteenth- and early nineteenth-century speculative housing development. The earl's financial involvement was limited but, as a measure of his interest in the artistic aspects and aspirations of the estate, he retained the right to approve and reject designs. This was also, presumably, a reflection of his astute appreciation that good and up-to-the-minute design could add value to the estate.

When the company was in place things started to move fast. The opportunity to improve the estate came not only from rebuilding swathes of late eighteenth-century houses in Sloane Street and Hans Place – houses that were then generally regarded as not only old-fashioned architecturally but also too cramped, too repetitive in their constrained plans and too hemmed in by the area's later growth. There was also the chance to open up new land for development. Henry Holland's detached villa – the Pavilion, sub-divided by the 1870s – and its generous grounds to the south of Hans Place were easy targets for redevelopment. However, there were also the market gardens and paddock to the west, bordering on the land of Smith's Charity Estate. All this represented a magnificent opportunity to greatly expand building on the estate and to increase its value almost beyond measure, if the planning and architecture were right. The planning was brilliant in its bold simplicity. Existing urban arrangements made by Holland – notably Hans Place and Cadogan Place – were not to be disturbed, just enhanced by new, larger buildings where appropriate. This generally was to happen in Hans Place and generally not to happen in Cadogan Place. Pont Street, laid out in the 1770s as a short street east of Cadogan Place, was to be extended far to the west as the estate's new east–west thoroughfare, communicating with Walton Street and the smart new streets to the west around Brompton Road. The new street – broad and straight – was also, of course, to provide a large number of building plots. It had the potential to be a most generous avenue, with a fine prospect. South of the extended Pont Street was to be the new main urban feature of Hans Town, created partly on the site of Holland's Pavilion and its grounds. This was Cadogan Square, and its creation in the late 1870s marked an historic moment in the architectural history of London. As Alan Powers has observed, 'this was the last [square] to be built at the top of [London's] domestic property market' because 'after 1900, the very rich who wanted to build looked beyond London to Surrey or the Thames Valley' (*Cadogan & Chelsea: The Making of a Modern Estate*, p. 139).

So Hans Town acquired two new splendid locations for high-class residential buildings: the broad western extension of Pont Street and Cadogan Square. The latter was substantially larger than Sloane Square, under 2:1 in proportion and with a generous private garden for the occupants of the square.

The convenient function of the enlarged Hans Town was evidently most carefully considered with a good deal of thought going into the manner in which the new houses and their occupants could be best serviced. Stabling was of prime importance because most residents would keep their own horses and carriages, so the narrow 'New Road' shown on Horwood's map of 1799–1819 became of vital importance. It had been created by Holland to serve stabling behind the houses on the west side of Sloane Street and to connect with the gardens of houses on the east side of Hans Place. As the main service road of the expanded Hans Town, it was to contain not only additional stabling but also a variety of mundane uses, and low rent accommodation, essential to the smooth running of the big houses. However, the stabling provided by Pavilion Road – as the 'New Road' was renamed – was inadequate. It is a curiosity of Cadogan Square and the houses on Pont Street that, grand as they are, they have virtually no private gardens of any significance. Holland had provided his large houses with generous rear gardens, but in the extended Hans Town, density was increased, the demand for the provision of the maximum number of large house plots became paramount, and conveniently located stabling was evidently seen as essential. So the large houses have mews to their rears where gardens could have been; a good example is the long Clabon Mews, set behind the west side of Cadogan Square but with two outriders entering the square itself, and Shafto Mews between the north side of the square and Pont Street. The compromise, most obviously apparent at Cadogan Square, was to provide curious small communal gardens behind some of the houses and, of course, to compensate occupiers by making available the large communal garden, essentially a small private park, in the centre of the square.

The very distinct architecture of the new parts of Hans Town – so radically at variance with the established built character of the area – captures the mood of the moment. The Gothic Revival, growing in strength from the 1830s, had not made a profound difference to the design of London's domestic architecture. It was the style of churches, some public

91. Above
A charming moulded brick detail on the
porch of 30 Pont Street, built in the
mid-1880s to the design of Stephens.

and institutional buildings, some railway stations and hotels from the 1840s or occasionally for country houses, but London's residential street architecture remained firmly classical. The re-fronting of the houses of c. 1805 at the south end of Cadogan Place makes the point. They were overhauled in the 1850s in a thoroughly classical manner with architraves added to their windows and uniform Doric porches to their doors. However, in the 1870s tastes started to change. The Arts and Crafts phase of the Gothic Revival came to maturity, and with it came not just an appreciation of individual and hand-crafted design in opposition to the mechanical mass-produced classical details evident in such elevations as those grafted on to Cadogan Place, but also of vernacular design, and solid and traditional building materials and construction techniques. History remained a key inspiration, but the historic buildings that were particularly regarded as exemplary were those with open and flexible floor plans that possessed large internal volumes and in which windows were designed to let light flood inside. So fifteenth- and sixteenth-century English architecture, with its double-height and open great hall lit by large oriels or mullioned and transomed bay windows were much admired, as were Dutch seventeenth-century urban terrace houses with their often huge windows and narrow areas of wall. Such buildings were, of course, seen as historic but also modern, or rather timeless in their essential qualities of open space and generous light. From this emerged – in the early 1870s – a confusingly termed style known as the 'Queen Anne Revival'.

As all architectural history books will tell you, the Queen Anne Revival has little to do with architecture produced in England during the first decade or so of the eighteenth century. It is a composite style – a distinct fusion of historic prototypes, not a revival – that is a mix of north European vernacular Renaissance architecture of the late sixteenth to the early eighteenth centuries, particularly seventeenth-century Flemish and Dutch. From genuine Queen Anne – itself a product of Dutch influence – comes a regard for large sash windows, vigorous, inventive and characterful hand-made classical detail, and a palette of mellow red brick, off-white painted joinery perhaps combined with white Portland stone. There is also, in the architecture of the Revival, a joy in strange juxtapositions in dramatic contrast in scale and in materials, and a sense of playfulness and often undisguised theatricality.

The Queen Anne Revival was first used on a large scale and consistent manner in a residential area in Bedford Park, Chiswick, that got underway in 1875. The planning is picturesque and the architecture – although tame and low-rise in comparison with what was about to happen in Hans Town – represents a start. More important, from 1877 the estate architect was Richard Norman Shaw, who was to play a most influential role in Hans Town's architectural destiny.

Who precisely made the decision to go for what Girouard called the 'hyper-concentrated canal-side' permutation of the wide-ranging Queen Anne Revival style is hard to say. Presumably the Estate believed that the fashionable look would give the area visual distinction and attract wealthy tenants who wished to take leases on sites and commission architects of their own choice, as well as attracting speculating builders. In time-honoured tradition, much of the estate was to be developed by speculators building houses they hoped to sell-on for a profit, as lease holds, or to let to tenants willing to pay handsome rents. The look and the architecture on offer was not just to do with style but also about changing ways of life and about the communal activity of living in cities.

Of course the two – look and life – were profoundly connected and to understand

how, it is important to reflect on the nature of the change that was taking place. Architecture was a great public art, even if realised through private funds, and in seventeenth- and eighteenth-century London the creation of communal architectural harmony was more highly valued than individual display. In addition, since London was a city built overwhelmingly on leasehold, with houses generally run-up by speculating builders, occupants – even if they so desired – had little opportunity to personalise the exterior of their homes. Holland's Hans Town was the epitome of all these time-honoured principles – and now all was being overturned.

As in the great seventeenth-century north European merchant cities that provided the key artistic model – Antwerp, Amsterdam or Rotterdam – individuality of exterior architecture became desirable on the Cadogan Estate, indeed de rigueur when the lessee employed an architect to design his home. This itself was a novelty because in the past in London even grand tenants tended to occupy ready-built speculations, or speculations built to standard patterns. Very few clients, usually only wealthy members of the aristocracy, had their homes purpose-designed and built.

In 1868 the English poet and essayist Matthew Arnold had adopted the phrase 'sweetness and light' in his book Culture and Anarchy (published 1869) to represent beauty and intelligence. He argued that the desire for one and the application of the other has through time formed the bedrock of culture. As he put it, culture 'seeks to do away with classes; to make the best that has been thought and known in the world current everywhere; to make all men live in an atmosphere of sweetness and light'.

The enthusiasm for beauty – either to behold it or to create it – became part of the Aesthetic Movement of the 1870s and the notion of 'Art for Art's sake' was promoted by the epicurean Walter Pater and in the early 1880s personified by Oscar Wilde. The movement held that beauty was more important than practical or moral concerns – a seemingly amoral attitude that predictably worried Evangelical Christians, who can hardly have been reassured when, in his 1891 essay *The Critic as Artist*, Wilde stated that 'Aesthetics are higher than ethics,' and that a 'colour sense is more important ... than a sense of right and wrong'. So, as one might expect, what was sweet for some was bitter for others.

The 'light' of intelligence was another aspect of the same ideal. It was the expression of the enlightened intellect, of the enquiring, caring and compassionate mind that would 'dissolve ugliness ... smooth away intolerance and bigotry' (Mark Girouard, *Sweetness and Light: The 'Queen Anne' Movement*, 1860–1900, Oxford: Oxford University Press, 1977). The hallmarks were charity, a concern for the welfare of the poor, the promotion of health and education, of free libraries and of temperance.

Together, the vision of 'sweetness and light' gave an intellectual direction to the Queen Anne Revival. Compromised and absurdly hypocritical as it may seem – naturally only the rich could indulge their taste of Queen Anne architecture – this was nevertheless an artistic movement that, at one level, embodied a philosophy and a morality. Girouard argues that the phrase had the meaning that taste and beauty and happiness need not be confined to the wealthy but when 'light' was applied 'sweetness' could be available to all – and benefit all – society. The 5th Earl Cadogan presumably had this notion in mind when he sacrificed a portion of his profits to provide decent working class homes on his Chelsea land.

Since the 5th Earl Cadogan had the power to approve or reject designs submitted by architects, their clients or by speculating architects and builders for plots in Hans Town, he must have had a significant role in promoting the Queen Anne/Flemish Renaissance Revival styles. However, Alan Powers suggests convincingly that the 'switch to the new style was owed to Colonel W.T. Makins (1840–1906). The Chairman of the new Cadogan and Hans Place Estate Improvement company, an M.P. and contemporary in age to Lord Cadogan' (*Cadogan & Chelsea: The Making of a Modern Estate*, p. 143). In 1873 Makins' brother had commissioned architect J.J. Stevenson to design Queen Anne Revival houses in Palace Gate and in 1877 to design a house in Princes Gate for Makin himself. Stevenson was one of the main practitioners of the Queen Anne style and, as we will see, worked extensively on the Cadogan Estate, eventually designing most of the south side of Cadogan Square between 1879 and 1886.

A brief tour through Hans Town, as remade from the late 1870s, reveals the practical expression of this maelstrom of ideas. However, first it is worth collecting a few earlier reactions to this remarkable architectural ensemble. As you have read, in the 1970s Girouard, the authority on the Queen Anne Revival as he is on most aspects of British nineteenth-century architecture, compared the gabled architecture of Pont Street and Cadogan Square to the canal-side architecture in Antwerp. This analogy with the Low Countries was honed by the jovial architectural pundit and cartoonist Osbert Lancaster, who delighted in coining pithy phrases to sum up different types of architecture, for example 'Stockbrokers Tudor' to describe the fashion for mock Tudor and stick-on timber framing that enjoyed a vogue in the interwar Home Counties. Similarly, in 1938, in his satirical architectural guide, *Pillar to Post*, Lancaster defined the dominant architecture of

Hans Town as 'Pont Street Dutch', and with an ironical twinkle, gushed that, as the 'cultured frequently pointed out ... a wayfarer in that high-class residential district might easily imagine himself to be in Vermeer's Delft' (Osbert Lancaster, *Pillar to Post, or the Pocket-Lamp of Architecture*, London: John Murray, 1938, p. 54). This theme was continued by Bridget Cherry, in the 1991 edition of Nikolaus Pevsner's *The Buildings of England*, where she observed of Cadogan Square that the 'generous fronts and expressive gables provide a vision of prosperous burghers of Bruges or Amsterdam' (*The Buildings of England, London 3 North West*, p. 579).

So Antwerp, Delft, Bruges, Amsterdam ... all very different cities, and all defined by water, mostly by extensive canal systems. There are no canals in Hans Town and anyone who knows these cities also knows that despite superficial similarities – notably the sense of architectural individualism and the use of gables – the architecture of Hans Town is distinctly different. It is a direct copy of nothing specific but a fusion of much, and at its best a very creative and original fusion. This is not to be pedantic but to make the point that the architecture of Hans Town can be confusing and can make one search for generic models in an attempt to categorise and comprehend what is going on. Cherry says it offers a 'vision' of Bruges and Amsterdam, not that it is a copy but an evocation, and that – a subjective view – is fair enough. When you walk through Hans Town you are indeed walking through a vision, through a dream-like atmosphere of sweetness and light made manifest, given tangible form, by extraordinary architecture.

Pont Street

We start our tour on Pont Street, west of Sloane Street. The street is wide, the houses tall – many with a variety of curvaceous gables – elevations are generally diverse and there is some asymmetry.

However, it is clear that most of the houses were built as speculations, so there is some of the economy and repetition that are part of the business-side of large-scale building operations. There is also the hint of the penny-pinching that comes from speculative building, which is an especially risky business, of course, when the speculation involves the construction of large houses that – by their nature – demand a relatively large amount of ornate decoration. The building material is – overwhelmingly – red brick. *The Buildings of England* observes that the street is 'enjoyable in the aggregate' but since the houses are nearly all speculatively built groups, they tend to be 'individually of less interest' (*The Buildings of England, London 3 North West*, p. 580). Completely correct. And does the street look like 'Vermeer's Delft'? Hardly.

Numbers 26 to 30 and numbers 32 to 40 on the north side are fairly representative. They are two speculatively built groups dating from the mid- to late 1880s designed by Charles William Stephens, a former London Board School architect who went on to become the architect to Harrods from 1892 and to design its Baroque-style Brompton Road façade completed in 1905 (*The Buildings of England, London 3 North West*, p. 580). The houses are individual in superficial details and plans but generally permutations of the same theme. Numbers 26 to 30 all have canted bays rising to second-floor levels, and crowning gables above their third floors; numbers 34 to 40 have ornamental brick panels above their first-floor window containing tracery that is a strange mix of Gothic and peculiar Renaissance strapwork that is almost Art Nouveau.

These two groups of C.W. Stephens designed houses frame two other blocks, divided by a short road leading into Hans Place. These houses are in fact entered from and numbered with Hans Place although they present significant

92. Above
Numbers 34, on the right, 36 and 38 Pont
Street, dating from the mid- to late 1880s
and designed by Stephens. These houses sport
ornamental brick panels above their first-floor
windows that are a most individual mix of
Gothic tracery and Renaissance strapwork.

93. *Above*
On the left, part of 65 Pont Street, designed
by E.H. Boucher, and number 67, that faces
largely on to Lennox Gardens. Designed in
1884 by Stephens, the elevation of number 67
is an intriguing and lively display of vernacular
materials and building techniques, including
tiles that look like timber shingles and timber-
framed and pargetted gables.

elevations to Pont Street. They are numbered 17 to 27 (inclusive) Hans Place, number 17 bears the date 1888, others are perhaps slightly earlier and Stephens was probably involved in their design. Each of these Hans Place groups is asymmetrical in design yet virtual mirror images of each other, with each framing the entry to Hans Place with a slender tower and each terminating at east and west ends with two-storey crowing gables embellished with large curvaceous Baroque scrolls picked out in a red brick of darker hue.

Within all these groups windows are generally wide, joinery is painted white (this is part of the aesthetic – any other colour would be unthinkable) and they include casements incorporating arched mullions made of timber set above central windows. This was one of the favoured *leitmotifs* of the Queen Anne Revival and seems to have been devised – or at least promoted – by Norman Shaw in the early 1870s, inspired by vernacular precedent, notably the mid-seventeenth-century oriels on Sparrowe's House in Ipswich. This arch-mullioned oriel became a favoured Shaw detail and in various forms entered the vocabulary of the movement, with many examples present in the terraces of Hans Town.

The ornament of number 30 is generally wrought of fine quality rubbed red brick, with the usual motifs of swags, bunches of flowers, large rosettes and cherubs' heads. Good as these are, they were mass-produced and more or less bought of-the-peg, perhaps sized to a specific location but not specifically designed for the house they adorn. They are most rewarding all the same. The brick-built porch of number 30 is particularly delightful with its piers topped by moulded brick capitals of broadly Ionic form, but with the volutes formed by luscious leaves from which peer mask-like faces, seemingly evocations of the Green Man (see page 208).

On the south side of Pont Street, numbers 31 to 39 form a speculative group, started in 1876, so one of the first in this part of the street, designed by G.T. Robinson. It is defined by essential uniformity relived by a sprinkling of varied details. Not very exciting but – by contrast – the slightly later (1886) numbers 49 to 53 by E.T. Hall are a splendid example. Once again, each house is pretty much the same but with mirrored plans that offer the opportunity for monumental shared entrance porches, which the architect exploits to the full. One porch (to 49 and 51) has a dentilled cornice supported by huge bare-breasted winged sphinxes of a most muscular kind, while another (to 53) has a cornice supported by winged lions. Each house has a two-storey bay, packed with mullioned windows, a scattering of diminutive but most mannered pediments and terrific crowning gables formed by generous scrolls supporting small semi-circular pediments. To the west, numbers 55 to 65 of the 1880s by E.H. Bouchier are relatively tame, and by their basic uniformity reveal themselves to be a speculatively built group. Details and composition of the façades vary slightly but all are united by a continuous first-floor balustraded balcony sporting ball finials.

Number 67 of 1884, facing largely on to Lennox Gardens and also by C.W. Stephens, reveals another strand of the Arts and Crafts Queen Anne Revival. Red brick is reduced in its visual dominance – and a variety of vernacular materials and building techniques are on display. Arts and Crafts architects loved to use building materials made on, or from, the site on which they built their houses, or at least to utilise local and time-honoured building practices. These options were not really available, in a useful way, to Stephens on Pont Street in the 1880s, so he made do with a little invention and fantasy. The ground floor is red brick, the first and second floors are clad with tiles designed to look like timber shingles, and the array of crowning gables

94. Right
A visionary elevation from Richard Norman Shaw's office of the Shaw-designed number 68 (right) and 72 Cadogan Square, of 1877–8. They are a superlative expression of the Flemish Renaissance-influenced Queen Anne Revival. Number 70, designed by A.J. Adam and in reality set between the pair of Shaw houses, has been omitted in this perspective.

contain what looks like timber framing topped by raking entablatures decorated with an idiosyncratic permutation of late seventeenth-century floral motifs. Note the towering chimney stacks typical of this overtly vernacular version of the Revival.

Cadogan Square

To the south of Pont Street is Cadogan Square, the great showpiece of the revamped and extended Hans Town of the 1870s and 1880s. First the east side, which is by far the least interesting. It was constructed in 1879 by G.T. Robinson as a speculation. The houses are tall, of dark red brick and wonderfully gloomy. They are broadly uniform but enlivened by the addition of a scattering of classical details and a few gables, that on number 51 being the best by far – a composite affair, with a scroll, swan-necked pediment interrupted by a smaller triangular pediment thrusting up though its centre.

The south side gets better, mostly with individual-looking houses designed by J.J. Stevenson, with numbers 63–73 from 1885 and numbers 75–79 from 1879. There are two- and three-storey bays, some modest gables and restrained classical details. Number 73 has a very large fanlight above its door in the Dutch Rococo style of the 1760s that was most popular in Delft.

So Osbert Lancaster is – to a degree at least – vindicated. However, much of the variety here is little more than skin deep because plans are generally similar as most of these houses were built as speculations.

Now for the west side of the square that was the favoured side and is – in its way – the great showcase in London of the affluent – indeed luxurious – manifestation of the Queen Anne and Flemish Renaissance Revival. When in 1952 Pevsner wrote of Cadogan Square that there 'are few other places in London [where] the prosperous 80s [can] be studied more profitably', it was this run of houses that he had in mind (Nikolaus Pevsner, *The Buildings of England, London 2*, Harmondsworth: Penguin, 1969, p. 100).

At the south end, on the corner with Cadogan Gardens, is 'Stuart House' – number 84 – a big block of a building of c. 1880, quite dull with its exterior high-points being terracotta reliefs showing scenes from the lives of Mary Queen of Scots and James I, commemorating a distant connection through marriage between the Cadogans and the Royal House of Stuart. This house was purpose-designed for O.L. Stephen, the Director of the Great Northern Railway. The architects were F.G. Knight with Hunt and Steward. The adjacent houses, across from Clabon

Hovses·in·Cadogan·Sqᴱ·Chelsea·
R·Norman·Shaw·RA·ARCHITECT·

Mews – numbers 76-82 – were also probably designed by Knight, but this time as a speculation. Then, moving north of Clabon Mews, we get into the square proper and for these prime sites things start to become more interesting.

Number 70 (now somewhat confusingly numbered 72 and 70 because it is linked to 72, which has lost its front door) was designed by A.J. Adam, who also designed number 74. Number 70 is large, restrained and a text-book example of the low-key side of the Revival. The elevation possesses a sense of symmetry, except for the two-storey canted bay that rises to one side and is furnished with a first-floor balcony supported by large, white-painted, serpentine-profile brackets. These are a favoured motif in and around Cadogan Square. The windows of the second and third floors are framed by brick-wrought Ionic pilasters, which frame a shallow arch, within which is a display of luscious fruit and flowers suspended from lions masks, all rendered in red moulded and rubbed brick. And above all is a wide gable with an ogee profile and crowning pediment. It really is a most competent piece of work, and is revealed to be no more than that by the neighbours on each side of it, numbers 68 and 72. Both are by Richard Norman Shaw, one of the prime authors of the Queen Anne Revival and an architect of genius, and his two houses are having a conversation with each other as if number 70 did not exist. In fact, that seems to have been Shaw's intention because he produced a perspective of his two houses – nesting together to form a fascinating single, asymmetric composition – with the inconvenient and interloping number 70 entirely removed.

Shaw's houses were designed between 1877 and 1878, number 72 first, while number 68 bears the date 1878, in moulded red brick, set below a pomegranate tree and a scallop shell, both also made of moulded brick. Shaw had been active in Chelsea

before working on these two houses – notably on the newly created Chelsea Embankment (see page 76) where in 1875 he designed number 17 – Swan House – which is a power-house of Shaw's favoured motifs and essentially a declaration of his architectural intent that drove the eclectic strand of the Queen Anne Revival. There are three oriels, each with arched-mullions of Sparrowe's House-type with – lighting the floor above – long and narrow oriels, that became standard, alternating with large 'Queen Anne' sashes. And, most dramatic perhaps, floors project one above the other, in the manner of medieval jettied buildings, to give the elevation a most dynamic quality. The look of all is red and white – red brick walling with white painted joinery and pargetted plaster around the oriels. In fact, Chelsea Embankment in the 1870s was something of a repository of avant-garde architecture, much of it proto-Queen Anne, such as G.F. Bodley's The River House of 1876 at number 3, numbers 9-11 of 1879 by Norman Shaw and E.W. Godwin's White House for James Whistler of 1878 near the junction of the Embankment with Tite Street (see page 186). Some of these ideas found expression in Hans Town when building got underway in the mid-1870s.

In Cadogan Square, number 68 is the most striking of Shaw's pair of houses. It is six storeys high, four windows wide, with very large second-floor sash windows – like seventeenth-century Amsterdam houses – with all joinery painted white for maximum contrast with the dark, smouldering red of the brickwork. The first floor is treated like a mezzanine, with almost continuous glazing – incorporating a ubiquitous central arch – topped by a deep, coved cornice. Below the mezzanine, and centrally placed, is a brick-built pedimented entrance porch. On the north side of the elevation rises a four-storey bay – rather like an attached tower – which is richly ornamented. Above it all sits a wide, inhabited gable containing the windows that light the top storey of the house. Number 72 is broadly similar in design, although its gable also dated 1878 contains a projecting, white-painted oriel window and a horizontal sliver of a window above. According to design drawings, this house had a porch similar to that on 68, but it is entirely missing and the door has been made into a window.

A few doors to the north is number 62 – on the corner with Milner Street – also by Shaw. It is of the slightly later date of 1881–3 and its elevation to the square is simpler in design, but generally there is a strong family resemblance, and this time the asymmetrically placed tower-like bay is used to turn the corner. A nice touch. Superficially, the most noticeable difference is that – for this house and for no obvious or rational reason – Shaw decided to go for seventeenth-century-style casement windows rather than sashes, but still painted white.

The secondary elevation to Milner Street is fascinating because here Shaw goes more decidedly free-form. A quest for formalism drives the design of the elevation to the square, but the driving force for the side is function. There is a formal central portion, with windows grouped below a gable, but to the east of this windows appear to be placed where interior arrangements dictate. The result is an asymmetry driven by function rather than by artful contrivance. This is both in the true Gothic spirit of the past, but also anticipates the functionalism of twentieth-century Modernism. And it is because Shaw was a bridge between worlds – between the architectural past and the architectural future – that his work is so interesting. Like so many of the more talented architects of his generation, he was trying to forge a modern architecture appropriate to Britain from an eclectic and inspired interpretation of its architectural history.

On the facing corner of Milner Street is a less inspiring composition. Numbers 54 to 58 Cadogan Square were designed in 1877 by William Young in a solid and stately Queen Anne style with tall brick-made Ionic pilasters and dainty gables. Their interest lies in the fact that they were a speculation by Lord Cadogan himself and their early date suggests that they were intended not just to kick-start the development of the new square but also to be model houses. Number 60, the corner house, was not completed until 1888 by F.G. Knight (although the listed building description suggest Norman Shaw was the architect, which seems hardly likely). It is less interesting and seemingly intends to visually balance Young's buildings without competing with them.

Fortunately, few buildings in the square fall below the somewhat stolid if grand standard set by the earl's trio while several rise high above it. And the one that rises highest – in almost every sense – stands right next door. Number 52 is one of the most extraordinary houses in London, ablaze with energy and inventive detail, and utterly – and almost unbelievably – romantic in its intentions. Bridget Cherry calls it 'a glorious apotheosis of Flemish Renaissance' (*The Buildings of England, London 3 North West*, p. 580) and she is right. The building is truly amazing and a feast for the eye and imagination – indeed, perhaps, too rich for some. The house was designed in 1885 by Ernest George – of George & Peto – and completed in 1886 (as a date in the gable proclaims) for T.A. de la Rue, and was very evidently a one-off bespoke design. The house is built of red brick, with a huge amount of biscuit-coloured terracotta moulded detail and decoration combined with some spectacular moulded and rubbed red brick ornament. The composition is asymmetrical with two bays of different heights and forms – although both most ornate – framing the centre of the façade, which is crowned by an all-embracing gable of complex and curvaceous Baroque form and two storeys high. The decoration represents a fairyland of bizarre creatures; some delightful, others sinister.

95. *Far left, left and below*
52 Cadogan Square, completed in 1886 to the designs of Ernest George for Thomas Andros de la Rue, a high-class paper manufacturer and printer of bank notes and stamps who was made a baronet in 1898. The house, with its astonishing array of fine but often peculiar detail, is one of the most glorious Flemish Renaissance Revival buildings in Britain.

The arched entrance porch, set within the southern bay, is made of terracotta and is framed by exquisitely moulded male and female Caryatids, or Terms, grasping volutes above their heads, both in an over-heated seventeenth-century Flemish Mannerist style. The female face on the keystone of the arch gasps – open-mouthed and looking down – at all who enter.

The north bay displays, at ground-floor level – below terracotta mullions and transoms of its tall window – moulded and rubbed red brick panels depicting youths disporting themselves amongst swags and strapwork, while side panels contain grinning, long-eared demons with disturbing eyes. At first-floor level there is another large brick panel, this time showing a satyr and satyress or fauna (observe her cloven foot) playing instruments while putti cavort among swags of fruit, including vines. The side panels here also show putti playing pipes. Presumably the room behind was used for dining or dancing. At second-floor level, above the north bay, is a pair of windows with Shaw-style arched mullions – here made of terracotta – that are accompanied by three Caryatids, two male and one female, smiling in most unsettling manner while they play musical instruments. The female Caryatid is being particularly energetic as she clashes away on symbols. Above and around the Caryatids are grimacing masks and the heads of putti or cherubs that look decidedly unhealthy as they smirk in a maniacal – even diabolic – manner, like angelic beings possessed.

What is one to make of all this? At the very least it suggests that the architects and clients of the Queen Anne and Flemish Renaissance Revival were not strait-laced, puritanical or conventional late Victorians when it came to matters architectural and artistic. Things quieten down after this, as you head north, but that is not to say that the buildings become architecturally dull. Far from it. Number 50 is also by George, a

year or so later (it was completed in 1887) and far more reserved. The client was a Colonel A.W. Thynne, who was either not such an artistic free spirit as T.A. de la Rue, or not as wealthy, as the high-quality terracotta and brick ornament on number 52 would not have been inexpensive.

And now come numbers 28 to 36 that are – in their own way – the most memorable group on and around Cadogan Square, not necessarily because they are architecturally the best examples, but because they are the ultimate expression – the epitome – of what is now generally taken to be the 'Pont Street Dutch' variation of the Queen Anne Revival. They really are a glorious group, with a superb array of Baroque gables – one with crow-steps – and lots of early seventeenth-century Dutch details. This is the nearest Hans Town comes to authentic canal-side architecture of the Low Countries. The architect was George Devey, who died in 1886, the year in which these houses were designed. He was sixty-six years of age and during his career had done much to establish the use of vernacular, regional architecture – particularly timber frame – as a legitimate source for modern domestic architecture. It is significant that both Norman Shaw and Charles Voysey had worked for him and of course both – in their separate ways – carried on Devey's experiments with history. The group was built in 1888–9.

There is one more surprise left, and it is not the north side of the square despite the fact that it is – in its own way – most surprising. After all the individuality, invention and display of the Gothic spirit in classical garb, the north side is a simple, straight up-and-down, largely uniform, neo-Renaissance composition. The houses are pretty well uniform, designed in the Georgian tradition with first-floor *piano nobile* and square attic windows. The dominant feature is the linking of porches to form a ground-floor colonnade supporting a first-floor terrace.

It is a visually strong idea providing a pleasant amenity for the occupants of the houses, but the colonnade plays no public role in the life of the square, since there is no route through it nor reason for being in it unless you are entering or leaving a house. The terrace was designed in the 1880s by G.T. Robinson.

At the east end of the terrace is the real surprise – a Gothic-detailed intruder in an overwhelmingly Renaissance domain. Number 4 was designed in 1879 by the great Goth George Edmund Street, commissioned by the Misses Monk who evidently wanted something a little different. And they got it and – being by Street – there are a few most original twists. How do you make medieval Gothic, largely an ecclesiastical architecture, relevant to the design of a large and comfortable late nineteenth-century home in a grand residential square? Well, this is Street's answer, and it is pretty good. The front façade – asymmetrical, red brick and gabled – has enough in common with its neighbours to fit in, although, of course, its details are Gothic, but in a quiet way. Street was a Gentleman, as no doubt the Misses Monk were Gentlewomen, and they did not want to be bad mannered or do anything to upset the visual harmony of the square or frighten the neighbours nor affront the Earl. However, the side elevation is a little more radical. It is more strikingly asymmetrical with two gabled bays of different heights and different designs. One incorporates a very fine stone-built loggia with a Gothic shaft and capital that helps supportes wide pointed arches. Above, in the gable, is tall and narrow blank Gothic arcading with moulded brick tracery that has a distinctly European look, like the Gothic of the Baltic states or Poland. And as you pass, take a look inside through the windows. The main ground-floor rooms, at least, are decorated in a robust seventeenth-century classical manner. How very odd were these late Victorians – Goths outside, but classicists

inside. Just one more set of houses to see in the square. Numbers 22 to 26 are built of the usual red brick and buff stone but at upper levels and in the gables include a mix of vernacular roughcast, tile-hanging and half timbering. You have seen it all before, but this is a most pleasing example of the mid-1880s by E.T. Hall. Particularly good is the abstract sculptural treatment of the flue of number 26, set on the corner with Clabon Mews. As it rises the flue gets wider floor by floor by means of concave, convex and ogee profiles. A lovely Gothic project, where function becomes the primary ornament and dictates form, but here realised with classical details. A typical Arts and Crafts solution.

One last word about Cadogan Square: it is intact. There is not one significant intrusion that is later than the date of its initial completion. So the picture of the past, of its architectural and social aspirations, is complete. That, of course, is what Pevsner meant when he observed that there are few places in London where the architecture of the prosperous 1880s could be 'studied more profitably'. The trees in the square and in the patches of communal rear gardens have grown during the last 130 years but, otherwise, the world is largely unchanged. This is true of few other squares in London.

Hans Place and Hans Road

Hans Place, mostly rebuilt at the same time as Cadogan Square and west Pont Street were created, has little to compare with the majority of buildings in these two showpieces. Clearly all was ratcheted down in expense and scale, as well as in ambition. Numbers 14 and 15 make a charming pair. Number 15 is an original corner house – of the 1780s or 1790s – but heightened in the later nineteenth century by the addition of a fourth-floor gable containing a large tripartite Venetian window. Number 14 is a good, relatively small, Queen Anne house of the 1880s. It has a three-storey oriel – with pargetting

– set to one side of the elevation, within a tall arched recess. On the other side of the façade is a doorcase, with a large late seventeenth-century scallop shell hood. Number 47 is also pleasing, with a corner tower furnished with Gothic detailing, and set on the corner of Hans Road. You are now nearly in Knightsbridge, the Brompton Road is a just a minute or so away, but in Hans Road – on the Goddard Estate – are two of the most intriguing late nineteenth-century houses in the area.

Numbers 14 and 16 Hans Road were designed by Charles F.A. Voysey in 1891. He was in his early thirties so these houses are not from his mature period, but they are marvellous. They are marvellous not just in themselves but because they make crystal clear where the Queen Anne Revival, and the architecture of George Devey (with whom Voysey had trained) and Norman Shaw, were heading. Superfluous ornament and most of the cosy but confusing historicist detailing – and associations with the past – have been stripped away, while vigorous composition and the essential functionalism of Shaw and the Queen Anne Revival are retained, but now displayed in a wonderfully spare and almost abstract setting. You really can believe these two houses represent the basis of a modern British architecture that – emerging from the morass of historic styles and details – is fit for purpose and for the coming machine age of the twentieth century. The houses are built of red brick with dressings of Ketton stone, each has shallow canted bays with mullioned windows and little ornament. At fourth-floor level is a row of attic windows with the traditional arrangement and designs of stone lintel cills and jambs rethought to make a strikingly original version of a familiar form. A subtle but most effective reworking of history, going back – as it were – to first principles. Nothing here is a slavish or thoughtless copy. In the centre of the shared elevation are three tall and narrow oriels, of Norman Shaw type and asymmetrically arranged, that suggest that the outside has been ordered from within, that the house is becoming a functional machine in which to live. Voysey's design drawings show a more symmetrical treatment. There were two narrow oriels in the centre of the façades – one per house – not the irregular grouping of three as built. So, as the design was refined, asymmetry increased.

The main external ornament is reserved for the interior of the matching entrance lobbies. Both contain relief panels by the favoured Arts and Crafts sculptor and potter Conrad Dressler. One shows a crouching and beckoning guide holding a lantern, about which flutters a dove. The other shows a lioness, standing still below the spreading branches of a tree. It seems that originally these reliefs were intended to be displayed more openly above the porches.

Internally the houses are practically and ingeniously planned, with generous top-lit centrally placed staircases and split level floors for the main reception rooms – an emerging idea in the early 1890s. Number 12, immediately to the north, is also a significant building. It dates from 1893–4 and was designed by Voysey's friend, Arthur H. Mackmurdo. The design is more evidently Queen Anne than Voysey's buildings, with a conventional classical porch and cornice, but it also possesses a Shaw-influenced deep and narrow central oriel that gives it a distinct identity.

The client for all three houses was Archibald Grove, a progressive Liberal MP who liked to dabble in property speculation and investment. His plan was to commission Voysey to design all three houses with numbers 14 and 16 let to tenants while Grove himself lived in number 12. However, by 1892 client and architect had fallen out, with the issue of fees even going to court. When the unpleasant business was settled –

96. *Above*
Numbers 28 to 36 Cadogan Square, designed
in about 1886 in an almost antiquarian and
archaeologically correct seventeenth-century
Dutch Renaissance gabled style by George
Devey. The group was built in 1888–9. The
display of varied gables is particularly fine.

a compromise solution was finally agreed which left neither side particularly happy – Grove did not want to use Voysey's design for number 12 and instead commissioned Mackmurdo. When all three houses were completed in 1894, Grove decided to live elsewhere. Presumably the sweetness and light had – for him – moved on from this particular project (*Survey of London: Volume 41*, pp. 9-32).

The domestic architecture that matured in Hans Town during the 1870s and 1880s became the vernacular style for much of late Victorian and Edwardian Chelsea. It started early. Lennox Gardens, laid out in 1885 to the west of Cadogan Square on Smith's Charity Estate land, was soon lined with tall, gabled Queen Anne and Flemish revival houses. Similar houses appeared south of Cadogan Square, notably in Cadogan Gardens and the style continued to flourish along the Chelsea Embankment – for example Garden Corner at number 13 Chelsea Embankment, that was designed in 1879 in the Flemish Renaissance style by Edward l'Anson for railway engineer James Staats Forbes, with the interior redesigned in 1906 in most ingenious manner by Charles Voysey. And in Cheyne Walk, from 1894–1900, C.R. Ashbee designed numbers 38 and 39 in a simplified Queen Anne Style, with formal yellow brick elevations topped by a roughcast third floor, all enlivened with Art Nouveau ironwork. The best was 37 – the Magpie and Stump – built in 1895, with a three-storey multi-curved oriel. That was Ashbee's own home but it was demolished in 1969.

Taken together, Chelsea has an internationally significant body of late nineteenth-century architecture, pioneering in many respects and of the highest quality. It did not start with the Cadogan Estate's rebuilding and enlargement of Hans Town but this bold initiative did give Queen Anne and Flemish Renaissance Revival architecture a tremendous showcase, an impetus and an opportunity to develop, to display its qualities and to flourish city-wide.

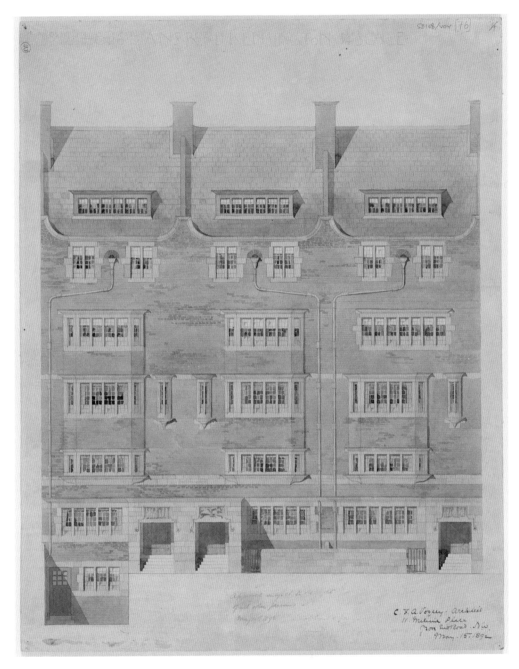

97. Left
A relief panel – showing a beckoning guide – by sculptor and potter Conrad Dressler that was to be fixed above one the entrance porches to the three houses in Hans Road. Ultimately it was fixed within one of the porches.

98. Above
Charles F. A. Voysey's design of 1891 for 12, 14 and 16 Hans Road, commissioned by Archibald Grove. Here history and functionalism fuse to create a modern domestic architecture. Unfortunately Voysey and Grove fell out, so only two of the three houses were built.

OUT ON THE TOWN

The darker side of Ranelagh Gardens as a hunting ground for criminals and harlots reinforced the character of Chelsea's meaner streets.

Convivial Chelsea has a curious history. When documented in the seventeenth century, Chelsea was a place of rural and riverside retreat with, from the 1690s, the barrack-like character of the Royal Hospital exerting a strong influence to create a dubious drinking environment in and around the northeast end of what is now Royal Hospital Road. This character was sustained when the Ranelagh pleasure gardens opened nearby in 1742. Then during the nineteenth century entertainments in Chelsea became more metropolitan, with architecturally significant public houses being built along, and just off, the King's Road and in 1888 a West End-style theatre, the Royal Court, in Sloane Square.

The ancient taverns and inns of Chelsea were almost invariably located in the village, near the church and mostly on the river – along what is now Cheyne Walk – although there were a number in Church Lane (now Old Church Street). These included the Black Lion, drawn by Walter Greaves, and long demolished (see *Chelsea Society Report*, 1939–40, p. 12). John Rocque, on his small-scale London map of 1746, names a few of the Cheyne Walk taverns when he shows 'stairs' leading down to landing stages in the Thames – the Feathers (on the site of what is now number 49 Cheyne Walk), and the Magpie, latterly the Magpie and Stump. There was

also the Three Tuns, with its bowling green. They are shown on one of Dr King's surveys of around 1705. The bowling green was to go in 1708 for the construction of Cheyne Row, and the Three Tuns was demolished by 1711. Numbers 46 to 48 Cheyne Walk now stand on its site.

In their watercolours of the 1850s and 1860s, Walter and Henry Greaves show views of Cheyne Walk, giving a little more detail. Most memorable is Walter Greaves' perspective of the Adam & Eve tavern (see page 78), just west of the Old Church, with a gallery supported on stout posts that rise out of the river and stairs leading from a mooring directly to the tavern's Thames-side bar. Basil Walters suggests this was the 'most interesting' of the old taverns, with the walls of its bar 'garnished with fowling pieces' (Basil Waters, *Chelsea Society Report*, 1998, pp. 47-8). Walter Greaves also drew the Old Swan, operating under the sign of 'Eliot Watney', purveying 'Old Ales' and with a charming two-storey bay window perched over the river, stairs leading down to a mooring, and a malt house or brewhouse adjoining.

The Old Swan seems to date from around 1780, established after the earlier Swan or White Swan was turned into a brewhouse (see pages 68-9). This, located to the east at the river end of Swan Walk,

100. Above
The Old Swan, painted by Walter Greaves in the late 1860s. Thompson's Chelsea map of 1836 records that the tavern was located at the southwest end of Paradise Row, with a courtyard, an outbuilding containing bars and a malt house fronting the Thames. All were destroyed in the early 1870s for the construction of Chelsea Embankment.

101. Above right
A game of skittles called 'Four Corners' being played at the Swan. The watercolour was made by Robert Dighton in about 1784, so presumably it shows the court of the 'Old Swan' which moved from the south end Swan Walk to Paradise Row in 1780.

was a riverside tavern, with a bowling green, and of mid-seventeenth-century origin or earlier because Samuel Pepys on 9 April 1666 mentions it in his diary in a somewhat sinister manner: '... thinking to have been merry at Chelsey, but being come almost to the house ... near the waterside, a house alone, I think the Swan; a gentleman ... called to us to tell us that the house was shut up of the sickness [the plague] so we with great affright turned back' (*Diary of Samuel Pepys*, ed. Robert Latham and William Matthews, Vol. VII, London: G. Bell and Sons, 1970, p. 95).

Since 1715 the Swan had been famous along the river because it was the finishing post in the epic rowing race between six young watermen from the Old Swan next to London Bridge. The race had been inaugurated in 1715 by Thomas Doggett

Jour Corners Played at the Swan Chelsea.

in honour of the recent Hanoverian accession and it was held on 1 August against an outgoing or ebb tide. It was a gruelling affair and one of the great annual events on the Thames. The race, about 4½ miles in length, was known as Doggett's Coat and Badge, and the victor was indeed awarded these baubles, and carried in triumph into the Swan to be regaled.

However, the real prize was life-long respect along the Thames and among fellow watermen and river folk, and a guarantee of employment as a ferryman (Holme, pp. 187-9). The race is still run, but now in July, with an incoming or flood tide, and ends at Cadogan Pier near the east end of Cheyne Walk. Virtually all the Cheyne Walk riverside taverns that survived into the nineteenth century were destroyed

in the early 1870s for the construction of the Chelsea Embankment. And even those set on the north side of Cheyne Walk, rather than on the river's edge, and which survived the 1870s purge – such as the Bell on the corner of Danvers Street and the Dog on Lombard Street – have long since gone. One old pub that does survive in Cheyne Walk, located on the corner with Cheyne Row and once known as the King's Head and Eight Bells, is now in fact no longer a pub. It is 'Fifty Cheyne', a very smart restaurant, but it retains a bar of sorts on the ground floor and the building has a charming early nineteenth-century elevation, sporting a good display of pilasters. So something of a miniature palace that, with flickering gas lanterns, was just the thing to attract early Victorian riverside custom – and still a most pleasing place.

Don Saltero's Coffee House

The most famous of Cheyne Walk's convivial establishments was Don Saltero's Coffee House, which in 1717 or 1718 was installed in a building on a fine site in Cheyne Row – the future number 18 – adjoining the New Manor House. The presence of the coffee house did much to make the village of Chelsea – then rapidly expanding – feel like a self-contained community with a rather urbane and cultured identity.

Daniel Lysons, in the Middlesex volume of his *Environs of London* of 1795, explains that Don Saltero's was 'well known' and had been 'opened ... by one Salter, a barber, who drew attention of the public by the eccentricities of his conduct, and by furnishing his house with a large collection of natural and other curiosities, which still remain in the coffee-room, where printed catalogues are sold, with the names of the principal benefactors to the collection'.

James Salter was at one time a servant of Sir Hans Sloane, which probably explains how he was able to accommodate his business on such a prime riverside site in 1717 or 1718 on land that had been acquired by Sloane in 1712 when he bought the Manor House and its grounds. Salter had been running a coffee house, combined with cabinet of curiosities, in Chelsea for many years – perhaps as early as the 1670s – but this must have been a relatively modest affair with his endeavours only blossoming into a masterpiece of eccentric self-promotion after he acquired the well-located Cheyne Walk establishment. His son was baptised in the Old Church in 1682, in 1684 he appears in rate books as the occupant of a house in Lombard Street (as a western portion of Cheyne Walk was then known), in 1695 he was located in Prospect Place, next to the church, and from 1708 to 1717 in a corner house in Danvers Street.

According to the *Survey of London* Chelsea volume of 1909, the first dated reference to Salter's coffee house is in a letter from a Chelsea resident, Anthony Cope, who wrote from Venice to Moses Goodyear in 1697, asking him to 'forget me not at Salter's in the next bowl' (*Survey of London: Volume 2*, pp. 61-4). As might be expected, Sir Hans Sloane became one of Salter's patrons and, as Lysons puts it, 'contributed largely' to Salter's collection 'out of the superfluities of his own museum'. In addition, 'Vice-Admiral Munden, and other officers who had been much upon the sea of Spain, enriched it with many curiosities'. It was by the wit of these Spanish veterans that Salter was given the name of Don Saltero (*Environs of London*, pp. 77-8).

DON SALTERO'S TAVERN and COFFEE-HOUSE Cheney Walk, CHELSEA

If this name sounds somewhat condescending, it is, because – if the *Tatler* is anything to go by – some found Salter's affectations extremely annoying. The *Tatler* edition of 28 June 1709 recounts a journey from the metropolis to the 'Village of Chelsea' – for the sake of fresh air – and offers a description that suggests some sophisticated city dwellers viewed upstart Chelsea as faintly ridiculous in its rustic pretentions. *Tatler*'s reporter, in his 'description of the Village', characterises it as the place spanning from the 'Five Fields where the Robbers lie in wait, to the Coffee-house where the *Literati* sit in Council' (the Five Fields was the name of the long road leading north–east from the Royal Hospital, now Ebury Street). The reporter – the playwright, former soldier and future Whig politician Richard Steele, writing under the pseudonym of Isaac Bickerstaff – tells his readers that as soon as he entered the coffee-house his 'Eye was diverted by ten thousand Gimcracks round the Room, and on the Cieling [sic]'. He then recounts his first meeting with the 'Tooth-Drawer', as he insists on calling Salter, which prompts him to ponder why 'of all the lower Order, Barbers should go further in hitting the Ridiculous, than any other set of men'. What seems to have particularly annoyed the sardonic Steele is that Salter took the 'Liberty' of describing his collection as a serious affair when it was nothing but an 'Abuse of the good people of England' and an 'imposition upon the World ... under the specious Pretence of Learning and Antiquity' (*Tatler*, No. 34, pp. 205-7 of 1754 edition, vol. I, London).

Although Salter's combination of coffee house and museum of curiosities did not appeal to the *Tatler*, it became a popular London destination and the heart and soul of convivial Chelsea after it moved to its larger Cheyne Walk premises. Here Salter strove hard to please and to increase his reputation as an eccentric collector of curiosities of all kinds. Salter died in 1728

but his coffee house continued, largely unchanged until 1799 when it was turned into a tavern and its collection dispersed. 'Mr Salter's Tavern' closed in 1867. The house of 1717–18 survives, although significantly altered, with a first-floor balcony added, soon after it ceased being tavern (see page 100).

Ranelagh Gardens
Don Saltero's reputation as Chelsea's best known place of public resort was somewhat eclipsed in 1742 when Ranelagh Gardens was opened. The gardens occupied the land, immediately to the east of the Royal Hospital, that had been acquired on leasehold from the hospital in must dubious circumstances by the errant Earl of Ranelagh, who in 1685 had become the hospital's Paymaster-General. By 1688 Ranelagh had built himself a house on the grounds – seemingly using embezzled hospital funds – which he turned into a fine private estate (see page 140). The roguish Ranelagh eventually fell into debt but at the time of his death in 1712 the estate was still in his possession. His daughter, Lady Catherine Jones, managed to remain in occupation despite her father's colossal debts, until 1730. At this time she vested the estate in trustees who three years later divided it into ten lots that were put up for auction. One of these – of 3 acres – was acquired by the hospital but the rest were snapped up by a body of speculators who recognised the commercial potential of the riverside site in a London village that had long been enjoying something of a property boom (see pages 83–4). However, there was a problem for the speculators, and that problem was the Royal Hospital. The land the speculators had acquired was held leasehold from the Crown and there were restrictions in the Crown lease that prohibited 'incommodious new buildings near the Hospital'. The challenge for the speculators was to find a way around this restriction, by fair means or foul.

In 1737 a successful London speculative builder named Benjamin Timbrell bought the 1680s Ranelagh House and erected a new house near it. In 1741 Timbrell became part of the syndicate of speculators, led by James Lacey, a former business partner of actor David Garrick and co-patentee of the Theatre Royal, Drury Lane, Covent Garden that included Sir Thomas Robinson, a Member of Parliament, an amateur architect who designed his home – Rokeby Hall in Yorkshire – in grand Palladian style, and an extravagant socialite and collector, who in 1742 was appointed Governor of Barbados.

This syndicate resolved to turn Lord Ranelagh's former estate into an exotic and exclusive pleasure ground, incorporating a vast rotunda 56 metres in diameter. How the syndicate imagined it could carry out this project without being in breach of the Crown lease remains a mystery. Self-evidently, the tranquillity of the Royal Hospital would be compromised and its architecture upstaged by an ostentatious new amphitheatre that could not be construed as anything but 'incommodious'.

However, presumably the syndicate knew something that we do not. No doubt arrangements had been made with some members of the hospital which – in the end – would be the body to decide if the new buildings were 'incommodious' or not. With great haste that was little short of pure impudence, the syndicate started to raise the rotunda, built by Timbrell and designed by William Jones, the surveyor to the East India Company. When, too late, the hospital objected, it did not do so vigorously or in a sustained manner. Terms were agreed, disadvantageous to the hospital, and the syndicate continued with construction. The hospital did not argue that the rotunda and pleasure ground were 'incommodious', nor did it use its power under the Crown lease to stop works, or to have the rotunda torn down. Presumably strings were pulled behind

the scenes and persons in power in the hospital had something personal to gain by the construction of the rotunda and the development of the pleasure grounds proceeding.

The speed of the enterprise was astounding, so that with the hospital unwilling or unable to take action, the rotunda and pleasure ground opened for business in April 1742, with Robinson appointing himself director of entertainments. He also managed to squeeze a house for himself – called Prospect Place – on to the pleasure ground, which he seems to have used for elaborate entertainments. By August 1742 Robinson was in Barbados but his habit of running-up excessive expenses ensured that he did not stay long.

The rotunda – although grotesquely out of sympathy in its design, scale, siting and purpose with Wren's hospital buildings – was nevertheless a fascinating structure. Its wide-span roof – famed as an ingenious piece of carpentry – had only one interior support, a central colonnaded pier that doubled as a stack for a massive fireplace. Around the wall of the rotunda was an arcade supporting boxes used by diners with – on one side – a large stand for the orchestra. Outside were tree-lined walks, pavilions and a canal. To the north of the rotunda, and connected to it by an arcade, was Ranelagh House that had been obliged to play a role in the festive pleasure ground that now engulfed it.

To the southeast the pleasure ground was bounded by the canalised course of the River Westbourne, as it found its way to the Thames, while southeast of the river, adjoining the Thames, were the reservoirs of the Chelsea Waterworks Company. Visitors to the grounds who came by boat had to use stairs almost adjoining those serving the Royal Hospital and then stroll to the pleasure grounds along a path set between the Westbourne and a hospital meadow.

An Inside View of the Rotundo in Ranelagh Gardens

London Printed for & Sold by Rob

72

Vüe de l'Interieur de la Rotonde dans le Jardins de Ranelagh.

he Golden Buck, opposite Fetter Lane, Fleet Street.

N. Parr Sculp.

104. *Previous page*
A view of the interior of the rotunda in Ranelagh Gardens, engraved by Nathaniel Parr, hand-coloured and based on Canaletto's painting of c. 1754. Note the central massive chimney stack that also helped to support the wide-span roof.

105. *Above*
A 'Juvenile fete' and balloon race at Cremorne Gardens, as presented in the *Illustrated London News* in 1859. The gardens were a popular pleasure ground at the west end of Cheyne Walk and flourished from 1845, inspiring local artists such as James McNeill Whistler, until its closure in 1877.

106. *Above right*
Female figures seemingly floating in spectral manner through the pleasure ground of Cremorne Gardens, as painted by Whistler in about 1870.

It must have been delightful, no doubt lit at night by lanterns or flickering oil lamps. Almost as soon as it was opened Ranelagh Gardens became one of the sights of London, and quickly more popular than the long-established Vauxhall Gardens, just across the river. Crowds flocked to it, happy to pay ticket charges that were high, up to 5 shillings on fireworks' nights or when elaborate masquerades were arranged, at a time when the average weekly salary for a skilled London tradesman was no more than £1 a week. George II was a regular visitor, Mozart performed in the rotunda and Canaletto painted its interior twice. It was also – as with all of London's places of pleasure – an alluring mix of high and low life, a place for king and commoners, for aristocrats and men and woman of fashion, but also of predatory rogues and women of the town, happy to invest in a ticket as the means of securing a profitable assignation.

This darker side of Ranelagh Gardens as a hunting ground for criminals and harlots reinforced the character of Chelsea's meaner streets. These had grown up immediately to the north of the Royal

Hospital, at the same time as smarter streets and houses had appeared to its west and south. To a large degree the hospital was the direct cause of both. With its noble architecture and its disciplined veterans patrolling the streets, the hospital had ensured tranquillity and stability, and had encouraged investment in Chelsea. However, the hospital's influence was more than just the creation of a sense of security. The pensioners themselves were a potent economic force. They were steady customers at local taverns and many a Chelsea boarding house thrived on the business generated by the fact that old soldiers had, until 1845, to apply in person for admission to the hospital, and even to claim a pension. The King's Road, as a private royal road until 1830, was not a popular location for taverns and inns, although there were one or two, notably the Six Bells (now number 195–197 King's Road) that had a bowling green and was in operation in the late eighteenth century, if not earlier.

Instead, taverns tended to be located to the south, along what was called Jew's Row, opposite the hospital's burial ground. However, Jew's Row was not just a favoured location for taverns, alehouses and cheap lodgings for old soldiers who found it convenient to live near the hospital but also for brothels and all manner of bawdy houses. Between Jew's Row and Turk's Row to its northwest, a series of narrow alleys and courts lined with small cottages took form from the 1740s to create the sort of netherworld found within the environs of most British barracks. Neither Jew's Row nor Turk's Row are shown on William Hamilton's map of 1717 but both appear on John Rocque's large-scale map of 1746, although the alleys and courts do not. However, Rocque's map does show that the buildings forming the Jew's Row frontage were divided, in an unusual manner, by a series of closely spaced blind alleys, some leading to small blind courts. The claustrophobic and tight grain of the development between the rows that followed long and narrow garden plots is well illustrated on Richard Horwood's London map of 1799–1819. The image is strange. Between these rows a piece of city had evolved that – in stark contrast with nearby gardens, Sloane Square and the spacious grounds of the

107. Above
The Chelsea Physic Garden showing its direct,
intimate and highly romantic relationship with
the river before the construction of the Chelsea
Embankment in the early 1870s. Note the noble
cedar of Lebanon trees, the Chelsea boys or
mudlarks frolicking on the riverbank and, to
the left, the malt house and entrance to the
court of the Old Swan tavern, see page 232.

Royal Military Asylum – was as cramped as anything in the more desperate corners of Whitechapel (*Victoria County History*, pp. 41–7). That such a seamy world grew in the shadow of the Royal Hospital is hardly surprising since the hospital was, in many respects, a barracks, and a large proportion of the old soldiers who lived within it were neither ancient nor terminally infirm.

On the other hand, it does seem strange that such a quarter would grow immediately to the south of Chelsea House, a Cadogan home on the estate. The proximity is made clear on Richardson's map of 1769. Chelsea House was demolished for the construction in 1801 of the Royal Military Asylum; indeed it was perhaps the presence of the sordid courts that made occupation of Chelsea House untenable and its demolition inevitable.

This licentious quarter can only have been confirmed in its character and expanded in its size and influence upon life in Chelsea by the underworld characters attracted by the nefarious opportunities offered by Ranelagh. Many Chelsea residents became exasperated. Thomas Faulkner, for example, in 1810 condemned the Jew's Row area as a disgrace to the Parish. Sustained criticism ensured that little of the area would long survive, even though its rowdy and potentially criminal character must have been greatly reduced by 1829 because a significant change had taken place in riverside Chelsea. One of the oddest of the many odd things about the Ranelagh enterprise is that the ruthless syndicate – skilled in pushing the difficult project forward at great speed – proved unable to do the basic arithmetic. Despite Ranelagh's great popularity, the pleasure ground failed to cover its costs. The syndicate soon faced bankruptcy and was only saved when Robinson became principal shareholder and pumped money into the enterprise. He died in 1777, after which decline became gradually irreversible. In 1803 the gardens were closed and in 1805 the rotunda, the pavilions and Ranelagh's 1680s house were all demolished. The setting of the Royal Hospital was restored, tranquillity returned and presumably the dubious habitués of the Turk's Row area were significantly reduced in number. Today the former pleasure ground is part of the hospital's gardens. It is as if the rotunda and its fantasy world had never existed. The final odd twist in the tale is that the demise of Ranelagh Gardens did not mark the end of the pleasure ground in Chelsea. Cremorne Gardens, just beyond the west end of Cheyne Walk, enjoyed a brief moment of London fame as a colourful, noisy and popular pleasure ground incorporating restaurants and dancing, and featuring balloon ascents and firework displays. Cremorne sparkled between 1845 and 1877, capturing the imagination of the capital and the artist James McNeill Whistler (see page 74) but annoyed some of Chelsea's grander residents, and its execution was organised by the orchestrated refusal to renew the garden's entertainment licence. Any chance of a reprieve was ruled out because the ground was quickly let to house builders.

Chelsea Physic Garden

While the Royal Hospital had to contend with Ranelagh Gardens on its east side, there was, to its west, a garden of quite a different stamp: the medicinal garden of the Worshipful Society of Apothecaries, more generally known as the Chelsea Physic Garden, founded in 1673. Its history is not, perhaps, an obvious part of the story of Chelsea's convivial life, not least because the garden did not open to the public until 1983. However, the garden did bring a select few people 'out of town' to Chelsea, to see it plants and natural wonders or to seek a possible cure for whatever aliment was afflicting them.

The aim of the Worshipful Society was to gain a source for medicinal plants and to create a training ground for its apprentices, allowing them to study the healing qualities of plants. It chose the location carefully – south facing and not too exposed to wind, removed from the smoke of the city but not too distant, on the river to make transport of plants easier, and a well-drained soil. Riverside Chelsea was ideal and a 4-acre site, with a 100-metre frontage to the Thames, acquired on leasehold. The site was improved by the construction of a tall, enveloping wall, most portions of which faced southeast and southwest to create a warm microclimate that would allow a wide range of exotic plants to flourish. John Watts, an apothecary, was appointed the garden's first director in 1680. The ground was divided by paths in a geometric manner to create a number of rectangular-shaped 'teaching beds' and the garden's seed collection was launched, working in collaboration with such prestigious institutions as Leiden University.

However, at first things did not go well. Watts was dismissed in 1692 because the garden had become neglected. Money was becoming a pressing issue and in 1706 a committee was set up to oversee the garden and to fundraise. A subscription was launched and people were invited to contribute, but this did not work. The future of the garden was in serious doubt.

However, in 1712 Sir Hans Sloane came to the rescue. In that year he purchased the New Manor House and its grounds from Charles Cheyne (see page 46) and these included the ground on which the Apothecaries' Garden was located. He gave it support, stability and – not least – security. The land was, essentially, made over to them. All the Worshipful Society was required to do in return for the gift was to pay Sloane or his estate £5 a year in perpetuity and to supply the Royal Society annually with fifty 'specimens; grown in the garden until the total of 3,000 was reached' (Holme, p. 178). The £5 per year rent is collected to this day.

In 1722 the Deed of Covenant between Sloane and the Society was signed and in the same year Sloane appointed Philip Miller as head gardener, who remained in the post until the late 1760s. The choice was inspired. Peter Collinson – a botanist, avid gardener and Fellow of the Royal Society – inspected the garden in 1764 and concluded that Miller had 'raised the reputation of the Chelsea Garden so much that it excels all the gardens of Europe for its amazing variety of plants of all orders and classes and from all climates' (see 'Philip Miller: A Portrait', by Allen Paterson, *Garden History*, 14, (1), 1986, pp. 40–41). More specifically, Miller did much to make the Apothecaries' Garden not only one of the most important centres of botany and plant exchange in the world but also a forerunner of 'economic' botany – where plants were collected and nurtured for their commercial value – that was so successfully developed late in the eighteenth century at Kew Gardens. Sir Joseph Banks, a leading botanist who became President of the Royal Society, was instrumental in the development of Kew's potential, but he also collaborated with the Apothecaries, perhaps partly because his mother Sarah lived nearby in the long-lost Turret House on what is now Paradise Walk.

Miller's most notable success in his endeavours with 'economic' botany came in 1733 when he sent long-strand cottonseed to the newly founded American colony of Georgia, where it launched a most valuable industry. It was, of course, hardly Miller's fault that his cottonseeds were ultimately to play a crucial role in the wickedly exploitative slave-based economy of much of the New World.

The Apothecaries' Garden continues to thrive, in every sense a living museum, with many of its plants, like its large and fruit-bearing olive tree, demonstrating on an annual basis the wisdom of the sheltered and sunny location as well as the successful creation, within the garden's

tall, sheltering and heat-trapping brick walls, of a most nurturing microclimate. The influence of the Physic Garden on the growth of Chelsea is intriguing. It arrived early when much of Chelsea was still open ground, before the Royal Hospital to its east and before the grand terrace houses on Cheyne Walk had been built to its west. Its significant near-neighbours, when it arrived, were the New Manor House to its west, the Swan tavern immediately to its south, and King James' College at Chelsea to its east, soon to be demolished for the construction of the Royal Hospital. However, the garden, because of the delightful prospect it offered, became something of a focus for house building. Paradise Row, defining the garden's northwest edge, was lined with buildings by the 1740s with those opposite the garden enjoying a fine view over it towards the river.

To the northeast of the garden's wall stands Swan Walk, on which in 1717, according to Hamilton's map, stood one large building, centrally placed, and another near the river. This no doubt was the Swan tavern, after which the walk was named. Horwood's map of 1799–1819, shows four houses, all set back from the road, and the large Swan Brewhouse next to the river. These houses mostly survive. Best is number 3. Five windows wide and three storeys high, it is set back from the walk and takes the form of a glorious brick box that appears to date from around 1700. Its porch is particularly fine, incorporating free-standing fluted Corinthian columns supporting an entablature featuring a carved architrave that – in splendid Baroque style – ramps up through the frieze to join the carved cornice. Number 4 Swan Walk was occupied in the 1730s by the redoubtable Elizabeth Blackwell. After her husband, a doctor, was jailed for debt she contrived to make money to support her children and herself and to pay off the family's debts by drawing specimens from the Apothecaries' Garden.

108. Right
Within the river gate of the
Physic Garden looking north
through a late seventeenth-
century wall and rusticated gate
piers, towards the famed pair of
cedar trees, planted in 1683 with
the last dying in 1903. The print,
dedicated to Lord Cadogan, is
based on a painting of c. 1835
by James Fuge.

Printed by Jas. Fuge.

NORTH VIEW OF THE CEDAR TREES

Dedicated by Permission

Lith? by H.Warren.

GARDENS OF THE APOTHECARY'S COMPANY, CHELSEA.

R? Hon?le the Earl Cadogan.

hed by G.F.Fuge, 13.Sloane Square.

These she engraved and coloured, and published in weekly parts between 1737 and 1739, along with a text describing the plants, their medical preparations and listing the aliments each plant could be used to treat. Bound together plates and text formed a most beautiful and useful book entitled *A Curious Herbal*. The project did raise enough money to secure her husband's release, but the story does not have a happy end. He went to Sweden, where he was executed for treason, and two of her children that she had been toiling to support died before the book was published.

Victorian pubs
During the latter part of the nineteenth century a number of taverns and public houses opened along the King's Road as it became a more public and busy thoroughfare, echoing the increase in Chelsea's population and urban growth (see page 101). Some of these pubs are – or were – architecturally very good. The White Hart, on the corner with Royal Avenue, appears to have been built in the 1890s as a modest 'Gin Palace' affair, nice and showy on its corner site with an attempt at a turret. It had ceased trading as a pub by 1968 when the Chelsea Drug Store was installed on the ground floor, behind a futuristic Pop-Art fascia. It is now a fast-food outlet.

Another good pub was the Markham Arms, at 138 King's Road, dating from 1856 and domestic in scale but with lavish stucco ornament and a splendid ground-floor bay window, dressed with Corinthian columns, to distinguish it as a place of conviviality and pleasure. Its interior was fitted up in excellent and erudite Victorian style in the 1970s by the eminent architect and architectural historian Roderick Gradidge, but that did not save it. The pub closed in the early 1990s, after which it housed a building society that, needless to say, did not make the best use of the lavish bay. At the time of writing, it is empty, awaiting its next tenant. Perhaps it will be a pub again.

The architecturally most impressive of the King's Road pubs is the Six Bells, at numbers 195–7. It was designed in 1898 by G.R. Crickmay and Sons (the Dorset architects for whom Thomas Hardy had worked before giving up architecture for writing), a wonderful Arts and Crafts extravaganza with Tudor arches and two-storey oriels with rich pargetting and the sort of early seventeenth-century style arched casement promoted by Norman Shaw (see page 215). Particularly good are the four carved brackets perched above the ground floor. With the wicked humour that was, ironically, part of the 'sweetness and light' of the Arts and Craft Movement and Queen Anne Revival (see page 209), these posts take the form of grimacing winged devils, presumably personifications of the 'demon drink' on sale inside. This pub was a prototype of the 'Olde Worlde' or 'Mock Antique Tavern' that – according to the Licensing World of 14 March 1914 – had replaced the ornate 'Gin Palace' pubs so popular from the early 1880s (see Mark Girouard, *Victorian Pubs*, London: Studio Vista, 1975, pp. 111, 189). Alas, the Six Bells is also a pub no more but a chain restaurant with flats above.

This leaves the Chelsea Potter, at 119 King's Road, which is a decent late Victorian corner pub with a good curved corner window. The interior originally had the usual compliment of saloon, public and private bars, and a snug, calculated to serve the varied strata of Victorian society. Virtually all has been swept away to create a more democratic – and far less interesting – interior into which more customers can be squeezed. However, at least the Chelsea Potter is still a pub.

The Royal Court Theatre
The most important example in Chelsea of Victorian architecture of leisure, pleasure and conviviality is the Royal Court Theatre on Sloane Square. Indeed, it is important on a national level. The theatre opened in September 1888 as the New Court

Theatre. By the standards of the time it is a fairly modest affair, constructed of red brick with a certain amount of moulded red brick decoration and designed in a free Italianate Renaissance style that is most compatible with the Queen Anne and Flemish Renaissance Revival styles being applied nearby on Pont Street and in Cadogan Square (see page 212). The building was at least partially financed by the Cadogans. The designers were the leading theatre and music hall architects Walter Emden and Bertie Crewe. Emden was productive and able – the Garrick of 1889, designed with C.J. Phipps is probably his best work. Crewe was prodigious as a theatre architect, displaying a genuine talent for producing, at speed, designs that both delighted and functioned. He had trained with the great Frank Matcham, studied and worked in London and Paris and – when the movies became big – transformed himself into a leading designer of cinemas. The ornate Shaftesbury Theatre of 1911, at the east end of Shaftesbury Avenue, is one of Crewe's most ostentatious designs.

Early productions at the New Court Theatre tended to be light entertainment – operettas and farces – but matters changed soon after 1900, at which point the theatre's name also changed to the Royal – as opposed to New – Court Theatre. Harley Granville-Barker became manager and he presented more thought-provoking plays, notably by George Bernard Shaw. This was presumably a reflection of Chelsea's evolving character as an enclave of artists, writers, intellectuals and individual thinkers. Granville-Barker was a most interesting and mercurial character who became a leading figure in the Edwardian theatre world. Born in 1877, he flourished as a playwright, critic, theatre manager and director, and as an actor, notably in early plays by Bernard Shaw.

One of Granville-Barker's most successful early plays was The Voysey Inheritance,

written in 1903 and first staged at the Royal Court in 1905. As a playwright, Granville-Barker liked to tackle tricky and controversial subjects, and this play was no exception. It portrays a family adrift in a crisis triggered by financial fraud and dishonesty that implicates, in different ways, not only all members of the family but also the institutions and assumptions that were taken to form the economic bedrock of Edwardian society. The choice of the family's name cannot surely have been pure chance. Presumably Granville-Barker was aware – as were many members of his educated and professional audience of local residents – of the recent bitter dispute over money that had taken place between the architect Charles Voysey and the speculator and Member of Parliament Archibald Grove.

The dispute was apparently over the payment of fees for the design of a group of houses that Voysey had designed for Grove in nearby Hans Road (see page 224). However, the play makes one wonder if there was more to it. Certainly the dispute was not resolved to anyone's satisfaction, and Grove, who had intended to live in one of the houses he paid for, eventually lived in none of them. The Royal Court closed in 1932, became a cinema in 1935, but closed again during the Second World War when it was damaged by a bomb that landed on the Tube station next door. However, it opened again as a live theatre in 1952, its interior largely rebuilt and made more commodious, and in 1956 came under the control of the English Stage Company. Its remit was to operate as a subsidised theatre company largely producing new British and foreign plays. Inevitably – given the time and place – these plays were, quite rightly, to be as challenging as possible in their content and in their production. Chelsea was, after all, about to be the vanguard of the social and artistic avant-garde in Britain. George Devine was appointed artistic director and one of the first plays staged was Look Back

109. Left
Sloane Square looking east to the Royal
Court Theatre. Built in 1888, the theatre
thrived initially but in 1935 was converted
into a cinema. The film being shown
when this photograph was taken was
The Key, a romance set during the Irish
War of Independence of 1919–21 and
starring William Powell and Edna Best.
The film was released in 1935, which
dates this photograph. The Royal Court
reopened as a live theatre in 1952.

in Anger, directed by Tony Richardson and
written by John Osborne, who was soon
tagged by the media and critics as one of
England new wave of 'Angry Young Men'.
This was followed in 1957 by Osborne's *The
Entertainer* – essentially commissioned by
and starring Laurence Olivier and, at one
level, a play about angry old men.

In the mid-1960s the theatre took the lead
in the challenge to censorship imposed by
the Lord Chamberlain's Office, thrusting
Chelsea into the forefront of the battle to
forge a 'liberated' society, one free of the
legal and cultural shackles that had, as
the argument went, stifled art and society.
This, of course, became – overtly or covertly,
consciously or subconsciously – one of the
great cultural projects of 1960s Britain.

The battle was intense and in 1965 involved
the theatre turning itself into a 'private
members club' so it could stage Osborne's
A Patriot for Me about homosexual intrigue
in the Austro-Hungarian empire of the
1890s, and Edward Bond's *Saved*, set in
a grim and impoverished dead-end council
estates in 1960s London. Both plays had
been refused performance licenses by
the Lord Chamberlain, who even went
so far to prosecute those involved in the
production of the play. Devine avoided
prosecution as he had died of a heart
attack while performing in *A Patriot for Me*.

However, victory ultimately went to
the Royal Court and its allies when the
Theatres Act was passed in 1968 that
abolished censorship on the stage.

The Royal Court remains in the forefront
of theatre in Britain, still experimental and
still controversial. For example, in 2009
Jerusalem by Jez Butterworth and *Seven
Jewish Children* by Caryl Churchill were
both premiered at the Royal Court, and in
2017 Butterworth's *The Ferryman*. It is still
the living heart that all city quarters, with
history and character, deserve to have.

MODERN VISIONS

110. Above
Syrie Maugham, photographed by
Cecil Beaton as a study in white.

Avant-garde architecture started to stalk the streets of Chelsea in earnest in the late 1920s.

The architectural revolution started, as it so often does, with the interior and with decoration. However, first a little background. By the time the First World War started in 1914, western architecture had – for as long as anyone could remember – been a series of recyclings of the past. Historic styles and ornament had, by convention, been utilised in modern design for many reasons: to give new work a sense of pedigree, a veneer of culture, a vocabulary of decoration and to make architecture legible to the layman. For example, a large portico marked a building of importance and probably gave a good idea about the location of the main entrance. The practice of adoption and adaptation is ancient. The Greeks, 2,500 or so years ago, took inspiration from Egypt, the Romans from Greece and Egypt, the fifteenth- and sixteenth-century Renaissance from Rome, and so it went on with, for example, Britain's beloved Georgian architecture being an inspired reworking of the Renaissance, adapted beautifully to the life and conditions of the nation at the time. The great debate in nineteenth-century Britain was not about whether or not to refer to history when designing new, but about which history

was relevant, superior and appropriate – Greek, Roman, Renaissance or Gothic – to forge the right style for the age.

However, as the twentieth century dawned, matters started to change. New materials – cast iron, wrought iron and steel, and from the mid-nineteenth century large sheets of plate glass – made new structures possible. Notable were wide-span station sheds required to house the incredible machines of the new railway age, and wide-span bridges, such as the Brooklyn Bridge, New York of the 1870s, with suspension cables woven of steel thread, and the steel-built Forth Railway bridge of the 1880s in Scotland. The early 1890s saw the steel-framed skyscrapers in Chicago, such as the Reliance Building. Should not these new materials and means of construction express themselves and form the aesthetic of the building they created rather than be obscured or denied by a veneer of increasingly irrelevant history-derived ornament or proportional systems? It was a good question and was increasingly asked by many, especially when such structures as the Forth Bridge abandoned history and made the ruthless and honest expression of its technology of construction its primary ornament.

In 1892 the young North American architect Louis Sullivan – later to be termed one of the early fathers of the skyscraper – wrote a seminal article entitled 'Ornament in Architecture' in the *Engineering Magazine*. In it he stated that 'a building quite devoid of ornament may convey a noble and dignified sentiment by virtue of mass and proportion' and argued that 'it could be greatly for our aesthetic good' to produce buildings that are 'comely in the nude'. Sullivan developed this idea in an article published in 1896 in *Lippincott's Monthly Magazine*, where he made a statement that was to become one of the theoretical principles of twentieth-century Modernism: '... form ever follows function'. In this view there was no room for superficial history-based ornament. Instead Sullivan argued for a new type of organic ornament that almost grew out of the structure.

Under the influence of Sullivan, the Vienna-based architect Adolf Loos published an article in 1908 entitled 'Ornament and Crime'. Loos's article can be seen as anticipating an aspect of early twentieth-century Modernism defined by functionalism, minimalism and the machine-age aesthetic. However, it was a little more complex than this. As with Sullivan's writing, Loos's article was not an attack on ornament as such but just on 'illegitimate' or 'degenerate' ornament derived directly from historic styles.

These ideas were developed in a forceful manner immediately after the First World War by Le Corbusier in France and in Germany by Mies van der Rohe and Walter Gropius. In 1919 Gropius became director of the highly influential Bauhaus school of design, and architect of its functionalist and seminal new building, completed in 1926.

In Chelsea the seemingly unlikely initial breeding ground for the new aesthetic was 213 King's Road. Unlikely because it is one of a pair, with adjoining 215, of modest brick-built terrace houses constructed, behind generous front gardens, in about 1720 (see page 102). In 1926, however, number 213 was acquired by Syrie Maugham, who was then a newly successful interior designer starting to introduce a pioneering sense of minimalism into an interior world still cluttered with the ornamental debris of Victorian and Edwardian taste.

Maugham is a strange character. She was the daughter of Thomas Barnardo, the self-promotional showman of a philanthropist and an astute professional fundraiser who, in the 1860s, launched a charity to care for destitute children. In 1901 – at the age of twenty-two – Syrie had married the forty-eight-year old industrialist and pharmaceuticals tycoon Henry Wellcome. However, she was to prove an unfaithful wife and after becoming pregnant in 1915 with a lover's child, divorced Wellcome to marry the lover. The lover was the novelist W. Somerset Maugham.

Syrie had been toying with interior decoration as a pastime since 1910 but after her marriage to Maugham in 1917 she set about turning her interest into a serious career. She opened a shop at 85 Baker Street in 1922 and by 1930 had additional shops in New York and Chicago. As her business was taking off she decided to make as big a splash as possible with her new home in the early Georgian 213 King's Road. She beavered away and in 1927 had a grand unveiling with maximum publicity. It was a great success.

With a sense for visual drama, Maugham had left a small entrance lobby inside the front door of the modest house to beguile visitors, then, turning right and through a door on to a gallery, the interior of the modest house suddenly became the saloon of a country mansion. She removed the floor so that basement and ground floor became one lofty double-height volume, and had pushed out the rear wall to create a surprising sense of space. She clearly had

111. Above
A living room decorated in shades of white by
Syrie Maugham. Dated c. 1933 and alleged to
be inside her Chelsea home on the King's Road.

little regard for the Georgian structure but the surprise was baroque in its theatricality and grandeur, and spatially echoed some of the quality of Chelsea's late nineteenth-century studio houses (see page 188). All this did much to anticipate – and promote – the multi-use, open-plan of the modern home. However, the unexpected sense of space was not the only surprise. Far from it. Eschewing the traditions and conventions of grand interiors, Maugham had painted the interior only in white, or rather in subtle shades of white. She must have seen the surreal possibilities of this scheme because, to further stun and confuse the observer, she had dipped fabrics in white plaster so they possessed an unnatural stillness. In his dark, decadent and seminal Symbolist novel À rebours (Against Nature), published in 1884, Joris-Karl Huysmans had experimented with rooms of many strange colours, including black. Maugham now gave the world the totally white interior, enhanced at the opening by containing mostly white objects, notably huge arrangements of white flowers.

The artistic possibilities of simple white-painted interiors had been explored earlier by Arts and Crafts architects working under the influence of minimalist Japanese art and of seventeenth-century Dutch lime-washed rooms of the sort shown in most of Johannes Vermeer's paintings of interiors. Indeed, the shock of the white had reverberated around Chelsea almost seventy years earlier when local artist James McNeill Whistler had, in 1863, exhibited his Symphony in White, No. 1 showing his then mistress, the red haired Joanna Hiffernan, dressed all in white, holding a white lily, in a white draped room and standing on a pale coloured wolf skin. However, these earlier representations of white interiors were not accompanied by the publicity-seeking showmanship displayed by Syrie Maugham. The world – or rather the world of interior decoration and of elite Chelsea fashion that had been invited to the opening – was most

satisfactorily stunned by her evocation of a white world.

Within her exclusive sphere of decoration the ambitious Syrie Maugham became a phenomenon. As Cecil Beaton observed, 'with the strength of a typhoon she blew all colour before her', and in 1930 she decorated the gothic revival Fort Belvedere in Windsor for the Prince of Wales (see Malcolm Burr, Chelsea Society Report for 2014, pp. 43–7).

The Maughams divorced in 1928. In all likelihood he could not stand their home – much too showy in its painful simplicity, almost vulgar. Syrie died in 1955, at which time the house came into the possession of the film director Sir Carol Reed.

Syrie Maugham's radical transformation of the interior of 213 King's Road, despite being hidden to most and so limited in its influence, formed the hinterland for the revolution of taste that was to take dramatic expression in Chelsea during the following ten years. The physical extent of the revolution was small but the works were, in their ideas, big and extremely influential. The first more public expression of the coming storm was modest – deceptively so perhaps – and can be still seen today in Chelsea Square.

Architect Oliver Hill was a friend of Syrie Maugham, and is said by some sources to have worked for her on the adaptation of 213 King's Road. He was no doubt present at the revelatory opening of the house. In 1930 he was commissioned to design number 40 Chelsea Square. Hill was soon to become the leading light of a particularly British brand of Modernism that was formed by Art Deco with its simple, abstract, classically derived ornament being combined with the simplicity of the flat-roofed, white-box architecture that had been promoted vigorously from the early 1920s by Le Corbusier. Hill's most characterful works are the Surrey country house Joldwynds, completed in 1932 for the eminent lawyer named Lord Greene, that was white-painted, abstract and curvaceous with a glazed staircase bay, and the Midland Hotel, Morecombe of 1933, also with a glazed staircase bay and dramatic, curved façade. Curiously, with these buildings Hill had contrived to produce Modernism without its social message or its morality about the honest expression of materials or means of construction. He had reduced Modernism to a mere style. And the style he had chosen as his guiding light for his Chelsea Square building was significantly different.

In the late 1920s and early 1930s Le Corbusier and the Bauhaus were not the only inspirations for young architects with modernising tendencies. An alternative influence was Scandinavian minimalist stripped classicism, sometime known at the time as 'Swedish Grace'. This was modern in its simplicity yet with a cultural connection to the classical traditions. The most able exponent of this Nordic variation of classicism was Erik Gunnar Asplund, famed in 1930 for his Stockholm Public Library, begun in 1922, with a reading room of vast cylindrical form and doors of primitive Grecian type set in rendered and colour-washed elevations. Hill had visited the Stockholm Fair in 1930, which was a significant cultural moment in inter-war Europe, promoting functional design and the public benefits of the machine-ethos and mass production. Asplund had been one of the leading architects for the fair, working in a stripped-down functionalist manner that marked a move from the neo-classicism of the library to the more overt Modernism that marks his later works.

Hill had evidently been impressed by what he saw and seems to have taken Asplund's stripped classical manner – modern yet rooted in history – as the appropriate model for a new house in the traditional urban setting of Chelsea Square that had been laid out in 1812 and then known as Trafalgar Square (see page 109). So he designed a freestanding pedimented pavilion simple in form and detail and painted white in the Modernistic manner but with clear references to the work of Edwin Lutyens, who Hill greatly admired and who had helped him launch his architectural career. Four years later, in 1934, Hill designed the adjoining 41 Chelsea Square. Despite his embrace of flat-roofed Art Deco Modernism that had taken place between these two projects – best exemplified by Joldwynds – with number 41 Hill remained true to the classical tradition. Like number 40, this house is also pedimented and painted white, but its planning is more daringly modern, with a cruciform plan and with one of the 'wings' flanking the pedimented entrance pavilion being, in fact, a screen wall concealing an inner court. Both houses are best when seen from their gardens but, alas, this viewpoint is not available to all.

This pair of buildings, essentially traditional, well mannered and merely fluttering around the perimeter of Modernism, are immensely small beer in comparison to what happened next in Chelsea.

In the same year that Hill started to work on number 40, a young architect named William Crabtree set up office in Chelsea. His story is odd in the extreme. He produced only one building of significance during his lifetime – and that at the very start of his career – but it was to be, and to remain, one of the outstanding monuments in Britain of pre-war, functionalist Modernism.

The building is the Peter Jones department store, at the junction of Sloane Square and the King's Road, and to understand the oddness and the unconventional nature of the pioneering qualities of Crabtree's design, it is necessary to understand the unconventional nature of his client.

112. Above
The west-facing garden elevation of 41 Chelsea
Square, designed in 1934 by Oliver Hill and no
doubt inspired by the contemporary fashion for
'Swedish Grace' that he had experienced during
his 1930 trip to Stockholm. The photograph was
taken in 1935.

Peter Jones, a Welsh draper, had established a store on Sloane Square in 1877, stretched across several buildings leased from the Cadogan Estate. In 1905 Jones's business was taken over by John Lewis, which had started on Oxford Street in 1864 as a drapery store but had expanded into an American-style department store as introduced to Britain by Selfridges. In 1914 John Spedan Lewis – the elder son of John Lewis – took over Peter Jones as his personal project and it was he, who in 1929, after his father's death, revolutionised the company – and, to a degree, retailing in Britain – when he initiated a more egalitarian system of management throughout John Lewis, making all employees 'partners' in the business and sharing profits. Thus, the John Lewis Partnership was born.

When in the late 1920s Spedan Lewis contemplated rebuilding and expanding Peter Jones, it was inevitable that he would turn to Modernism. They were natural bedfellows. During the 1920s, in continental Europe at least, many had come to regard Modernism as not only aesthetically and technically progressive but also representative of 'progressive' social and political aspirations. It was viewed as an architecture with a social message and purpose, an architecture liberated from associations with traditional social hierarchies and from ornament and history. Modernism in the right hands – brave architects and enlightened clients not afraid to use new technologies – was, some believed, capable of the mass-production of bright, elegant, functional and hygienic homes, places of work and stores; indeed of entire city quarters, all fit for purpose. There were of course, in England in particular, many with traditional artistic tastes and conservative social attitudes who viewed continental Modernism with deep suspicion. John Spedan Lewis was not one of them. In March 1970 Crabtree was interviewed by the *Architects' Journal* about the making of the Peter Jones store and confirmed that 'Speedan [sic] Lewis, the chairman, was the prime mover' (*Architects' Journal*, 'Historic Pioneers' by Sam Lambert, 11 March 1970, pp. 595–7). Crabtree began research work for the John Lewis Partnership on 1 January 1930, appointed because 'I had done a thesis on department stores at Liverpool where Reilly was teaching.' Charles Herbert Reilly, head of the Liverpool School of Architecture when Crabtree was a student in the 1920s, was a forceful promoter of international Modernism. He built up a strong and loyal following among many of his students, and brought in well-known Modernist architects to lecture, such as Erich Mendelsohn who visited the school at least twice. One of Reilly's early students was Maxwell Fry, who was to leave his mark on Chelsea soon after work started on Peter Jones.

According to Crabtree, 'it was due to Reilly the thing got off the ground. He was a great talker and backed me up in the design.' This is something of an understatement. In 1928 Lewis had organised an introduction to Reilly and appointed him architectural advisor to Peter Jones. It was Reilly who recommended his former pupil for the job, no doubt on the basis of his thesis and a final year project for the design of a department store on Oxford Street (see Alan Powers's essay in *Cadogan & Chelsea: The Making of a Modern Estate*, pp. 155–6). However, even with Reilly's involvement Lewis remained cautious about the practical ability of his protégé. He insisted that Crabtree – still only in his twenties – team up with a firm of established architects, so he worked not just under the wing of Reilly but with Slater & Moberly, who had some experience working on large stores. In 1933 Spedan Lewis had secured agreement from the Cadogan Estate to rebuild the Peter Jones store in three unified stages, and by 1934 the designs had been completed. They were, for their time and place, remarkable. As Crabtree remembered in 1970, 'we were pioneering

and we had to work it out from first principles. This was the first curtain wall building anywhere....' Crabtree is getting carried away here. The term 'curtain wall' is imprecise but is generally taken to refer to the elevation of a building in which the main load-bearing role is performed by a structural frame, be it of wrought iron, steel or steel-reinforced concrete. In such buildings the outer skin is like a curtain drawn around the structural frame and with no role beyond keeping out the weather, supporting itself and being as fireproof and secure as possible. Usually such façades – relieved of a major structural or loadbearing role – have been extensively glazed to let light flood inside.

The first phase of Peter Jones was completed in 1936, and in June 1939 the building was assessed by *The Architectural Review (AR)*, a most prestigious cultural publication of international significance, which admired the functional success of the building achieved by the rational application of modern building technology. In 1923 Le Corbusier had proclaimed in his influential book *Vers une Architecture* (retitled *Towards a New Architecture* in the 1927 English translation) that 'une maison est une machine-a-habiter' (a house is a machine for living in). The new Peter Jones was a machine in which to shop. As the *AR* observed, in the modern department store the 'primary requirement' in planning 'is the ability [to] permit any number of different arrangements of its selling space, with equal ease of access at all times'. In addition to 'flexibility of sales areas', the *AR* noted the need for 'natural lighting and ventilation wherever possible' to make a deep plan attractive, and the economic necessity 'to make use of as much floor space as possible'. These aims were achieved to the *AR*'s satisfaction by the use of a minimal structural frame of steel that allowed flexibility and adaptability of plan, and the 'tight-skin' of the generously glazed form of curtain wall that stretched around the building, slightly cantilevered out from the structural frame to let light flood in and to maximise usable floor area. The *AR* concluded that Peter Jones made 'a mature contribution to modern architecture' (*The Architectural Review*, June 1939, pp. 291–8).

The store's tall and curvaceous but essentially blank and certainly repetitive glassy façade must have been a shock to most Londoners, especially the laymen who were used to department stores looking more like the be-columned Selfridges, ornamental and full of historic references. However, if the case, the shock does not appear to have been generally unpleasant, at least according to the *Architects' Journal*, that in January 1939 (see also *Architects' Journal*, 9 February 1939, p. 233) asked its readers 'for names of well-known people in whose judgement of architecture they would have confidence' and then to 'ask each of those thus nominated to list the six recent British buildings which they considered of the greatest merit'. Thirty-six celebrities were invited to participate, all non-architects, including Kenneth Clarke and Charles Laughton, the popular actor. The *AJ* published the results in May 1939. Of the thirty-six people asked, fifteen nominated Peter Jones as the new building of 'greatest merit', which was far more votes than any other building received (*Architects' Journal*, 25 May 1939 pp. 851–62). The store numbered among its champions John Betjeman, Lord Berners ('composer, artist, connoisseur'), Osbert Lancaster, James Lees-Milne (representing the National Trust), Henry Moore, John Piper, Herbert Read (author and critic) and Rebecca West (journalist, critic, travel writer and long-time companion of H.G. Wells).

Peter Jones has stood the test of time. Its precocious sense of modernity in 1936 and its machine-like but sensible functionality has not yet aged, although the huge extent of its external glazing was probably not necessary, nor entirely practical. More to the point, however, it is still doing the job it was designed to do (admittedly after a number of major overhauls) and it continues to look almost shockingly modern, if in a slightly bizarre way. In 1970 Crabtree told the *AJ* that he thought the building had done 'moderately well' but was 'just a bit coarse and clumsy in places' (*Architects' Journal*, 11 March 1970, pp. 596–7). He is right, of course. The bronze vertical mullions of semi-circular section set between windows, presumably intended to counteract the horizontal emphasis of the strips of glazing, now look a trifle out of place because such curtain-walling exercises became much slicker after this early effort. On the other hand, this ornamental and slightly Art Deco detail, combined with the building's double curve as it hugs the street line – indeed the determined way in which it reinforces rather than degrades the established street frontage – gives Peter Jones individual character, an admirable urban presence and even a sense of charm rarely found in Modernist buildings of its generation.

As the construction of the first phase of Peter Jones was nearing completion, some of the protagonists in its story and influences in its making appeared on the streets of Chelsea. Again Reilly appears to have played the key if shady role of the *éminence grise*. Erich Mendelsohn – who Reilly had invited to Liverpool to lecture and whose Columbushaus in Berlin had so influenced Crabtree and the design of Peter Jones – arrived in London in the spring of 1933, having fled his native Germany and increasingly intolerant Nazi regime. Mendelsohn was then aged forty-six and at the height of his creative powers but suddenly his successful architectural career seemed to have stalled, his assets seized by the Nazis and his name removed from the German Architects' Union. He had to find work in this new county and fast. Almost upon arrival he formed an architectural practice with Serge Chermayeff, aged thirty-three and Russian in origin but who had lived in Britain since a child.

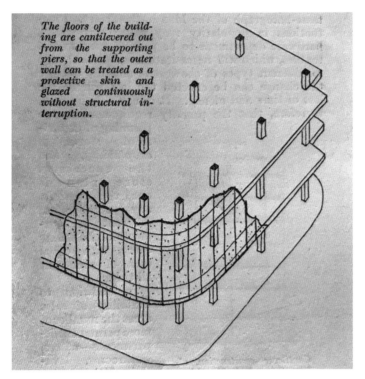

The floors of the building are cantilevered out from the supporting piers, so that the outer wall can be treated as a protective skin and glazed continuously without structural interruption.

113. Far Left
The King's Road elevation of Peter Jones, built in phases after 1934 to the design of William Crabtree with C.H. Reilly and Slater & Moberly. Particularly striking is the sinuous form of the store's extensively glazed curtain as it hugs the line on King's Road as it turns into Sloane Square.

114. Left
Illustration of the store's curtain wall construction from the *Architectural Review* of June 1939.

115. Below
Peter Jones store under construction in August 1935, showing the steel frame construction that allowed an open interior and a flexible and adaptable plan.

Berlin. Potsdamer Platz - Columbushaus.

Syrie Maugham's transformation of the interior of 213 King's Road ... formed the hinterland for the revolution of taste that was to take dramatic expression in Chelsea.

116. Above
The Columbushaus, Berlin, completed in 1932 to the designs of Erich Mendelsohn, was an office and shop complex that stood on Potsdamer Platz. The building had a profound influence on Crabtree. It was demolished in 1957.

Their partnership was brief but together they designed a number of significant Modernist buildings in England, including the De La Warr Pavilion in Bexhill, built in 1935, and number 64 Old Church Street, Chelsea.

The Old Church Street client was a publisher named Denis Cohen who wanted to construct an architecturally progressive house in Chelsea, tailored to his family's particular requirements and which would make the most of the site that had a large garden to its east. In 1935 he commissioned Mendelsohn and Chermayeff to realise this brief.

However, there was another element to this project. Cohen's cousin was Benn Wolfe Levy, a future Labour MP, playwright and screenwriter, and he bought the adjoining house, numbered 66 Old Church Street. Originally all the land, including that fronting on to Chelsea Square, had belonged to one house. Levy also wanted to construct a new house – along the same broad lines as his cousin – with the pair agreeing, in line with the Modernist principle of 'collective' living, to unite and share their gardens. In 1935 Levy commissioned Walter Gropius and his young English friend and partner Maxwell Fry. At the time Gropius was an architect of huge reputation. He had designed major and pioneering buildings before the First World War and had served in the German army during the war. In 1919 he had been appointed director of the epoch-making Bauhaus design school in Dassau and in 1925 designed its new building, again with a form of curtain walling. In 1934 Gropius fled the Nazis and, with the help of Fry, made his way to England.

Both houses were on site by late 1935 and both were completed in 1936. It is fascinating to speculate about the connection between these buildings and Peter Jones, the first phase of which was also nearing completion in 1935. Reilly, after all, knew Mendelsohn and had taught Fry. There must have been site visits, discussions and advice offered. Alas, nothing – as far as we know – was recorded, and no traces of crosscurrents left behind.

That these progressive, artistic, ambitious and successful individuals should choose to employ such renowned Modernist architects is easy to understand. They had been washed ashore in Britain by brutal times and despite international reputations were finding it hard to win commissions, which explains why they took these relatively modest jobs. We know little about the personal relations that developed between the families and their architects. Levy was a glamorous figure – he had been a screenwriter for Alfred Hitchcock and in 1933 married the famed American-British film star Constance Cummings, who played a key role in the evolution of the brief for the house. We do not know if Gropius was impressed with all this. He probably bonded more with Levy over their shared experiences, albeit from different sides, of the ardours of trench life during the Great War.

The houses make an interesting pair. Both were built largely of brick, but rendered and painted white so many people assumed they utilised the modern technology of reinforced concrete construction. Their white façades appear to proclaim these houses the progeny of Le Corbusier's 'white box' architecture of the 1920s – notably the Villa Savoye at Poissy, France of 1929 – which would suggest that they reflect his belief that a house should be a machine for living in. They are, in fact, far more subtle. For example, the white façades can be read as a reference to Chelsea's stuccoed Regency and early Victorian architecture, and their relationship to the garden is in the tradition of the English picturesque, with houses organised to offer the most favourable prospects. A key strategy in the co-ordinated planning of these two houses is that they are set at right angles to each other to maximise the potential of the site and garden. Both, in their internal planning and in their external details – such as balconies, viewing platforms and terraces – favour the garden. This is reasonable but means that the more utilitarian elevations – especially that of the Mendelsohn and Chermayeff house (number 64) that stretches its full width along Old Church Street – are presented to public view, while the best elevations are concealed and essentially for family enjoyment only. This, while nice for the clients, did the public no favours, nor has it done much for the reputations of these buildings. A common criticism is that number 64 looks industrial, or perhaps like a small school. The somewhat unprepossessing street presence of this pair of houses probably explains why the Mendelsohn and Chermayeff house received no votes from eminent laymen in the 1939 *Architects' Journal* survey to identify buildings of 'merit', while the Gropius and Fry house received only one. This was from Anthony Bertram, author and art and design historian who in 1935 had written a book that rather reveals his preference. It is entitled *The House: A Machine for Living In*.

A more intriguingly titled Bertram book, published in 1937, is *Ode to a Bulging Member* (*Architects' Journal*, 25 May 1939, pp. 851–62).

Internally, both houses display the usual concerns of Modernist architects and their clients. Main floors with open and adaptable plans make much use of double doors or sliding partitions, there are long vistas through the house, large windows let light flood in and offer pleasing prospects, and large and modern kitchens are placed in convenient locations.

Both houses were published in the *Architectural Review* in November 1936. The magazine was enthusiastic in its written description that – no doubt inadvertently – reveals a disparity in 1930s Chelsea between egalitarian orientated Modernist architecture and modern privileged middle-class life.

Of the Gropius and Fry house we are told it was designed as 'accommodation for parents and three children, a butler and two or three maid servants' and that 'the living rooms are well lighted by large sliding windows' (*AR*, November 1936, p. 249). Of the Mendelsohn and Chermayeff house the salient point the *AR* makes is that 'the accommodation includes a squash court, with its playing floor below ground level so that an extension to the dining-room becomes a spectators' gallery'. This is perhaps more Hollywood then Chelsea, and possibly an indication of a commitment to healthy and sporty 'collective' living, although it is doubtful if the court was open to the wider community of Old Church Street.

The architects' engagement with the construction of these houses was probably minimal. Even before he become involved in the design of the Cohen House, Mendelsohn – ambitious and thrusting – had rekindled his relationship with Chaim Weizmann, later the first President of Israel,

and by early 1934 had started to work on projects in Palestine for Weizmann. In 1935, while 64 Old Church Street was on site, he opened an office in Jerusalem, although it was not until 1938 that he gave up practice in London and moved to Jerusalem full time. He managed to create some highly significant buildings in Palestine, but was soon disillusioned and disappointed. In 1941 he moved to the United States, settling comfortably in California where, as far as we know, he gave little or no thought to his Chelsea creation.

Walter Gropius stuck it out in England a little longer but with war looming and commissions hard to secure, departed in early 1937, also choosing the United States for his new home and place of work.

In 1970 Benn Levy reflected on the making of 66 Old Church Street, that he still occupied. It was, he said, '... a first rate house to live in ... a pioneering job in its day', but rather ruefully conceded that because 'a great deal of the structure and material was experimental and not always wholly successful [t]he point has now arrived where pretty radical repair work has to be done if the building is to be saved'. However, Levy did not seek to blame Gropius or Fry: 'We were ... willing guinea pigs and we went into it with our eyes open' (*Architects' Journal*, 11 March 1970, p. 596).

Maxwell Fry, pondering the adventure of 1930s Modernism in general terms, admitted in 1970 that it was 'more notable for courage than discretion in its use of materials', and that, 'as with all revolutionary movements you had to make a noticeable break with the past' (*Architects' Journal*, 11 March 1970, p. 596).

The consequences of this 'not ... wholly successful' experimentation with structure and materials, and the triumph of courage over discretion, has – in the long term – had serious consequences for these two houses.

117. Top
64 Old Church Street (right foreground),
designed by Erich Mendelsohn and Serge
Chermayeff, with, in the distance, number 66
designed by Walter Gropius and Max Fry. Both
houses were completed in 1936. The ground-
floor windows on number 64 light the kitchen
and the first-floor windows light bathrooms,
the staircase and the maid's bedroom.

118. Above
The garden elevation of number 66, with large
windows lighting the dining room, living room
and main first-floor bedroom and study.

119. Left
Curvaceous corner detail of 66 Old Church
Street. The window lights the 'day nursery'
with a door opening on to a first-floor terrace.

They were both listed by the government in 1970 as buildings of historic or architectural interest, and correct too. Since then the Mendelsohn and Chermayeff house has been kept in very good order and near authentic condition, still painted a crisp white, but with a conservatory added at its south end. By contrast, the Gropius and Fry house is virtually unrecognisable. Levy was right to worry about its future but presumably the 'radical repairs' that have been carried out are not quite what he had in mind. The upper-level viewing gallery has been walled over and the entire building clad in what looks like grey-coloured artificial slates.

There are salutary and somewhat conflicting lessons here about 1930s Modernism in Chelsea. The pair of houses on Old Church Street continue to look alien because their back-to-front arrangement – with their service uses and rear elevations pushed on to the street – contradict Chelsea's long-established urban tradition of presenting best elevations to the main frontage. Even buildings as intimate as private houses do have public faces, and these really do need to be presentable and legible. Surely these eminent architects knew this. Interestingly, Peter Jones, although almost equally Modernist, does not have this problem because it holds the edge of the streets and relates to its neighbours, has a lively ground floor and does most certainly present its best face to the public. And, of course, Oliver Hill's two houses, which in fact back on to 64 and 66 Old Church Street, have no problem at all fitting in because, although modern in certain respects, their pediments and spare classical detail made them instantly a part of Chelsea's established architectural character. Modernism with a human face and with a dash of Art Deco panache. They were never truly cutting edge but were, and remain, much admired.

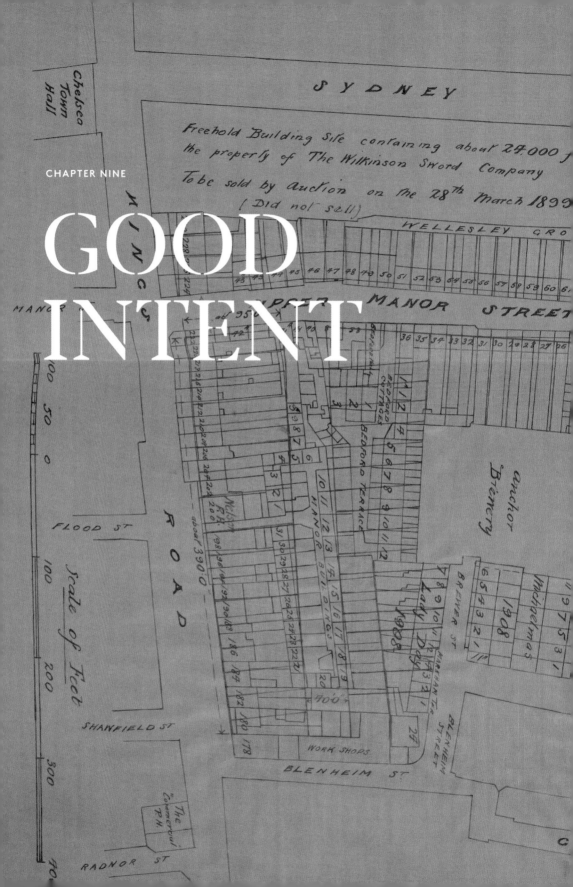

GOOD INTENT

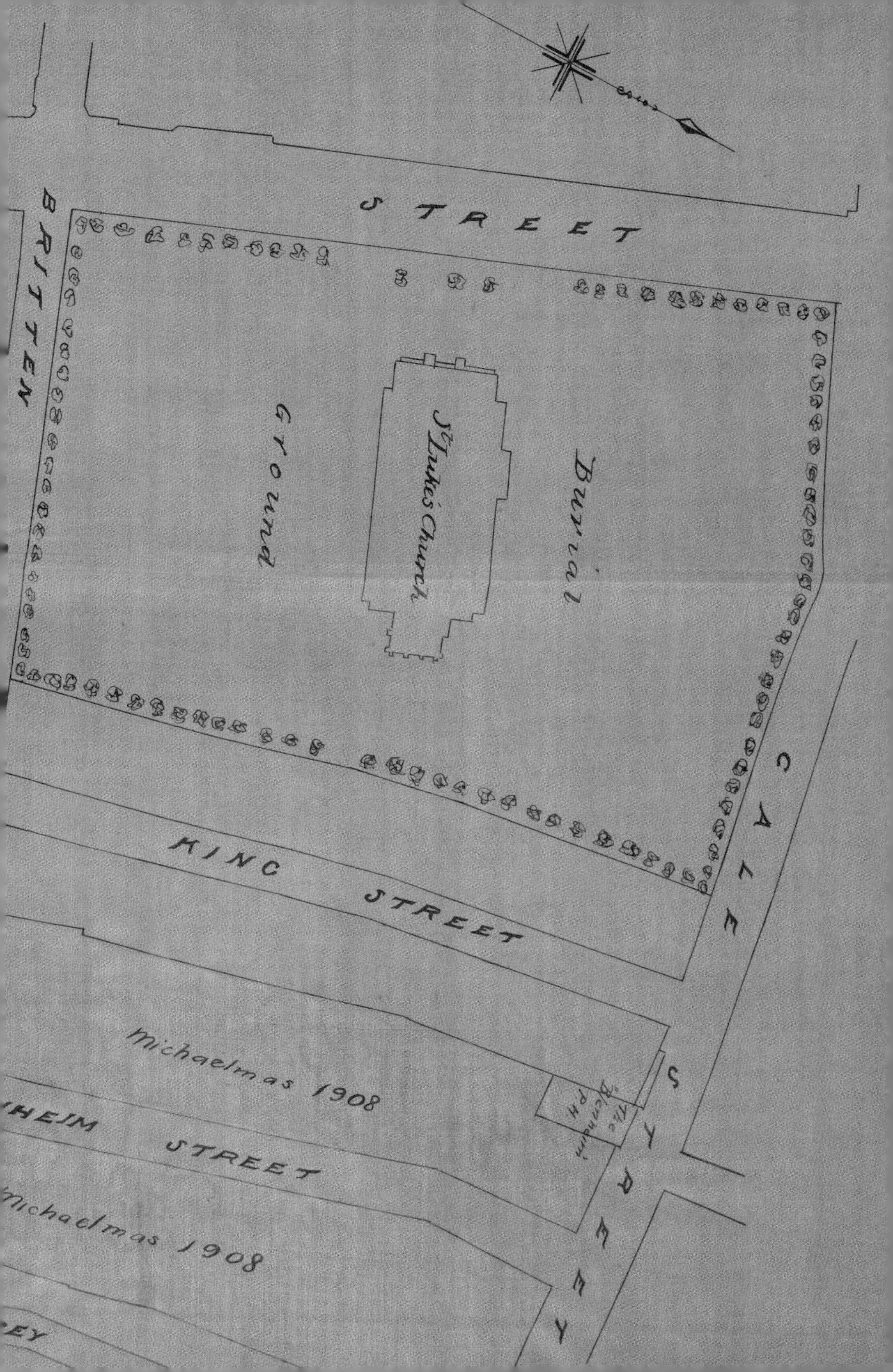

STREET

BRITTEN

Ground

St Luke's Church

Burial

CALE

KING STREET

Michaelmas 1908

STREET

NHEJM STREET

The Reading Rm

Michaelmas 1908

EY

Running through Chelsea's history is the continuous thread of stewardship in the hands of the Lord of the Manor. Born out of the duties and responsibilities imposed by the traditional system of land ownership is a paternalistic care for the wellbeing of the community, as well as the environment and character of the area.

120. Left
The Vestry Hall, King's Road, designed for
the Metropolitan Vestry of Chelsea in a fine
Italianate style by William Wilmer Pocock.
The building opened in 1860. This photograph
was taken soon after 1900.

When in 1712 Sir Hans Sloane purchased Chelsea Manor House – called Chelsea Place – and its grounds from Charles Cheyne (see page 46) he was not just buying real estate. He was also buying civic power and status, for along with ownership of the manor house and its lands went possession of the Lordship of the Manor of Chelsea.

The rank of Lord of the Manor dates from the Anglo-Saxon feudal world and carried with it certain rights and powers. However, it also brought with it responsibilities, some religious or charitable in nature, and an obligation of service and loyalty to those higher in the feudal hierarchy as well as a duty of care to those below.

In the Middle Ages the Lord of the Manor could be a tenant-in-chief if he held the manor directly from the Crown or a 'mesne' (intermediate) lord if he was the vassal of another, higher lord. In either case the Lord of the Manor would generally function as head of his own fiefdom within his own enclosed world, owing allegiance to the greater lords above while ruling the lives of those within his power. Almost invariably he would control the largest amount of land within his manor, including the 'demesne'– wood and parkland used for his own pleasure – and with much of the manor's population being his tenants of various types.

The Lord of the Manor would also usually have control over the rights of usage of the Common Land within the manor and over the tenants' rights to exercise certain privileges, notably their use of the Common Land, their rights to collect firewood or building wood, and the degree to which they might live off the land. In addition, the Lord of the Manor had the responsibility to impose the law of the land and the power to adjudicate in disputes and, as a vassal, was obliged to raise levies of peasant soldiers or taxes from his manor lands when required.

The manorial powers had, of course, to coexist with other powers, both spiritual and temporal. Primarily there was the church. The boundary of the manor might be contained within the boundaries of a single parish, or it might overlap several parishes. And the parishes were within a diocese. Parish and diocese could assert great power and pressure within a manor, not least of which was economic power with the right for the church to collect tithes – meaning one tenth – of the valuable products or wealth created within the parish. Temporal powers included not just those of the royal court, but also the county or urban authorities within which the parish might be located. This meant, for example, that more serious legal cases were heard and decided not

121. Above
The south elevation of the 1886 Vestry Room or
Town Hall extension designed in a splendid neo-
Baroque manner by J.M. Brydon. The pediment-
topped and pilastered elevation distinguishes
Brydon's most handsome municipal great hall.

in the Lord of the Manor's court in his great hall or more latterly by justices of the peace in petty sessions, but in the Courts of Assize and of Quarter Session. The title of Thomas Richardson's 1769 map of Cadogan-owned buildings in Chelsea is revealing. Richardson had been, according to Thomas Faulkner, the 'Steward to the Lord of the Manor' – the Earl Cadogan – and he chose to describe his map as depicting the 'Estate and Manor of Chelsea'. This suggests the two were synonymous and both within the overarching power of the 'County of Middlesex'. Usually the relationship between overlapping powers was subtle and modulated by tradition. For example, while the Lord of the Manor might be subservient to the power of the church, he very often possessed the advowson of the parish churches or chapels within his manor, which meant he had the power to recommend – in practice, appoint – clergymen to these livings. So, through the power of patronage, the Lord of the Manor's influence in church affairs could be tremendous. This was the case in Chelsea.

The Manor of Chelsea

The powers and functions of the Manor of Chelsea are recorded in some detail. From the twelfth century the feudal overlord for the Manor was Westminster Abbey (see page 153), and it is known that in the fourteenth century the 'leet' – the manorial court that dealt with feudal rights and obligations and not criminal acts – elected two constables, two 'headboroughs' (broadly speaking eminent men of property residing in the manor who were responsible for administration and the application of its laws) and two 'aletasters' (no doubt a pleasurable but also most important post ensuring that the ale made and sold in the manor was not watery or adulterated). In 1379 a bailiff was also mentioned.

Most of these posts continued into the nineteenth century. The relationship between the manor and the parish evolved in Chelsea in the post-medieval period, as it did on the periphery of all cities, which invariably had their own municipal charters defining their rights and powers. By the beginning of the nineteenth century the parish had in Chelsea – as generally elsewhere – long been the dominant power and the key unit of local government. Vestrymen (usually eligible property owners in the parish who gained office through appointment or through election by their peers) had the power to impose and raise local taxes, and duty to watch, light and cleanse the streets, and to appoint and pay parish officers. The vestry room of the parish church had, to all intents and purposes, the function of a town hall, with vestrymen working through various sub-committees.

In London the situation changed significantly after the mid-nineteenth century. The Metropolitan Local Management Act of 1855 created the concept of 'inner London' and set up the Metropolitan Board of Works (MBW). The MBW was given powers to oversee strategic road construction and infrastructure throughout 'inner London' – as, for example, expressed through the construction of Chelsea Embankment and related developments such as Tite Street (see page 183) – that overrode the authority of the vestries and lingering manorial rights. In Chelsea this led to the creation of a Metropolitan Vestry, which inherited the powers of the traditional vestry but with added responsibilities.

Notable among these was the responsibility for public health, which became a major preoccupation in the nineteenth century as the understanding of the spread of contagious disease grew along with urban populations. The parish as overseen by the Metropolitan Vestry was divided into four wards: Stanley, Church, Royal Hospital and Hans Town, with sixty elected vestrymen. In 1894 Church ward was divided for the creation of Cheyne ward. The rector and churchwardens were ex officio members of the vestry, and the vestry elected the parish's representatives on the MBW. By 1856 the Metropolitan Vestry had appointed a clerk, surveyor, foreman of the roads and medical officer of health. Four main committees were set up and in 1856 the vestry met 130 times. The vestrymen were mainly shopkeepers and tradesmen who were anxious to serve (*Victoria County History*, pp. 210–17).

The first meetings of the Metropolitan Vestry were held in the vestry room of St Luke's parish church but this proved impossibly inconvenient and the Vestry, enlarged in size, was obliged in 1856 to build its own Vestry Room. In 1857 it acquired a leasehold on part of Manor Terrace – a gift from Lord Cadogan – on the south side of the King's Road, looking along Robert Street, now Sydney Street. The building was to contain offices for the clerk, surveyor and medical officer, committee rooms, a hall, a hall-keeper's apartment, a fire-proof store room and cellarage. The building was designed, in an Italianate style, by William Wilmer Pocock and completed in 1860.

However, all did not go well. By 1885 the Vestry Room had become structurally unsound – clearly a major problem had occurred during construction when the builder went bankrupt – and in 1886 the vestry was obliged to repair or substantially rebuild it and at the same time add a larger hall and more offices to the south. The new buildings were designed by J.M. Brydon, with the hall being particularly handsome (see page 199). In 1906 the Vestry Hall, by then commonly called the Town Hall, was demolished and by 1908 replaced by the existing Old Town Hall. The 1886 hall and offices, with splendid Baroque-style elevations to the south, were retained (*Victoria County History*, pp. 210–17).

The 1888 Local Government Act created the County of London and the London

County Council (LCC), a strategic authority responsible for London as a whole. However, perhaps the most dramatic change came in 1899 with the London Government Act, which came into force in November 1900. This created Metropolitan Boroughs, which shared functions and powers with the LCC. The new boroughs, with democratically elected councillors, replaced Metropolitan Vestries as mechanisms of local government, along with various boards, such as the London School Board (LSB) that since 1870 had responsibility for school building in London. Some of the functions fulfilled by the boards were absorbed into the new boroughs, others into the LCC with the LSB's responsibilities passing in 1902 to local education authorities. The new Metropolitan Borough of Chelsea had six aldermen and thirty-six councillors representing the same five wards as the Metropolitan Vestry.

The story of these evolving and emerging civic powers is very much part of the history of Chelsea and of its Lord of the Manor. When the Metropolitan Borough of Chelsea was created in 1900, the Lord of the Manor – the 5th Earl Cadogan – became the new borough's first mayor and, in a bold gesture of civic responsibility and generosity, gave the land on the King's Road for the architecturally impressive and large-scale replacement and extension of the 1860 Vestry Hall. The new building completed in 1908 (see page 198) and incorporating the 1886 hall, is now known as the Old Town Hall.

The Cadogan family and the Lordship of the Manor of Chelsea
Through marriage and inheritance, Sir Hans Sloane's Lordship of the Manor of Chelsea passed to, and remains with, the Cadogan family. Arguably the traditions of the manorial system – with its concept of the duties and responsibilities imposed by land ownership – formed the framework within which the Cadogan Estate

evolved in the late nineteenth and early twentieth centuries. It is most revealing that the earliest surviving record book in the Cadogan Estate archives, dating from the late 1830s and documenting the 'particulars of leases', is titled 'The Manor of Chelsea', confirming that the estate and manor remained essentially the same thing. By the later nineteenth century the comparable books are titled merely 'Cadogan Estate'. The visionary 5th Earl, the man responsible for extraordinary changes that did much to transform Chelsea physically and socially in the latter nineteenth and early twentieth centuries, seems to have operated as a benevolent Lord of the Manor with an almost chivalric regard for the well-balanced exercise of power. The Earl's commission to rebuild Holy Trinity Church, Sloane Street in ethereal style, and the rebuilding and enlargement he promoted from the mid-1870s of Hans Town into an aristocratic and intensely romantic – and in many cases palatial – Renaissance revival fairy land are told in earlier chapters in this book.

However, while these architecturally and socially elevated projects were proceeding, the 5th Earl also pondered the means by which the lives of the poorer occupants of his manor, primarily those living on the Cadogan Estate, could be improved. The reasons for him to take action were numerous. The most cynical interpretation is that streets of dilapidated and desperately occupied houses in the centre of Chelsea lowered the tone of the area and undermined the value of ambitious new developments.

There is, of course, another interpretation, suggested by the Cadogan Estate Agenda and Minute Books that record in great detail the regular discussions that took place between the 5th Earl and his estate advisors, and the decisions that the Earl took. What comes across is a sense of stewardship. As proclaimed in the Old Town Hall (see page 290), the Earl seems to have

122. *Above*
George, 5th Earl Cadogan – the model of the enlightened landlord with a commitment to the well-balanced stewardship of his estate and one of London's great late Victorian philanthropists.

123. *Overleaf*
Detail of Charles Booth's 'Poverty Map' of London, as updated in 1898/9 and published alongside a revised edition of the *Life and Labour of the People in London*. Booth and his researchers walked and colour-coded the streets of London to suggest the financial and social status of the inhabitants and to imply the physical condition of their homes.

recognised that his duty, as Lord of the Manor and major local land owner, was not only to preserve and enhance the estate so that something of value would be passed on, but also to make efforts to improve the conditions for all living within the Cadogan boundary. The 5th Earl was a great tactician who looked to the long term. These same issues exercise the estate today.

Charles Booth's catalogue of poverty in Chelsea

Charles Booth, a philanthropist and social reformer, created a colour-coded 'Poverty Map' of London (see overleaf). It was first published in 1889 and revised in 1898/9 and showed there were isolated but significant areas of poverty and poor housing in Chelsea, some near the river towards the west end of Cheyne Walk (see page 79), and more north and south of the central portion of the King's Road. To the north there were streets of purple coded houses as well as some dark blue and some black along Manor Buildings running east off Upper Manor Street (now Chelsea Manor Street). And to the south, purple and light blue houses along Manor Street (now also Chelsea Manor Street), and dark blue and some black in streets off it, such as Manor Gardens (now Chelsea Manor Gardens), Alpha Street and Wellington Street. Black signified the worst streets and houses whose occupants were, according to Booth, the 'Lowest Class. Vicious, semi-criminal', while dark blue meant occupants were 'Very poor, casual. Chronic want'. Light blue streets were 'poor' while purple were 'mixed', with some households 'comfortable' but others 'poor'.

During the 1880s and 90s the Cadogan Estate evidently pondered how best to respond to the obvious hardships of many people residing either within the estate or very close to it. The obvious, broad solution was to work closely with the local authorities – until 1900 the Metropolitan Vestry in conjunction, after 1888/9, with the LCC – and with various industrial

dwelling companies. These companies were one of the wonders on nineteenth-century Britain. Their story is complex and most individual but essentially they were philanthropic organisations that worked for profit. This sounds something of a contradiction, and in a way it was. The object was to raise the money to build sound, hygienic but usually brutally economic working-class housing by borrowing money and promising lenders a return – but the return would be less than lenders might make if they put their money into less worthy causes. So the term 'five per cent philanthropy' (see J.N. Tarn, *Five per cent Philanthropy: An Account of Housing in Urban Areas between 1840 and 1919*, Cambridge: Cambridge University Press, 1974) was coined to describe this curious form of charity. Many of the dwellings companies sought to house particular sections of London's poor communities. The most obvious contribution the Cadogan Estate could make towards the pressing problem of housing the low-income working classes (if not the desperately poor and destitute) was to give land – either freehold or on long leases – for the construction of appropriate housing. This land could be given to the Vestry (and after 1900 to the Metropolitan Borough) or to industrial dwellings companies.

The issues involved were not straightforward. The gift of land of course reduced the size and value of the estate, so there were serious long-term implications to consider and – either gift or lease – the estate needed to be assured, in a legally binding manner, that the land would be used for the purpose for which the estate gave or leased it. Then there was the question of which parcels of the estate to turn over to working-class housing, and the implications for neighbouring streets of the construction of large blocks of industrial dwellings. It would seem to be best for the estate if existing poor or slum streets and houses were redeveloped, but sometimes there were complications.

THE STREETS ARE COLOURED ACCORDING TO TH

Lowest class.
Vicious, semi-criminal.

Very poor, casual.
Chronic want.

Poor. 18s. to 21s. a week
for a moderate family.

...AL CONDITION OF THE INHABITANTS. AS UNDER:—

	Fairly comfortable. Good ordinary earnings.		Middle class. Well-to-do.		Upper-middle and Upper classes. Wealthy.

...e comfortable,
...rs poor.

Perhaps leases had a long time to run, so emptying and demolishing the properties would be difficult. And it was clear that a large number of the more desperate poor squeezed into these mean streets could not be accommodated in new dwellings. This was partly due to the dilapidated nature and overcrowding of their current accommodation and the requirements of mains water and sewage systems, and because some were too poor to pay the reasonably high rents that 'five per cent philanthropy' demanded. And also there were just too many of the poor to fit into the regimented new accommodation that was proposed.

The *Victoria County History* reflects on the delicate situation. It notes that 'working-class housing was provided' in Chelsea 'by a number of agencies ... with some receiving assistance from local landowners, particularly the Cadogan Estate'. The gifts of land, were, the *VCH* observes, 'variously attributed ... to the desire to remove poor housing encumbering the estates while retaining some necessary local labour in the vicinity', and to 'guilt over displacing so many people as leases fell in'. Private estates could, if they so desired, radically change their social profile by ejecting poor or working people when their leases expired, demolishing their former homes and selling or leasing the land to aspirational speculative builders or to rich new tenants. There were no planning controls to prevent such social 'cleansing' and for ruthless or greedy landlords it must have been tempting. However, for landlords with a social conscience, with a deep-rooted connection to Chelsea and with a long-term interest in its survival as a vibrant and harmonious – and, by definition, mixed – community then such a simplistic and selfish short-term approach was not an option. The 5th Earl, as revealed by the series of discussions and decisions recorded in the Estate's Agenda and Minute Books, was the very model of the modern, enlightened landlord and

proved himself to be, all things considered, one of London's great late Victorian philanthropists who was resolved, as far as it was possible and compatible with his responsibility to safeguard the value of the estate he had inherited, to use his worldly possessions to help give working people decent homes.

The Agenda and Minute Books numbered 11, 12 and 13 and covering 7 September 1888 to 14 December 1891, in particular make fascinating reading. They not only touch on many of the main issues raised by the challenge of building 'working class housing' on the estate, but also offer a detailed 'case study' that illuminates many of the general points made by Charles Booth. His 'Poverty Map' – including Chelsea – was published at the same time as part of *Life and Labour of the People in London* (Volume 1 published 1889 and volume 2 published 1891 by Macmillan).

The Guinness Trust
An estate meeting at Chelsea House on Wednesday 5 May 1890 – attended by Earl Cadogan's surveyor and solicitor – records the discussion that took place about 'the gift to the Guinness's Trustees'. The book minutes the discussion on one page and on a facing page records the Earl's comments or decision for action, seemingly written in his own hand. The minutes record that 'the draft Conveyance of the land given to the [Guinness] Trustees was framed by Mr Wolstenholme so as to bind them to use the land as a site for Dwellings for the poorer classes for ever'. However, the Guinness Trust wanted the land conveyed to it without restrictions of use. The Earl was worried by this and replied that 'before I consent ... I should like to have a conference with the [Guinness] trustees' (Book 12, 5 May 1890, pp. 227–30). The Earl was right to be concerned. The Guinness Trust had just been formed and had, for the time being, no proven track record.

124. Above
Draycott Avenue artisan housing built in 1892 by the Guinness Trust on land made available by the Cadogan Estate and designed by Mervyn Macartney. This photograph was taken in 1950.

125. Overleaf
A delightful vernacular Baroque door surround (now framing a window), designed by Mervyn Macartney and built in 1892 as part of the Guinness Trust's Draycott Avenue housing scheme for the 'working classes'.

Charles Booth, a philanthropist and social reformer ... in 1889 ... showed there were ... significant areas of poverty and poor housing in Chelsea.

However, although a newcomer, the Guinness Trust had reassuring credentials and aims. Its founder – Sir Edward Guinness, the future 1st Earl of Iveagh and the beneficiary of brewing riches – had put £200,000 of his own money into the Trust, a truly princely sum in 1890. Its aim was to 'ameliorate the conditions of the working poor' in London and, unlike the usual industrial dwellings companies, it also attempted to help the more desperate, including the 'homeless', by making rents as low as possible. An additional £50,000 was soon put into the Trust to extend its work to Dublin. On Wednesday 13 August 1890 the matter is continued in the Agenda and Minute Book under the heading 'Gift to Sir Edward Guinness's Trustees' (Book 12, p. 325). The minutes record that 'Sir Edward Guinness's Trustees' had 'declined to accept a grant of the land offered them except ... without limitation'. It seems the Earl was satisfied, or at least reassured, by his 'conference' with the Guinness Trustees because the minutes record that 'your Lordship decided to make the Grant on the terms desired'. However, legal conditions had been hammered out, notably that in case of a subsequent sale of the land its estimated value '... should be ... appropriated to provide dwellings for the working classes in Chelsea'. The Guinness Trustees consented to this condition.

At an estate meeting a few days later, on 6 November 1890, the Earl was presented with the 'conveyance to the Trustees of Sir Edward. Guinness's Settlement of the site for the dwellings for the poorer classes given by your Lordship'. The Earl duly signed (Book 13, pp. 51–2). The Guinness Trust confirms that the 1 acre of land it acquired from the Earl was 'a free gift' and that it was to be used to provide 'dwellings for the poorer classes of the district' (see history. guinnesspartnership.com/timeline).

Minutes of an estate meeting held on 9 November 1891 (p. 311) reveal that the Guinness Trust's housing project was in Cadogan Street. Charles Booth's 1889 'Poverty Map' shows blocks of light blue near the open land where the Guinness Trust estate was to be built, with some of the streets immediately to the northwest also being coded light blue. So this was another pocket of poverty in the heart of rich and fashionable Chelsea, only a stone's throw from Cadogan Square and Lennox Gardens, both of which Booth had colour-coded gold, denoting the homes of 'Upper-middle and Upper-classes. Wealthy'. The discussion about the scheme minuted on 9 November was about 'rights of light' because the Earl had observed that 'some of the windows in the buildings now being erected by the Guinness Trustees overlook houses in Cadogan Street and will in course of time acquire rights of light at their expense' (Book 13, pp. 311–2). The Earl was ever a man for pertinent detail.

The Guinness Trust scheme consisted of eight five-storey blocks forming an estate arranged around courts and one large communal garden. The courts were entered from Draycott Avenue that was formed at the time and soon mostly lined with blocks of apartments in a belated Queen Anne Style tinged with bold Baroque detail. These were for middle-class tenants, so the Guinness Trust architecture had to fit in. Consequently the estate was reached through a large arch in a handsome red-brick block with a respectable scattering of Queen Anne detail. A large plaque, framed with palm or acanthus leaves, proclaims that this entrance block, along with the buildings beyond, are 'The Guinness Trust Buildings AD 1892'. This must have been a proud moment for the new Trust. The Draycott Avenue Estate, as the scheme was called, was only the second project it completed. The first, just a few months earlier, was in Brandon Street in Walworth.

The Draycott Avenue entrance arch is now not generally used but originally it led to a central court around which blocks were grouped in an informal manner with, to the south, blocks facing each other to define the garden. The estate contained 303 dwellings, so presumably housed around 1,000 people. By 1901 the Trust had built 2,597 homes for London's 'working class'; an impressive achievement by an enterprise that the Cadogan Estate did much to launch and to support.

Also impressive is the architecture of the Guinness Trust estate. After the entrance block, designed to fit into the setting of Draycott Avenue, the estate strikes a slightly more solemn tone. However, it is nicely done. The *Victoria County History* states that the Guinness Trust's Draycott Avenue scheme was designed by Joseph & Smithem (*Victoria County History*, pp. 66-78). These architects designed the Brandon Street scheme but according to the Guinness Trust the architect for Draycott Avenue was in fact 'M. Macartney'. This is fascinating. Mervyn Macartney was a major figure in London's late Victorian and Edwardian building world and was the consultant architect in London to the Guinness Trust. He trained with Norman Shaw, started in independent practice in 1880, was one of the founders in 1884 of the highly influential Art Workers Guild, which was set up to promote the 'unity of the arts' and the crafts in architecture. In addition, he was the surveyor to St Paul's Cathedral from 1906 to 1931, editor of *The Architectural Review* from 1906 to 1920, and the author of numerous books about English architecture – particularly Baroque architecture – and gardens of the seventeenth and eighteenth centuries. So Macartney's response to the challenge of designing – and creating a setting for – economic urban housing for the working classes within the historic heart of Chelsea is most interesting. He opted for simplicity and repetition – each block is essentially the same, for symmetry and for the diluted Queen Anne Style, or perhaps more correctly neo-Georgian of an early eighteenth-century sort with a touch of Baroque spirit.

Each block is crowned with a brick-made cornice, the centre windows on each floor have semi-circular heads in an attempt to give the elevations focus and to help relieve the inevitable sense of monotony that comes with repetitive design of large buildings. Best are the centrally placed doors in each block. Here Macartney indulged his passion for English vernacular Baroque, framing the doors with brick voussoirs, rustication and cornices, and embellishing them with hefty keystones. They are delightful, if slightly under-scaled for the massive load of building that rises above them. The estate now includes six blocks rather than eight, and its frontage to Cadogan Street is a long, low and architecturally undistinguished post-war block that serves as the main entrance. Perhaps war damage was responsible or the simple desire to extend the estate on to Cadogan Street. Whatever the reason, Macartney's vision of a secluded and self-contained world, entered in magical manner via the arch on Draycott Avenue, has been sadly diminished.

The Estate's Agenda and Minute Books regularly address the topics of 'Working Class housing' and 'Artisan Dwellings'. For example, at a meeting held on 18 February 1890 (pp. 161–3), sites were submitted 'suitable for the erection of dwellings for the poorer classes'. These included the 2¼-acre Blacklands where 'the principal advantages ... are its central position and its being practically vacant so that no clearance of occupants on a large scale will be required'. The main disadvantage noted was the site's proximity to 'better class property, and the large extent of the property'. The meeting wondered if this latter problem could be dealt with by 'limiting the gift' of the land to 1 acre, and then letting the remainder of the site, or 'by dedicating it as an open space'. This seems to be what happened, for it was part of the vacant Blacklands site that was gifted to the Guinness Trust.

A 1-acre site between Queen's Road (now Royal Hospital Road) and Christchurch Street – 'comprising very old property' – was also discussed. The advantage of redeveloping the site as 'Artisans' Housing' was its proximity to Turk's Row, a notorious slum street. Consequently, the site was in an already 'very poor neighbourhood' which some rebuilding could improve. In addition, most of the land was 'in hand' so that 'clearance would not involve disturbing more than one hundred people, whilst the site when rebuilt would accommodate 1,200'. The 'principal disadvantage' was that the construction of artisan dwellings on the site would 'perpetuate a poor district at the entrance to the Queen's Road' and 'tell against the development of the property immediately to the west, which is now coming rapidly into the market'.

Also on the agenda was a site in 'Manor Street', now Chelsea Manor Street. This site – to the south of what is now the Old Town Hall – seems to have been a long-running problem: 'The site is in the midst of a very poor and thickly populated neighbourhood' but some of the leases in 1900 still had fourteen years to run and to clear the site 'would probably displace several hundred people' (Book number 12: 18 February 1890, pp. 161–7).

Six months later, at a meeting held on 21 July 1890, 'Artisans' Dwellings' were again discussed and it seems a decision reached about at least one of the sites discussed previously. Proposals by William Willett – a regular builder on the estate – for 'Cadogan Building', Holbein Place were discussed (Book 12, p. 317), as were remaining parts of Blacklands and Whitelands. For these Willett offered £31,500 for the land. The Earl agreed the sale. A large and architecturally rather grim five-storey estate was eventually constructed in Holbein Place. It is now managed by Peabody and known as the Lumley Estate.

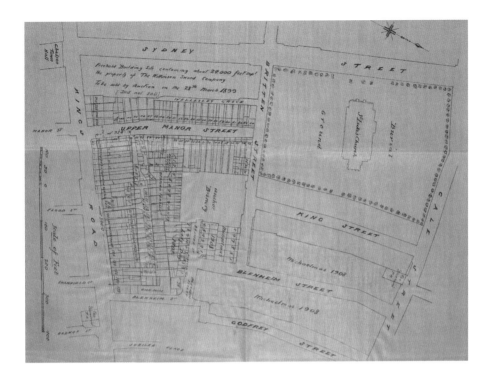

126. *Above*
A plan from volume 20 of the Cadogan Estate
Books of minutes taken recording poor quality
housing around Upper Manor Street and along
the narrow Manor Buildings to Blenheim Street,
now renamed Burnsall Street and Astell Street.
Manor Buildings were of some age, shown on
Horwood's map of 1799–1819 as a small group
of terraces set among the gardens and fields
north of the King's Road.

127. *Right*
Sample page from volume 21 of the Cadogan
Estate Minutes Books – covering late 1900
to early 1902 – dealing with the topic of the
'Housing of the Working Classes in Chelsea'.

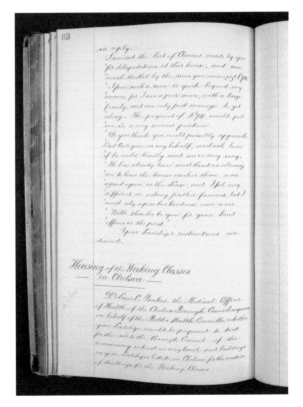

There were two William Willetts, father and son, the younger joining his father in the building business in 1880. Willett junior is now famed for inventing and promoting the notion of 'daylight saving', leading to the adoption of British Summer Time (*Cadogan & Chelsea: The Making of a Modern Estate*, pp. 152–3) The Willetts rebuilt most of Lower Sloane Street during the 1880s and 1890s, replacing speculative housing from Henry Holland's time and usually working with architect Harry Measures. The Holbein Place project was part of the Lower Sloane Street rebuilding campaign.

To appreciate the 5th Earl's continuing concern about the building of an adequate amount of 'working class housing' on the estate, it is only necessary to fast-forward a decade. In Agenda and Minute Book number 20, covering 14 July 1899 to 23 November 1900, there is a record of 'matters brought before Lord Cadogan' during a meeting at Chelsea House on Saturday 2 June 1900. The entry records that at a recent meeting of the Chelsea Vestry, the Public Health Committee submitted a report upon the 'Housing of the Working Classes in Chelsea'. Evidently the Earl's agent thought it useful to offer a bullet-point account to help focus the Earl and his advisors' minds on its future endeavours and obligations.

The report, the Minute Book records, 'pointed out that in course of next 10 to 12 years a large amount of Working Class property in the Parish would have to be dealt with, involving ... displacement of 12,000 to 13,000 people and that the new Borough Council, which will come into existence November next, would have powers far ampler and more effective to deal with the re-housing problem than those at present possessed by the Vestry'. The Vestry Committee requested that freeholders in the parish – such as Lord Cadogan – should not make 'arrangements for the releasing and rebuilding' of

properties until after the new Metropolitan Borough had been established. The agent pointed out that in fact no Cadogan leases in 'working class areas' fell-in until Lady Day 1902 – in the particularly dense and poor areas of Manor Buildings, just south of St Luke's churchyard and in Manor Gardens to the south of the Town Hall – while leases of poor houses around Chelsea Common did not expire until Christmas 1908. Consequently, the agent or the Earl's lawyer suggested that the Estate inform the Vestry of this and thus 'give the new Borough Council the assurance asked for without admitting their right to interfere with your Lordship, in the management of your property' (Book 20, pp. 105–06).

Subsequently, the Earl was approached by Dr Louis C. Parkes, the 'Medical Officer of Health' for the new Borough Council, to see if he would be 'prepared to treat for the sale to the Borough Council of the revisionary interest in any land and buildings ... for the erection of dwellings for the Working Classes'. Dr Parkes proposed, if the idea was in principle acceptable, to leave it to the Earl's 'initiative' to specify 'such sites and buildings as he might be prepared to sell'.

Various sites were considered by the meeting – Manor Gardens south of the Town Hall, Manor Street to Oakley Gardens – 'most suitable for the erection of Artizan Dwellings' – Beaufort Street and Chelsea Common (Book 21: 23 November 1900 to 17 January 1902, pp. 83–5). At a 'Special Meeting' on 13 July 1901, under the heading of 'Housing of the Working Classes in Chelsea', another site was considered, named the 'Crooked Usage' site (a long and narrow street just to the east of Manresa Road). It had been offered to and refused by the Board of Guardians (the body that operated the Workhouse near Arthur Street north of the King's Road) and was now considered 'the most suitable site for the erection of Artizan Dwellings'.

The Earl wrote his instructions on the page opposite the minutes: 'This site may be offered as proposed, but I would like to attach a condition that preference shall be given to inhabitants of neighbouring Districts when allocating habitations in the new buildings erected on this site.' The 1¼-acre site was offered to the Borough Council for £22,500 (Book 21 pp. 88–90). It would seem that the Earl now started to seriously consider the sale of Manor Buildings, with its bad buildings, when leases fell through in 1902. A few months later the possibility was discussed in some detail and the minutes record the agent's view that 'the only way to effect a sale of so large an area as Manor Buildings would be to put the property up to auction, and accept a smaller price than would be paid than by purchasers of individual plots' (Book 20: 11 July 1899 – 23 November 1900, p. 145).

Manor Buildings was a long narrow court approached off King's Road, to which it ran parallel. Its west and east ends were blind so the Buildings was in effect an enclosed world. It is shown on Horwood's map of 1799-1819, set next to gardens – so it was of early origin. To its east was Blenheim Street (now Burnsall Street and Astell Street) with small houses and almost equally troubled. A census return from 1911 for a single house in Blenheim Street – in the rather ominously named Omega Terrace – is perhaps typical. At number 3 on the day of the census were two family units. One comprised Mrs Francis Mary Clayton, a fifty-six-year-old widow with 'no occupation', her eighteen-year-old son, a 'motor cleaner' by occupation, and her three daughters aged twenty to twenty-three, two of whom were dressmakers and one a glass blower. Mrs Clayton appears to have been the head of the house, suggesting the other family were her tenants. This family consisted of thirty-one-year-old Mary Jones, with no occupation, and her sons aged four months and two years. No husband

is listed, although he could have been absent on the day of the census. But two other men were present, both listed as 'visitors' and both named Jones. One described himself as a 'dealer' and the other as a 'clerk'. The house is described as having four rooms. Houses of similar small size survive in Burnsall Street – perhaps including this specific house – so the extremely cramped nature of the accommodation is easy to visualise.

The debate about the estate's appropriate response to slum housing on its land and to the need to create decent low-cost housing continued into the twentieth century. The Cadogan Estate did eventually sell the 1.6-acre site on the east side of Beaufort Street to the Borough Council for just over half its market value on condition that it was used for working-class housing. The Council erected the six-storey Sir Thomas More estate on the site, containing 262 self-contained flats designed by Joseph & Smithem and completed by 1905. This was the Borough's first block of 'council' houses. In Manor Street Lord Cadogan gave a half-acre site to the Borough Council that in 1909, with some LCC funding, built Grove Buildings. The gift was on the condition that the tenants had incomes of less than 25 shillings a week. Fears that rebuilding the worst streets would mean a reduction in accommodation available for the poor were justified. 'Between 1902 and 1913 3,467 rooms occupied by working-class residents were demolished, and on the sites only 763 rooms were replaced by working-class dwellings' (*Victoria County History*, pp. 79–90).

The writing on the wall
A direct way to appreciate the physical presence of the Cadogan Estate in the fabric of Chelsea is to walk along some of the streets that were the subject of such earnest debate during the last decade of the nineteenth century and into the early twentieth century. In a sense the story is emblazoned on the wall.

128. Right
A group of small houses in Burnsall Street, formerly Blenheim Street, which in the late nineteenth century was one of Chelsea's more desperate slum streets. These small houses are not shown on Thompson's 1836 map and so presumably date from the 1840s or 1850s. A census return of 1911 reveals that one such four-room house in Blenheim Street was occupied by two families, totalling ten people, on the day of the census.

In Manresa Road, leading into what is now Chelsea Square, the decrepit houses and workshops have long gone, including the colony of artists' studios along the east side, near the junction with the King's Road. On the west side is the palatial public library, opened in 1890 and designed by Brydon in a Baroque style to match the Town Hall's hall and offices he had designed just few years earlier on the King's Road. The ground and building costs were the gift of the 5th Earl, and the story is told by the foundation stone that proclaims that it had been laid by 'Beatrix Jane the Countess Cadogan', the Earl's wife. So the library seems to have been very much a family affair.

Also, on Manresa Road, the Earl gave land for the building of the South-West London Polytechnic Institute, with the main building (1891-5) another J.M. Brydon endeavour. The Polytechnic used the Cadogan family arms on its documentation until 1949. (*Victoria County History*, pp. 187-190, King's College website: kingscollections.org/exhibitions/archives/ studentdays/chelsea-college/chelsea-college-through-the-years/chelsea-polytechnic-1922-1956)

After the library, walk south across the King's Road, past the Old Town Hall – the 5th Earl's premier civic gift to the people of the Borough of Chelsea – and then south down Chelsea Manor Street, formerly Manor Street, and in the late nineteenth century a place haunted by poverty and decaying houses. First on the left (east) is number one – Cadogan Hall – a jaunty little neo-Baroque gabled building with a 'memorial stone' laid in 1903 by Earl Cadogan. The architects were Sheppard and Burkinshaw. The area that so taxed the 5th Earl – to the south of the Town Hall's splendid south elevation by Brydon – seems to have been cleared and built upon soon after leases expired around 1902. However, the nearby Peabody Trust's Chelsea Manor Estate was not built until 1931.

It was designed by Victor Wilkins, and even at that late date its flats did not have individual bathrooms but instead sculleries with bathtubs that could serve as tables. The Peabody Trust had built its first working-class dwellings in Chelsea in Lawrence Street in the late 1860s (it was the Trust's fifth estate and the architect was Henry Derbishire) and it seems that they eventually provided a solution for this most troubling portion of Manor Street. South of the Peabody building, on the west side of Chelsea Manor street, are the somewhat grim Grove Buildings, erected, as a plaque proclaims, in 1909 by the Borough Council on land 'presented by Earl Cadogan'. The architects were Wills and Anderson. Chelsea Manor Street is awash with plaques. Opposite there is another, on a block of apartments on the corner with Flood Walk. It states that they were also erected by the Borough Council and opened in March 1939 by Reginald Blunt CBE, an historian, writer and Honorary Secretary of the Chelsea Society.

This makes a most interesting connection. The buildings on his estate that most distressed the 5th Earl were slums that were perceived to be unfit for human habitation. The accepted solution of the time was to clear them away and rebuild blocks of housing. In retrospect, it might be felt that upgrading the buildings, some of them historic, to serve as artisan housing could have been an option but demolition was, at the time, the usual approach to solving the problem of the slums.

Chelsea had seen many old and picturesque buildings replaced when the Chelsea Embankment was cut through in the 1870s (see page 76), and by the late nineteenth century some later regretted what had taken place. Alfred Beaver, in his *Memorials of Old Chelsea*, published in 1892, still saddened by the loss of the riverside palaces during the eighteenth century (see page 6), bemoaned the 'wave of destruction once more at the full'

The 5th Earl ... was the very model of the modern, enlightened landlord and proved himself ... one of London's great late Victorian philanthropists.

129. *Above*
42 Cheyne Walk, designed in early Georgian manner by Sir Edwin Lutyens for Lord Revelstoke and completed in 1933. Its construction involved the demolition of the ancient 43 to 45 Cheyne Walk. However, the Lutyens house was replaced in 1938 by the existing apartment block, named Shrewsbury House.

(*Memorials of Old Chelsea*, 1892, pp. 1–4). However, in the early twentieth century opinions against new developments hardened; too much of Chelsea's special character and beauty was being swept away and regrets were no longer enough.

The Chelsea Society

In 1927 the Chelsea Society was formed, and the initial moving force was Reginald Blunt, who became the Society's first Honorary Secretary. The aim was to protect the historic fabric of Chelsea and its special brand of beauty, to foster its amenities and to safeguard the interests of the people who lived there. Initially this was attempted through persuasion and through publicising threats and raising general awareness about Chelsea and its history.

The Chelsea Society was one of London's earliest residents' associations with a particular penchant for history and architecture, and with a readiness to campaign and lobby for what it believed in. The Society's first annual report – published in March 1928 – reveals much about what was then happening in Chelsea. Two entries are of particular interest.

One refers to Lombard Terrace, 'at the bottom of Church Street, close to Chelsea Old Church'. The Society 'greatly regretted that the effort made to save this interesting little row of old houses has proved unavailing'. Major Sloane Stanley, the owner, was also regretful, but nevertheless 'could not see his way to save the old houses'. The Society had circulated a paper stressing the 'historic associations of the terrace', and organised a 'petition for its preservation'. But to no avail. And it was not just history that was under attack. Sir William Orpen, painter and long-time Chelsea resident (he lived at Rossetti Studios on Flood Street), had appealed for the terrace to be spared because it was 'a thing of beauty in all lights and at all times of the year'. This really was conservation campaigning with a wonderful Chelsea twist. The terrace was important not just because it was old, architecturally significant and packed with history but also, quite simply, because it was beautiful – in all lights – and its loss would sadly diminish 'this typical corner of the old riverside'.

What sort of man was Major Roger Cyril Hans Sloane Stanley that he was not moved by these heartfelt appeals? He was a descendent of the 1719 marriage between Sir Hans Sloane's daughter Sarah, and George Stanley, and his family had been embedded in the fabric and history of Chelsea for generations, as landowners and architectural patrons. Paultons Square was named after the family's country seat in Hampshire (see page 105). It would have been reasonable to assume that he cared about the protection of Chelsea's history and possessed a sense of stewardship and thus not put personal convenience

or profits first. But something seems to have gone wrong. The situation is made more puzzling by the fact that elsewhere Sloane Stanley displayed an admirable appreciation of old buildings, as revealed by his most sensitive and thoughtful remodelling and extension of the late eighteenth-century Sloane House at 149 Old Church Street. The eminent historian John Ehrman, when writing in the *Chelsea Society Report* of 1969, characterised Sloane Stanley's works at Sloane House, executed in 1911, as 'a triumph' and 'one of the most successful conversions of a generally insensitive period'. It seems Sloane Stanley even salvaged and re-used old glass. He acted as his own architect but with the assistance of architects Elms & Jupp (Annual Report, 1927/8, p. 9; and article by John Ehrman in Annual Report, 1969, pp. 31–6).

The second entry in the 1928 report refers to '43-45 Cheyne Walk and Terrey's little old fruit shop' and it is an even sorrier tale. These buildings represented the 'substantial remains of the western wing of Shrewsbury House, built here in the 16th century and probably the oldest remaining house in Chelsea' (see pages 21-9). Inside, the Report noted, as had the *Survey of London* nearly two decades earlier, there was still surviving 'interesting panelling, doorways and a staircase'. The Society grabbed at straws: 'it would be fortunate for the lovers of old Chelsea if these could be incorporated in some way into the building destined to occupy the site'. They were not. The replacement building swept all memories and mementoes away, including 'Terrey's quaint little shop' (Annual Report, 1927/8, p. 13).

The replacement building itself has an extraordinary story that is told through the annals of the Chelsea Society. In its Sixth Annual report of 1933 the Society stated that the replacement building was designed by Sir Edwin Lutyens, and described by *Country Life* as 'a small county house in London' (Annual Report, 1933, p. 19 and *Country Life*, 14 January 1933 pp. 40–4, and 21 January 1933 pp. 64–8). The house was built and set well back from Cheyne Walk and designed in the early Georgian brick-built style that Luytens favoured at the time for domestic architecture. Three years later the Society announced, in its Ninth Annual Report for 1936, that 'Chelsea heard with some astonishment last January that the large house built by Sir Edwin Lutyens ... for the late Lord Revelstoke ... was to be pulled down and replaced by yet another block of flats (Annual Report, 1936, p. 19). The following year, 1937, the Society reported that the demolition of the Lutyens house had indeed taken place, and that 'the gaunt steel skeleton of yet another block of flats which is to replace it already towers above the neighbouring houses' (Annual Report, 1937, p. 14). The new apartment block was, rather shamelessly, named Shrewsbury House.

New buildings – luxury houses and apartment blocks as well as blocks of workers' dwellings – were impinging on Chelsea's character. This was clear. So it is curious that Blunt 'opened' the Borough Council's estate on Chelsea Manor Street and Flood Walk. It really is nothing special – four-storey slabs with access balconies and the most minimal of neo-Georgian detail. But the Chelsea Society was in its way socially progressive and perhaps relieved that nothing of historic significance had been destroyed for these slabs. In its Twelfth Annual report for 1939 the Society offered 'congratulations to the Borough Council upon the recent completion of the three large blocks of industrial dwellings to be known as Chelsea Manor Buildings', primarily because its ninety-four flats for 422 people incorporated 'playing grounds and grass plots' and because 'every flat' – unlike those in the nearby and slightly earlier Peabody dwellings – 'has its bath, its gas heater and its balcony ' (Annual Report, 1939, pp. 21–2).

Indeed, and possibly surprisingly, the needs of the working classes are still very much at the heart of Chelsea's stakeholders. The 2003 case – DANO vs CADOGAN saw the 8th Earl Cadogan take to court to defend the redevelopment of a particular piece of land in Chelsea Manor Street, originally sold by his predecessor, the 6th Earl, in 1929 to the Royal Borough of Kensington and Chelsea on the condition it was used for the benefit of working classes. This case would not see any financial gain, but it was a matter of principle to uphold the provision for social housing, aware that a mixed society is a healthy society and with concern that those key workers who enable the area function were being priced out (casemine.com/judgement/uk/5b46f1f42c94e0775e7eed61).

Nearly a hundred years after its foundation the Chelsea Society remains active, engaged and vociferous, and indeed is now campaigning to preserve architecturally significant and socially important examples of working-class housing. In late 2018 the Society played a key role in preventing the demolition of the large, neo-Baroque style William Sutton Estate, designed by E.C.P. Monson and located off Cale Street, just north of St Luke's churchyard, on land sold by Cadogan for the purpose of creating 'working class housing'. It was completed in 1913 to provide 'housing for the poor' and financed by the philanthropic entrepreneur William Sutton. The estate contains 674 dwellings for 2,200 people. It has now been designated a conservation area by the Royal Borough of Kensington and Chelsea to ensure that any changes reflect and enhance its architectural and social character. As the Society's Chairman, Dr James Thompson, explains, 'we believe there should be no loss of social housing in Chelsea, but we also believe that – when possible – priority should be given to "keyworkers" – nurses, firemen and so on. What the Society is against is people that buy but don't live in Chelsea. This kills community.'

130. *Left and below*
The future of Sloane Street envisaged. Computer-generated images show traffic reduced by management and a greater number of trees to help create a street that will be more pleasant to use and less polluted.

This sentiment is very much at the forefront of Cadogan's way of doing things too. Not only by being a strong, sometimes outspoken voice, lobbying local government, but also by its actions – committing over £1.3 million each year to subsidise affordable, community and key worker housing in the local area.

Celebrating and conserving heritage is not about being stuck in the past, but constantly assessing the relevance of historic buildings and the environment to people today.

The Future

The current Lord Cadogan is one of the Vice-Chairmen of the Chelsea Society and conservation is part of the bedrock policy of the Cadogan Estate. This concern is expressed in a number of ways - through maintenance and repair of the Estate's large stock of historic buildings, including the reinstatement of long-lost details, such as cast-iron railings in Oakley Street and Oakley Gardens that had been removed as 'salvage' (to contribute to the war effort) in the dark days of 1940.

There is also, in broader terms, the conservation and enhancement of Chelsea's established and special character, particularly the care and expansion of what is now commonly called the 'public realm'. For instance, with Chelsea's artistic legacy woven so deeply into the cultural and architectural fabric of the area (see Chapter Five), when the heavily dilapidated artists' studios 'Rossetti Studios' were recently put up for sale, it was important to Cadogan to purchase, restore and preserve the studios for their original purpose – home to practising artists. The £4 million invested in the restoration and renovation of the listed premises is not the act of a property developer looking for a return on investment, but as explained by Cadogan's Chief Executive Hugh Seaborn, part of Cadogan's Stewardship ' ...we feel it is essential that we contribute

to safeguarding the area's wonderful bohemian heritage'. Another angle is the particular care and expansion of the 'public realm'. The Estate's concern on this front is well expressed by two projects, one recently completed and one still in the future.

The first is Duke of York Square that nestles in what was once a desolate space between the rear elevation of buildings fronting on to the King's Road and an early nineteenth-century range that was once part of the Royal Military Asylum. The square – completed in 2003 – is traffic-free, lined with shops, cafés, restaurants, as well as office and residential accommodation, hosts a weekend food market and is a delightful space in which to sit, eat and reflect; a place in which to enjoy, in the current jargon, pleasurable 'dwell-time'. As the Estate explains, the square is the 'largest privately owned public space created in London in a generation'. It is also a space largely defined by new architecture. However, this architecture is not brazen nor provocative or self-assertive. Rather – in a most civilised manner – it follows the traditions established by the nearby big-player that sets the tone, the Military Asylum, now known as the Duke of York's Headquarters. The architects for the new square are Paul Davis + Partners.

This architectural approach is also in harmony with the Chelsea Society. As its chairman James Thompson explains, 'the Society supports new buildings in Chelsea, if they are right in design and use, and reinforce the architectural and social character of the area'. Duke of York Square would seem to be something of a model of this approach. It also probably passes Thompson's other test: 'we encourage not only conservation but the best new architecture, we believe new buildings should make people smile when they walk by'. The second project is the 'Greening' of Sloane Street. The Estate plans to spend £40 million making Sloane Street a far more pleasant and less polluted place. In collaboration with the Royal Borough of Kensington and Chelsea and Transport for London, the Estate proposes to reduce the drone of heavy, fume-gushing traffic by reducing the street from three lanes to two, with flow kept on the move by traffic management and the use of 'pull-in places'. Street-clutter and street furniture will be reduced and with greatly increased planting and seating the aim is to partly reclaim the street from traffic for people and to make shopping a somewhat less stressful experience. The scheme is bold and if it can be made to work, demonstrating that traffic flow can be reconciled with the creation of more pleasurable and habitable streets, then this could prove to be a model scheme.

Cadogan's desire to do its best to ensure that Chelsea remains a mixed and vital community enjoyed by all – and to address current concerns about urban pollution and sustainability – are given tangible expression in Sloane Street's parallel world to the west. Ever since Hans Town was created by Henry Holland in the late eighteenth century, Sloane Street has been a smart thoroughfare, with Pavilion Road to its west being a service road, originally a place of stables and modest accommodation. It is now the Estate's 'artisan hub', with cafés and curious shops creating, in current planning idiom, an environment bustling with local residents and visitors enjoying the special atmosphere.

Pavilion Road is also the location of a crucial experiment. Number 126 appears to be no more than a charming nineteenth-century mews building, one of the structures that justifies Pavilion Road's conservation area status. However, it is also a 'Passivhaus', retro-fitted with a sensitivity to history to make the building energy-efficient and carbon neutral. This means it makes no contribution to the clouds of pollution that still leak from the average home. This experiment demonstrates that, through sensitive design, an existing residential building in a conservation area can be, as the Cadogan Estate argues, 'updated to rigorous levels of sustainability whilst ... respecting its heritage'. The small house embodies a big idea. It has established, in its particular way, a new precedent in environmental performance. The Estate is closely monitoring the performance in terms of 'energy efficiency and wellbeing benefits for ... residents' to decide if it should 'roll out these measures' more widely within its bounds.

So sustainability, history, human wellbeing – and beauty – are all, perhaps, reconciled. Quite an achievement. The future prospects of the Cadogan Estate, and of the ancient Manor of Chelsea and its people, look most promising.

131. Above
Pavilion Road, laid out in the 1770s as a service
road behind Sloane Street, is now the Cadogan
Estate's thriving 'artisan hub', where cafés
and shops and traffic-free areas make it an
attractive place for people to gather and relax.

Acknowledgements

I would like to thank Ian Strathcarron and Lucy Duckworth of Unicorn for their guidance throughout the production of this book; Hugh Seaborn, CEO Cadogan, for initiating the project and Kira Charatan, of Cadogan Estates, for advice and invaluable help with the most rewarding estate archive; David Walker, the Local Studies Manager of Kensington Central Library, for his generosity in answering my many questions and for guiding me through the library's vast collection of relevant publications, manuscripts, prints and drawings; Ramona Lamport for her support, enthusiasm, efficiency and insights as a one-time Chelsea resident as she tackled my often over-long copy; Pauline Hubner for her skill and professionalism in the assemblage of images; Charlie Smith Design for the beautiful design of the book and – finally – to Dr James Thompson, Chairman of the Chelsea Society and Geoffrey Matthews, Secretary of the Chelsea Arts Club, for their most valuable contributions and for helping me resolve details of relatively recent Chelsea history.

Selected Further Reading

Beaver, Alfred, *Memorials of Old Chelsea: A New History of the Village of Palaces*, edited by Patricia Meara, Wakefield: E.P. Publishing, 1971

Britannia Illustrata: Views of Several of the Queen's Palaces and also of the Principal Seats of the Nobility & Gentry of Great Britain, 1707–09, folio of plates by John (Jan) Kip in collaboration with Leonard Knyff

Caesar, Julius, *The Conquest of Gaul*, translated by S.A. Handford, Penguin, 1965

Chelsea Society Annual Reports

Cherry, Bridget and Nikolaus Pevsner, *The Buildings of England, London 3: North West*, London: Penguin, 1991

Cox, Devon, *The Street of Wonderful Possibilties: Whistler, Wilde & Sargent in Tite Street*, London: Frances Lincoln, 2015

Davies, Randall, *Chelsea Old Church*, London: Duckworth & Co., 1904

Defoe, Daniel, *A Tour thro' the Whole Island of Great Britain*, London, 1724–7

Donald Insall Associates, 'Historic Building Report on Rossetti Studios, 72 Flood Street, Chelsea' for the Cadogan Estate, 2016

Eastlake, Charles, *A History of the Gothic Revival*, London: Longmans, Green and Co., 1872

Faulkner, Thomas, *An Historical and Topographical Account of Chelsea, and its Environs*, 2nd edition, 1829

Faulkner, Thomas, *An Historical and Descriptive Account of the Royal Hospital and the Royal Military Asylum in Chelsea*, London: T. Faulkner, 1805

Girouard, Mark, *Sweetness and Light: The 'Queen Anne' Movement*, 1860–1900, Oxford: Oxford University Press, 1977

Gotch, J.A., *Early Renaissance Architecture in England*, part II, 1891

Helmreich, Anne and Pamela Fletcher, *The Rise of the Modern Art Market in London 1850–1939*, Manchester University Press, 2011

Holme, Thea, *Chelsea*, London: Hamish Hamilton, 1972

Holroyd, Michael, *Augustus John*, London: Pimlico, 2011

Honey, W.B., *Old English Porcelain*, 3rd edition, Faber and Faber, 1977

John Rocque's 'Exact Survey of the Citys of London, Westminster and ye Borough of Southwark and the Country near London ten miles round', published 1744–6, see *The A to Z of Georgian London*, introduction by Ralph Hyde, London: Guildhall Library, 1981

Kroyer, Peter, 'The Story of Lindsey House', *Country Life*, London, 1956

Lancaster, Osbert, *Pillar to Post, or the Pocket-Lamp of Architecture*, London: John Murray, 1938

L'Estrange, Rev. A.G., *The Village of Palaces; or, Chronicles of Chelsea*, London: Hurst and Blackett, 1880

Le Lay, David, 'Danvers House', *Chelsea Society Report*, 2001

Lysons, Daniel, *Environs of London, Volume 2, Middlesex,* London: Cadell & Davies, 1795

Nairn, Ian, *Nairn's London*, London: Penguin, 1966

Orme, Kate, 'Artists' Studios, Supplementary Planning Guidance', 2004

Pennell, E. Robins and J. Pennell, *The Life of James McNeill Whistler*, 2 vols, 1908; 5th edition in 1 vol., 1911

Pevsner, Nikolaus, *The Buildings of England, London 2*, Harmondsworth: Penguin, 1969

Powers, Alan, *Cadogan & Chelsea: The Making of a Modern Estate*, edited by Anjali Bulley, London: Unicorn, 2017

Survey of London: Volume 2, Chelsea, Part I, edited by Walter H. Godfrey, LCC, London, 1909

Survey of London: Volume 4, Chelsea, Part II, edited by Walter H. Godfrey, LCC, London, 1913

Survey of London: Volume 7, Chelsea, Part III (the Old Church), edited by Walter H. Godfrey, LCC, London, 1921

Survey of London: Volume 41, Brompton, edited by F.H.W. Sheppard, LCC, London, 1983

Transcript of the Rev. Dr. John King's Manuscript Account of Chelsea, and the Receipts of the Rectory from the Glebe Lands and other sources during is Rectorship, 1694–1732, Chelsea Public Library, 1902

Victoria County History: A History of the County of Middlesex, volume 12, Chelsea, edited by Patricia E.C. Croot, London, 2004

Walkley, Giles, *Artists' Houses in London, 1764–1914*, Scolar Press, 1994

Weinreb, Ben and Christopher Hibbert, *The London Encyclopaedia*, 3rd edition, London: Macmillan, 2008

1 Courtesy Royal Borough of Kensington and Chelsea; 2 Coram in the care of the Foundling Museum, London/ Bridgeman Images; 3 Yale Center for British Art, New Haven; 4 Photo © Dan Cruickshank; 5 David Rumsey Map Collection (www.davidrumsey.com); 6 Courtesy Royal Borough of Kensington and Chelsea; 7 London Metropolitan Archives, City of London (COLLAGE: the London Picture Archive, ref. 23880); 8, 9 Courtesy Royal Borough of Kensington and Chelsea; 10 Photo courtesy alondoninheritance.com; 11 Courtesy Royal Borough of Kensington and Chelsea; 12 John Hammond/National Trust Photographic Library/Nostell Priory, Yorkshire/Bridgeman Images; 13, 14 Reproduced with permission of the Marquess of Salisbury, Hatfield House; 15 DK Photography/Alamy Stock Photo; 16 From *Gentleman's Magazine*, December 1833. London Metropolitan Archives, City of London (COLLAGE: the London Picture Archive, ref. 286266); 17 Courtesy Royal Borough of Kensington and Chelsea; 18 © British Library Board. All Rights Reserved. Image courtesy Matthew Sangster (romanticlondon.org); 19 Courtesy Royal Borough of Kensington and Chelsea; 20 Photo © Sir John Soane's Museum, London; 21 By kind permission of the executors of the Estate of David LeLay; 22 Courtesy Royal Borough of Kensington and Chelsea; 23 Photo © The Trustees of the British Museum; 24 Engraving by John Boydell. London Metropolitan Archives, City of London (COLLAGE: the London Picture Archive, ref. 313344); 25 Yale Center for British Art, New Haven; 26 Courtesy of Cadogan Estates Ltd; 27, 28 Courtesy Royal Borough of Kensington and Chelsea; 29 Private Collection. Photo Christies; 30 Tate, London. Photo © Tate; 31 Courtesy Royal Borough of Kensington and Chelsea; 32 Tate, London. Photo © Tate; 33 Manchester Art Gallery/Bridgeman Images; 34 Apsley House, The Wellington Museum, London. Photo © Historic England/Bridgeman Images; 35 Courtesy Royal Borough of Kensington and Chelsea; 36 London Metropolitan Archives, City of London (COLLAGE: the London Picture Archive, ref. 29125); 37, 38, 39 Courtesy Royal Borough of Kensington and Chelsea; 40, 41, 42, 43 Photos © Dan Cruickshank; 44 Private Collection; 45 Photo © Dan Cruickshank; 46 © British Library Board. All Rights Reserved/Bridgeman Images; 47 Photo © Dan Cruickshank; 48 © British Library Board. All Rights Reserved/Bridgeman Images; 49, 50 Photo © Dan Cruickshank; 51 © British Library Board. All Rights Reserved. Image courtesy Matthew Sangster (romanticlondon.org); 52 Photo © Dan Cruickshank; 53 Rijksmuseum, Amsterdam; 54 By permission of the Pepys Library, Magdalene College Cambridge; 55, 56 Photos © Dan Cruickshank; 57 Yale Center for British Art, New Haven; 58 © British Library Board. All Rights Reserved/Bridgeman Images; 59 London Metropolitan Archives, City of London (COLLAGE: the London Picture Archive, ref. 22734); 60 London Metropolitan Archives, City of London (COLLAGE: the London Picture Archive, ref. 7304); 60 Royal Hospital Chelsea, London/Bridgeman Images; 62 Courtesy Royal Borough of Kensington and Chelsea; 63, 64, 65 Photos © Sir John Soane's Museum, London; 66 Courtesy of Cadogan Estates Ltd; 67 Photo © Dan Cruickshank; 68, 69, 70, 71, 72 Courtesy Royal Borough of Kensington and Chelsea; 73 Photo © David Iliff; 74 Photo © Graham Lacdao;

75 Photo © David Iliff; 76 Courtesy of Cadogan Estates Ltd; 77 RIBA Collections; 78 Museum of Fine Arts, Boston. The John Singer Sargent Archive - Gift of Richard and Leonee Ormond/Bridgeman Images; 79 Courtesy Royal Borough of Kensington and Chelsea; 80 Metropolitan Museum of Art, New York. Gift of Irwin Untermyer, 1964 (Acc. 64.101.519); 81 Courtesy Royal Borough of Kensington and Chelsea; 82 Photo © Victoria & Albert Museum, London; 83 Library of Congress, Washington, DC (LC-DIG-ds-04741); 84 RIBA Collections; 85, 86 Photos © Victoria & Albert Museum, London; 87 Photo © Dan Cruickshank; 88 The Hunterian, University of Glasgow/Bridgeman Images; 89 Photo Historic England Archive. Courtesy Royal Borough of Kensington and Chelsea; 90, 91, 92, 93 Photos © Dan Cruickshank; 95 (far left) Martin Charles/RIBA Collections; 95 (left and below), 96, 97 Photos © Dan Cruickshank; 98 RIBA Collections; 99 Courtesy Royal Borough of Kensington and Chelsea; 100 Courtesy of Cadogan Estates Ltd; 101, 102 Yale Center for British Art, New Haven; 103 London Metropolitan Archives, City of London (COLLAGE: the London Picture Archive, ref. 20115); 104 Yale Center for British Art, New Haven; 105 London Metropolitan Archives, City of London (COLLAGE: the London Picture Archive, ref. 286383); 106 Metropolitan Museum of Art, New York. John Stewart Kennedy Fund, 1912 (Acc. 12.32); 107 Courtesy Royal Borough of Kensington and Chelsea; 108 Wellcome Collection, London; 109 John Lewis Partnership Archives; 110 © The Cecil Beaton Studio Archive at Sotheby's; 111 Chronicle/Alamy Stock Photo; 112, 113 RIBA Collections; 114 From *The Architectural Review*, June 1939; 115 John Lewis Partnership Archives; 116 akg-images; 117 Architectural Press Archive/RIBA Collections; 118 Harvard Art Museums/ Busch-Reisinger Museum, Gift of Ise Gropius. Photo © President and Fellows of Harvard College; 119 Photo © Jack Howe. From *The Architectural Review*, November 1936; 120 Courtesy Royal Borough of Kensington and Chelsea; 121 Photo © Dan Cruickshank; 122 Courtesy of Cadogan Estates Ltd; 123 Courtesy LSE Library; 124 Guinness Partnership; 125 Photo © Dan Cruickshank; 126, 127 Courtesy of Cadogan Estates Ltd; 128 Photo © Dan Cruickshank; 129 Photo A.E. Henson/Country Life Picture Library; 130, 131 Courtesy of Cadogan Estates Ltd

Chapter openers
pp. 9–10 Detail from John Rocque's small scale 'Exact Survey of the Citys of London, Westminster and ye Borough of Southwark and the Country near Ten Miles Round' (1744–6). David Rumsey Map Collection (www.davidrumsey.com)
pp. 80–1 Detail from Survey of the District of Hans Town, Chelsea, c. 1770 (fig. 48)
pp. 118–19 The Royal Military Asylum (fig. 66)
pp. 150–51 Interior view of St Luke's, looking east (fig. 73)
pp. 174–75 Detail from George R. Woolway, 'Literature', 1912. Chelsea Town Hall (fig. 89)
pp. 202–3 Architectural detail, Pont St (fig. 91)
pp. 228–29 Thomas Bowles, Ranelagh House & Gardens with the Rotunda at the Time of the Jubilee Ball, 1759. Yale Center for British Art, New Haven
pp. 252–53 64 Old Church St (fig. 117)
pp. 272–73 Plan from Cadogan Estate Book, volume 20 (fig. 126)